The Beautiful Side of Death

by

Floyd C. McElveen

DEDICATION

To my beloved Aunt, Velma 'Sunny' McElveen, whose generous support helped to make this book's impact possible.

To my dear Canadian friends, Richard and Alica Hughes, for the indispensable help in initiating, supporting, and correcting the book, and encouraging the Author.

To my wonderful Michigan friends, Roger and Dianne Hansen, whose tenacity, support, and constructive criticism helped make this a better book.

G.T.M.
Box 1015
Grand Rapids, Michigan 49501

This book contains several chapters taken by permission from books by Authors Dave Hunt, Johanna Michaelsen and Dr. Maurice Rawlings.

Table of Contents

CHAPTER ONE

The Ugly Side of Death

As a young boy, my interest in the supernatural side of death and dying was aroused by a story told me by Mr. Barton, a renter sharecropper on our Mississippi farm. "It *was* spooky," he said. "I can still see the coffin as clear as if it was sitting here in this room."

He chuckled as he noticed my uneasiness. Then he became serious again, musing into the past.

"The coffin I saw in my dream . . . or vision . . . was made of a certain material. It had several designs on it—designs I had never seen on any other coffin. It had a distinct color combination, outside and inside. I remember that I woke up with a deep sense that something was wrong."

Mr. Barton took a deep draw on his pipe. His jaw muscles tightened. "The next day," he said, "I got word that my brother had just died. I saddled up and rode over for the funeral. When I walked into the parlor where they kept the body, I almost went into shock. There, with my brother's body in it, was the exact coffin I had dreamed about the night before." Mr. Barton paused for a moment. "Every detail was exactly the same. The material of the coffin. The designs on it. The colors. It was," he declared, "exactly the same coffin!!"

Mr. Barton had reputedly killed three or four men, and had spent time in prison for one of these killings. This man

1

he claimed had opened fire on him from his field as he drove by in a car. Mr. Barton had jumped out and returned fire with his own pistol until the attacker was dead.

Years later I met the son of the man he had killed. He told me this was an absolute lie. As a little boy he had been out with his father who was working in the field. He claimed Mr. Barton had driven up, shot his father in cold blood, then finished him off with another shot while his father pled for his life. Whatever the facts were, Mr. Barton introduced me that night into one of my first encounters with the supernatural world, especially concerning death.

It was dark when he finished his story. To this day I remember running home, so fast it seemed to me that I floated over the ground.

To some degree all people are concerned or curious about death. I may have been thinking seriously about it at an earlier age than many people, as a consequence of its early intrusion into my life.

I remember my red-haired father. He was something of a local hero, having caught a person who was falling from the roof of a schoolhouse. At 5 foot 10 inches and one hundred and sixty pounds, he was one of the strongest men in the country. He was also quite intelligent, being one of the first college men in our area. He was a very good baseball player and also wanted me to love and play the game, I was told.

Fathers tended to be pretty stern and aloof in that day. One day when my dad was in his study, his brothers coaxed me into going into the room, getting his attention, and piping up in my shrill little three year-old voice, "Daddy, you're a pretty good guy from the top of your head up!"

I still remember the way he slowly turned from his studies and looked unsmilingly at me. I beat a hasty retreat.

One of the fondest memories of my dad, treasured in my heart for many long and lonely years, shows another characteristic of this man. We were at my grandmother McElveen's house, 3½ long graveled miles from the little town of Osyka, Mississippi. I had a sweet tooth from birth, always begging for homemade "teacakes" or a candy bar. In those days, candy bars were scarce, but my father had taken the logging truck to town for something and promised me that he would bring me back a candy bar. I couldn't wait. The hours dragged by. Would he bring me chocolate silver-bells? (Now better known as Hershey kisses.) Maybe a Baby Ruth. Or maybe even—and my heart danced—a Milky Way . . . my very favorite! Finally, the logging truck came down the road through clouds of dust. I tore out of the house into Daddy's arms. "What did you get me, Daddy? What did you get me?"

Slowly, it dawned on me that there was no response. I looked deep into my father's eyes. Shame and hurt seemed to shadow their normal sparkle. Taking me in his arms, he told me that he had simply forgotten my candy bar. I sobbed as if my world had caved in. To this day, memories of that disappointment tug at my heart. But it was more than that. Fathers kept their word in that day, at least mine did, and I believe most others did also. Mingled with the disappointment was an awful, empty feeling that my father had broken his promise. I was shattered. If I couldn't trust my father in my tiny world, what was left?

Suddenly, unbelievingly, I heard my father say softly, "Stop your crying, son. I'm going back into town to get your candy bar!!" Young as I was, I *knew* daddies simply didn't *do* that in those days of hard work, long hours, and little money. I never heard of it before or since. Most times, when you sniveled over some minor thing like a candy bar, you were told to "shut up" and spanked if you persisted. To spoil a child was one of life's greatest tragedies. Few people, especially dads, ever told children that they loved them.

Nevertheless, my father, tired and busy as he was, got in that old logging truck, drove back to town, and brought me back a candy bar. He won his three-year-old son's heart forever and gave him a warm, sweet memory to cherish.

A few months later, shortly after having been stabbed and cut unmercifully by a two-hundred pound man, in the act of defending an innocent woman's name, my dad came down with encephalitis, "sleeping sickness." He died in Shreveport, Louisiana, and was buried on my fourth birthday. A bright light went out in my life. From then on, death was a horrible thing to me, a wrenching pain, an aching loneliness, a dreadful fear.

My mother was unable to care for me and I was given to my grandmother and grandfather McElveen to raise. I had just gotten settled when death struck again. My grandfather was shot by a man who claimed grandfather's livestock had gotten into his field. (There was really much more to it than that, but that is all I knew about it for a while.)

At fourteen, I sat by the side of my beloved grandmother as she lay dying.

In 1943, at age seventeen, I joined the Navy. One of my best friends was a handsome boy, filled with dreams of returning home to his girl friend in New York. I will never forget the night his dream ended when a suicide plane slammed into our ship. It was just past midnight. We were near the shore of Okinawa. While fires and explosions consumed our small ship, I rushed over to my friend. He was seriously injured and bleeding profusely from his chest. Later I was told at least one hundred and twenty-five pieces of shrapnel had pierced his body.

He was screaming uncontrollably with unbearable pain and fear. His eyes seemed to look beyond me, seeing something I couldn't see. It wasn't long before he was dead. For years I shuddered at the horror in his voice, the fear in his face. I wondered what he saw beyond death.

We try to avoid the words death and dying by using other names—departure, deceased, and passing away. Burial becomes interment. Embalming preserves the body . . . for a while. Flowers smother the stench of death. Funerals become more and more sterilized. I read recently of a drive-in funeral home where one never has to get out of the car. Just drive through and view the coffin or remains, if it is an open casket. Then, of course, sign the guest book.

The sneaking suspicion in most of our minds, however, is that the epitaph W. C. Fields wanted on his tombstone might be most appropriate on many others, "On the whole, I'd rather be in Philadelphia."

None of this mutes in the slightest the reality that each of us must die. This may occur at any time, anywhere, anyplace. The age-old question persists. Why am I here? Where did I come from? What happens when I die? Is death really the end? Or the beginning? Or an altered state? Does anybody know? Can anybody know?

In the following chapters let us consider the answer from people who have been, or testify that they have been, beyond death. Can we get an answer from the spirit world? The occult? Man's inner being? The Force? What lies beyond death? Is there really a spirit world? Do they have the answer to life and death? Can we contact them? Is there really a way to transform into something beautiful this apparently ugly thing called death?

In the next chapter we begin our search for the answer with Dr. Maurice S. Rawlings, a medical doctor who has counseled and listened to the "beyond death" experience of hundreds of his patients. He, as well as other witnesses, will present the evidence. You will render the verdict.

CHAPTER TWO

The Reality of the Spirit World "After Death"[1]

Encounters in the next world are variously described as heavenly, pleasant, exhilarating, beyond expression. Most of these descriptions, of course, represent interviews occurring away from the scene of resuscitation, usually a few days later. Many who have had these experiences are sure they are headed for a serene afterlife. For some, this could be true; others could have received a false impression. Those who have had bad experiences do not remember them after being removed from the resuscitation scene, as evidenced by cases published thus far. We will discuss these bad episodes later, but now for the more pleasant ones.

Why should we publish all of the volunteered reports if some might not be representative?

First, we must document the reports as they come until we are able to get a more accurate accounting by recording them at the actual times they occur. Second, we are not primarily concerned as to whether they concur with any particular philosophical or religious belief. We first present them as they are. I will give you my observations. Your conclusions may differ entirely from mine.

Variable Experiences

Pleasant experiences have considerable variability. Although the sequence of events is very much the same, some of the details may be omitted or altered from one experience to another. The following report concerns a lady in her twenties who saw herself dying, then leaving the scene, but not quite making it through the "tunnel":

> I had lost a lot of blood. It was about an hour after I had delivered my only child. When they moved me from the stretcher to the bed to take me to surgery, I could see the blood pouring through the separation between the bed and stretcher. It seemed to spurt with each heart beat. The loss of blood was incredible. I was sure I would die.
>
> They rushed me to the operating room. But when I arrived, I suddenly wasn't in my body. I don't remember getting out of it. But at least it didn't hurt. I was floating in the left-hand corner of the ceiling, looking down at my doctor. I didn't like him. He was cursing and yelling at the nurses. I think he was panicked over my condition. Now I was sure I was going to die.
>
> They were getting ready to give me an injection of medicine to put me to sleep but I was sure I would die before they could stop my bleeding. I saw the faces of my mother, husband, and baby boy who were all living. They would be sad at my death but I didn't feel despondent. In fact, it didn't seem to make much difference to me at all! I wasn't unhappy and I couldn't understand why.
>
> Next, I was hurdling down this dark tunnel at a high speed, not touching the sides. It made a swishing sound. At the end of the tunnel was a yellow-white light. Then I said, "This must be what it feels like to die. I feel no pain at all." I was glad of that. But before I could get to the light and out of the tunnel, I found myself back in the recovery room that had four beds in it and I was in one of them.

I will never forget the peacefulness that I experienced. For some reason I was not afraid of this dying business, but I was glad to see my baby boy again!

Most cases have "indescribable" experiences: "I just can't find words to express what I want to say." Extremely pleasant feeling may be present despite coexisting discomfort from such things as head injuries, accidental crushing injuries, or gunshot wounds. At the moment of injury, for instance, there may be a flash of pain and then all pain may sometimes vanish:

> The pain left after the first bullet entered. I didn't feel the second or third. I had a feeling of floating in a dark space. In all this darkness I felt warmth and extreme comfort although my skin was extremely cold. I thought to myself, "I must be dead."

Astounding realizations and new concepts in life may occur, as they did in the following case. Mrs. S. was struck by lightning while on a camping trip:

> In the moment that I was hit, I knew exactly what had happened to me. My mind was crystal clear. I had never been so totally alive as in the act of dying. [Regrets of past actions together with things she wanted to do with her life filled her mind.]
>
> At this point in the act of dying, I had what I call the answer to a question I had never verbalized to anyone or even faced: Is there really a God? I can't describe it, but the totality and reality of the living God exploded within my being and He filled every atom of my body with His glory. In the next moment, to my horror, I found that I wasn't going toward God. I was going away from Him. It was like seeing what might have been, but going away from it. In my panic, I started trying to communicate with the God I knew was there.

She begged for her life and offered it to God if He would spare it. She recovered fully in three months.

"Floating" after separation from one's own body and the feeling of transition into a new dimension seem common in almost every case report:

> I had pneumonia and was getting more toxic. My temperature was 107 degrees. They told me later that I went into a coma for several days and they didn't expect me to live. I was packed in ice and given alcohol sponge baths. My family was told that nothing could be done and I would probably have severe brain damage if I survived.
>
> During this coma, I found myself floating in a valley. There was a light in the distance on a mountain and as I approached the mountain I noticed beautiful orchids and flowers growing on its rocky slope. Among the boulders I saw my grandfather standing. He had been dead several years. I didn't talk to him, but I knew I wanted to stay and I didn't want to come back.
>
> I also saw a cross that was on the side of the mountain and a figure was hanging on that cross, still alive. I know it was Jesus. I had the sensation that this was both the beginning and the end of the world. After that, I suddenly found myself back in my body.
>
> About three years ago, I had a similar experience when undergoing surgery for a degenerated hip joint. The joint degeneration seemed to be aggravated by cortisone treatment I had received. I was getting ready to undergo anesthesia when suddenly they thought I had died. I did not feel any separation of my spirit from my body nor did I recall any tunnel. I was just suddenly floating in the same valley that I had experienced previously. Only this time, both of my grandparents were there on the rocky mountain slope. My grandmother said, "You can't go with us. You have to go back." She was crying because I couldn't stay. I am not sure whether this was a judgment ground or what it

represented. I do know that it changed my whole life. I enjoy life more now because I don't dread the future.

Separation from the body may occur in stages:

I had been in the hospital several days and my chest pain had already subsided. I was forty-six years old at the time and they could not find the cause of my trouble. I started packing to go home when I developed recurrence of the same severe chest pains. I was pushing the nurses' call button when I collapsed. Someone came into the room and called for help. Several other people soon came in and starting working on me. One was pumping on my chest and another was getting oxygen.

About that time, I started to drift upward, leaving the discarded body behind and coming into the presence of a silvery, peaceful, brilliant light. I was not afraid and I wanted to stay. I then reentered my body suddenly and without explanation. There was simultaneous recurrence of the same severe chest pain. As the pain subsided, once again I drifted up and out of my body, free of pain and then I thought "now I am really gone." And yet, I felt peaceful, wonderful. There was no fear of death. I had no meeting of any other people and no "tunnel" or flashback of previous life events that I had heard about in others.

Panoramic recall or instant replay of one's life, however, is a commonly reported observation; it often resembles television flashbacks. It is not clear if this playback is a prelude to judgment or to something else, but it is thought provoking.

I recall a particularly sad case of a man who died with an experience incompletely revealed. This patient had a common cold. Although I had told him that penicillin did not help colds or other viral illnesses, he insisted that it always helped his own colds. After he reassured me that he had never had a reaction to penicillin, and upon his insistence, I gave him the penicillin injection.

Then it happened. He had what physicians call an anaphylactic reaction. Within five minutes of the injection, he crumbled to the floor unconscious, in deep shock, and without blood pressure. We started circulatory support with external heart massage until we obtained supportive drugs. Then an ambulance was summoned to transport him from the clinic to another hospital.

While awaiting the ambulance, he recovered his heartbeat and blood pressure, the latter with the help of a very powerful drug we were giving by intravenous drip method. This drug constricted the small arteries in his body, giving some support for blood pressure. He awoke and looked up into my face and said that he had just seen all of his life passing before him. Every important event seemed to be portrayed.

I was too busy to pay much attention at that time. For years I have been "too busy" to listen to my patients. Now it's too late in his case. He died with a cerebral hemorrhage as an indirect complication of the penicillin reaction. I actually broke down and cried.

Bliss, peace, and euphoria usually attend the descriptions of heavenly encounters. But seldom do we hear condemnations reported.

Many of the "radiant" descriptions do not necessarily relate to "heavenly" experiences. One patient who was revived from a no-pulse, no-respiration, and dilated-pupil condition suddenly had a "new knowledge" of his relationship to his environment and to the world. The transition from life to death had been easy with no time for fear. He did not see his past life flash before him. He described moving at high speed through what appeared to be a grid of luminous strands. After he stopped, this vibrant luminosity became blinding in intensity and drained him of energy. He felt no pain, no unpleasant sensation. The grid had transformed him into a form beyond time and space . . . a new being. Personal fears, hopes, and wants were removed. He felt he was an indestructible spirit. As he was waiting for something momentous to occur, he suddenly returned to his body on the operating table.

Another patient described similar feelings of painless bliss when dying:

> I lost so much blood I was becoming unconscious. I felt my body separate. I was lying beside my own body. I looked over and watched the nurses and doctors working on my dead body. I myself felt very content and peaceful. I was free of pain and had a very happy feeling. I thought, if this was death it is beautiful. Thinking of my family helped me to hang on to life, although I felt all my troubles were gone at the time. I couldn't feel a thing except peace and ease and quietness.

The experience seems uniform: actual death has no sting, no pain. A condition leading to death—the crushing auto accident, for instance—may be quite painful, but death itself is like a simple faint, a missed heartbeat, or going to sleep. These people with pleasant experiences do not fear dying again.

Angel of Light

In a few cases, whether pleasant or unpleasant, the person does not recall actually leaving the body or experiencing transportation through a tunnel or any other passage. Many of them recall, however, meeting a heavenly (or grotesque) being or some form of a "take-away" figure. Some will identify the take-away figure as Jesus or an "angel of light" or some "holy being." I have not heard of anyone claiming to have seen the devil. Interestingly, whatever "being" they encounter has usually not identified himself. Usually the person having the experience makes the identification. Thus, Hindus, Muslims, or Buddhists may claim that they see their respective deities while Christians identify him as Christ. The following is an example of the latter:

> Suddenly I felt relief from my terrible chest pains. Now I felt exhilaration. I can't fully express it. I was floating into an area that looked like heaven. It was wonderfully bright with buildings and streets of gold and I saw a figure with long hair in a brilliant white robe. A light radiated all about him. I didn't talk to him. I am sure that it was Jesus. As he took hold of my hand, the next thing I remember was a jerking on my body. You were shaking me and then the pain came back. But I was back on earth again! I will never forget that moment of happiness. I want to recapture that moment again. I am not afraid of death. I really am not! I look forward to seeing Jesus again.

Other encounters with an "angel of light" resemble this case:

> I knew I was dying. They had just gotten me to the hospital and then I felt this pain in my head and I saw a great light and everything was whizzing around and around. Then I felt free and at peace and just an uncanny sense of well being. I looked down on the medical people working over me and it didn't bother me a bit. I wondered why.
>
> Then I was suddenly enveloped in this black cloud and went through this tunnel. I emerged from the other end in a white light which had a soft glow. I saw my brother who

had died three years previously. I attempted to go through a doorway, but my brother blocked my view and wouldn't let me see what was behind him.

Then I saw what was behind him. It was a bright angel. An angel of light. I felt encompassed by a force of love from this angel that searched and probed my deepest thoughts. It searched me and then seemingly allowed me to sense the presence of spirits of some other loved ones who had died previously. Then my whole body jumped upward from the electric jolt they gave me, and I knew I was back on earth again.

Since I have recovered from this encounter with death, I no longer fear death. I have already been there. I know what it is like.

People commonly report this experience of meeting a "loving" or "searching" being of light in a beautiful environment. Even confessed atheists have told me of similar experiences; they say that this proves there is no hell, and that God, if He exists, loves everyone and therefore would punish no one.

In each account, however, the people are returned to their bodies before any decision is reached or any disposition is rendered. This initial encounter would conceivably represent merely a sorting ground. It could also represent a deceivingly pleasant situation that implies security and sanctuary and prevents a desire or need for changed lives. This could be a satanic deception according to Charles Ryrie, Billy Graham, Stephen Board and other Christian spokesmen. The following case involved a non-Christian patient:

It was the third night I was in the coronary unit with a heart attack and I was awakened by the nurses and one of the men in white. They had a shot ready for me and I asked,

"What's the trouble?" One of the nurses said my monitor had stopped completely. I remember I asked them not to call any of my relatives as it was nearing the second shift changing time and it was late. I held up my hand for the man to give the shot through the IV tube that was running in my arm.

Suddenly I started ascending upward rapidly through this huge tunnel, round and round, without hitting sides. I was saying to myself, "I wonder why I don't hit the sides of this?" Then this brilliantly lighted person stopped me. He knew my thoughts and reviewed my life. He told me to go back—that my time would come later. I felt welcome. I don't remember getting back into my body, but I remember them waking me up and telling me my heart had stopped and they had just started it up again.

I was reluctant to tell my family because I didn't want to upset them about this strange experience.

Sometimes this light seems to illuminate the whole environment. It is usually described as a dazzling, though not blinding, light. Some describe a "being" in the light and others do not. In either event they seem to sense a thought-communication that this light affords with the whole environment.

Changed Lives

Life-after-death experiences seem to produce profound effects upon the future of one's purposes and beliefs. They change lives:

I always thought about social status and wealth symbols as the most important things in life until life was suddenly taken from me. Now I know that none of these are important. Only the love you show others will endure or be remembered. The material things won't count. Our present life is nothing compared to what you'll see later. Now I'm not afraid to die again. Those that are afraid of dying must have a reason, or else they don't know what it's like.

During spiritual existence some people report that they have heightened senses of perception. They may, for instance, sense a sweet smell to the air or beautiful music in the background or a euphoric existence.

The day following a violent storm in our city a few years ago, a crew of men from the electric power company were throwing a grounding chain over some fallen electric lines. Someone had neglected to turn off the power, and the chain became entangled around the leg of one crew member. As several thousand volts went through him, he writhed along the ground, his body creating sparks. Even the grass under him burned in spots. His fellow workers cut the chain loose and began resuscitation after confirming no heartbeat nor breathing.

When I saw him in the hospital emergency room, he was alive but unconscious. His pupils were normal, but several disturbances in heart rhythm required correction. Plastic surgeons performed grafts to replace a large area of skin that had been destroyed by electrical burns on the ankle.

When he awoke the next day, he remembered hearing beautiful music and experiencing an aura of quiet and peaceful existence long before becoming conscious. The odd thing was, he could still hear the music after he awoke. It intrigued him enough to ask a visitor to find out from where the music was coming. But the visitor could hear no music!

He could not recall several other details, but this experience profoundly affected his whole life. Why music should have such an impact, I do not understand; however, since this experience he has lectured to almost any group or individual who will listen.

Encounters Beyond the Barrier

Entrance into hell (or what appears to be hell) may occur in a direct fashion, frequently bypassing most of the usual sequence of events. Similarly, persons may report a direct entrance into heaven (or what appears to be heaven), although they seem more likely first to travel through some type of sorting ground or over some type of barrier. The sorting ground is usually a meeting area (true in both good and bad experiences) and the barrier is usually a fence or a wall or some similar obstacle.

A middle-aged overweight male, who had multiple deaths and multiple experiences before his final death, reported that some of these episodes had taken him to heavenly places. His high blood pressure caused repeated heart attacks, which in turn caused repeated episodes of fibrillation and sudden clinical death. Usually a convulsion would occur and then total loss of consciousness. All breathing would cease in two or three minutes if nothing was done, and each time electrical shock and resuscitation would bring him back. These episodes of reversible death recurred every few days, and he reported an out-of-the-body experience each time. Only two of the experiences will be reported. The first illustrates a remarkable on-the-scene recall:

> I turned over to answer the phone and began to have another very severe pain in my chest. I pushed the button to summon the nurse and they came in and started working on

me. They put medicine in the IV bottle beside the bed, which ran into my arm. I was miserable lying there. It felt like an elephant's foot was standing in the middle of my chest. I was sweating and about to vomit when I noticed that I was losing consciousness. Everything was turning black. My heart stopped beating. One of the nurses dialed the phone to the hospital loud speaker to call for help. "Code 99, Code 99!" she shouted.

As they were doing this I could feel myself leaving my body from the headward portion, detaching and floating in the air without any sensation of falling. Then I was lightly standing on my feet watching the nurses push down on my chest. Two more nurses came in and one was wearing a rose on her uniform. Two more nurses and one orderly came in and then I noticed that they had called my doctor back from his visits in the hospital. When he came into the room I wondered why he was there, since I felt fine!

Then my doctor took off his coat and relieved the nurse pushing on my chest. I noticed he had on a blue-striped tie. The room started getting dark and I had the sensation of moving rapidly down a dark corridor. All of a sudden I felt this horrible shock in my chest. My body moved, my back arched, and I felt a terrible burning in my chest like somebody had hit me. Then I woke up to find myself back in my bed. Only two nurses and an orderly remained. The others had gone.

The specific things this patient saw, including the number of people, what they did, and what they were wearing were subsequently verified. Reconstruction of the time sequence indicated that he was without heartbeat or consciousness during this entire interval of recall.

In contrast to most people who have been revived from death, this patient had an after-death experience each time he was resuscitated. Each experience was different. Each one was pleasant.

The second experience suggests a transition into a heavenly realm:

> Again, that terrible pain returned in my chest. I knew it meant trouble. Maybe a faint. It had before. And I had been sleeping so nicely! I took my usual "dynamite" tablet under my tongue and yelled for the nurse. I pushed on the lights. The nurse came in quickly. The pain was worse. Suddenly the room turned black again. I didn't feel any more pain.
>
> The next thing I knew I was floating at the far end of the room near the ceiling, looking down on my body from the footward direction. The nurses were working on me again. I must have died! I saw them wheeling in the EKG shock machine. Tubes seemed to be all over the place, one of them going to my nose and another one in my arm. Meanwhile, I was floating up in the air with no way of falling. Then I heard them say, "I am not sure that he'll come back this time!"
>
> That's all I remember in the room. Then I went swiftly through a black tube, not touching the sides. Soon I was glad to see light again, but this time that wall didn't stop me. I actually flew over it. I was flying rapidly through space.
>
> Below me was a river. Dawn was approaching. Everything was getting brighter. I noticed that I was crossing over a beautiful city below, as I followed the river like a soaring bird. The streets seemed to be made of beautiful shining gold. I descended onto one of the streets. People surrounded me—happy people who were glad to see me! They seemed to be in shining clothes. Nobody was in a hurry. Some other people approached me. I think they were my parents. But just then I woke up, back in the hospital room. I was back in my body. This time I really wished that they hadn't brought me back. I was getting tired of going through all of this. I wanted to stay.

This patient always had good experiences. He said he

was a Christian, and he had already seen where he was going. He did not want to be brought back again. He had suffered enough from shortness of breath and chest pains. Between episodes he tried to tell everyone who would listen—whether hospital staff or visitors—about his experiences and about the next life. Then he got his wish. He didn't respond after the next episode.

Today cases recall the biblical descriptions of Stephen's, Paul's, and John's heavenly visions. One minister reports the following:

> I was called in the middle of the night by the hospital nurse who informed me that Mrs. D., one of my parishioners, was dying. She asked me if I wanted to be present at her bedside. I dressed hastily and went quickly to the hospital. When I stepped off the elevator, the nurse told me, "I am sorry I called you out of bed. Mrs. D. is dead." She then took me into the room where Mrs. D., a small, frail, silver-haired lady, had died from a terminal cancer. I was told that all vital signs had ceased. I then prayed out loud to God saying that Mrs. D. had insisted on my coming for a purpose; I asked the Lord to let that purpose come to pass if it be His will.
>
> Then I saw Mrs. D.'s eyelids fluttering. Some rustling and commotion occurred in the room. Then Mrs. D. opened her eyes wide and stared straight at me. She spoke in a whisper, "I thank you, Pastor Grogan, for your prayer. I was just talking with Jesus and He was telling me to come back and do something for Him. I also saw Jim" [her recently deceased husband]. Breathing softly, she turned on her side and drew her knees up almost to her chin, and slept.
>
> As I walked down the corridor to the elevator, I heard the sound of running feet. The nurse who had witnessed it all overtook me and said, "I'm afraid! What did you do? That woman was dead and she came back to life! I have

been a nurse for many years and I never saw that happen before. I've always been an atheist."

Mrs. D., after she had recovered, had many conversations in which she described to others what she had seen during her death: Jesus in His shining brightness and her departed husband Jim. She wanted to stay in heaven but Jesus had ordered her back to talk to others.

Then one day she told me that she was going that very day to the hospital—this time to go to heaven and stay. "Do not pray for me to live this time."

Another illustrative case is a patient who visited a heavenly city through angelic transportation:

My first pacemaker was inserted in March and it wasn't working well. I was in the hospital to get a new pacemaker. I asked my wife and brother-in-law to get the nurse. Something was going wrong with my heartbeat. I could feel it. Then I remember someone shouting "Code 99, Code 99." But I wasn't in the room after that. Encircling my waist with her arms, a nurse, it seemed, had grasped me from behind and had taken me out of there. We started flying out of the city, going faster and faster. But when I looked down toward my feet, I realized that it was not a nurse. Instead I saw the tips of some white wings moving behind me. I am sure now that it was an angel!

After soaring for a while, the angel sat me down on a street in a fabulous city with beautiful trees and buildings made of glittering gold and silver. A beautiful light shone everywhere—glowing but not bright enough to make me squint my eyes. On this street I met my mother, my father, and my brother, all of whom had died previously.

"Here comes Paul" I heared my mother say. As I walked to greet them, however, this same angel picked me up by the waist again and took me off into the sky. I didn't know why they wouldn't let me stay.

We approached the skyline in the distance. I could recognize the buildings. I saw the hospital where I had been as a patient. The angel descended and put me back in the very room where I had been and I looked up and saw the faces of the doctors working on me. I was back in my body. I will never forget the experience. I don't think anyone could be an atheist if he had an experience like mine.

I was able to tape record the following report made by a seventy-year-old accountant soon after he recovered his faculties. Most of his descriptions of heaven closely resemble those given in the last two chapters of the Bible. In rare cases similar descriptions have been given by some who had never previously known the biblical descriptions of the New Jerusalem:

They were rushing me from the emergency room to the intensive care unit because of my chest pain. They told me it was a heart attack. In the elevator I felt my heart stop. I stopped breathing and I thought, "This is it."

The next thing I remember was looking down on my body in the intensive care unit. I don't know how I got there, but doctors and nurses were working on me. A black fellow in a white uniform was doing most of the work on me. This black fellow was shoving down on my chest and someone else was breathing for me and they were yelling to get this and get that!

Later I learned that this black fellow was a male nurse on the ward. I had never seen him before. I even remember the black bow tie he was wearing.

The next thing I remember was going through a dark passage. I didn't touch any of the walls. I emerged into an open field and was walking toward a big white wall which was very long. It had three steps leading up to a doorway in the wall. On a landing above the stairs a man sat clothed in a robe that was glowing and dazzling white. His face also had a glowing radiance. He was looking down into a big book, studying.

As I approached him I felt great reverence and asked him, "Are you Jesus?"

He said, "No, you will find Jesus and your loved ones beyond that door." After he looked in his book he said, "You may go on through."

Then I walked through the door, and saw on the other side this beautiful, brilliantly lit city, reflecting what seemed to be the sun's rays. The city was made completely of gold or some shiny metal. Domes and steeples of buildings stood in beautiful array. The streets were shining and made of something I had never seen. Present were many radiant-faced people all dressed in glowing white robes. They looked beautiful. The air smelled so fresh. I have never smelled anything like it.

I heard music in the background that was beautiful, heavenly. I saw two figures walking toward me and I immediately recognized them. They were my mother and father who had died years ago. My mother had been an amputee and yet the severed leg was now restored! She was walking on two legs!

I said to my mother, "You and father are beautiful." And they said to me, "You have the same radiance and you are also beautiful."

As we walked along together to find Jesus, I noticed one building that was larger than the others. It looked like a football stadium with an open end from which a blinding light radiated. I tried to look up at the light but I couldn't. It was too brilliant. Many people seemed to be bowed in adoration and prayer in front of this building.

I said to my parents, "What is that?" They said, "In there is God."

I will never forget it. I have never seen anything like it. We passed many people as we went to see Jesus. All of them were happy. I have never felt such a sense of well-being.

As we approached the place where Jesus was, I suddenly felt a tremendous surge of electricity through my body as if someone had hit me in the chest. My body arched upward as they were defibrillating my heart. I had been restored to my former life! But I was not too happy to come back. I knew that I had been sent back, however, to tell others about this experience. I plan to dedicate the rest of my life to telling anyone who will listen!

Discovering cases of beyond-the-barrier experiences exhilarates me. In the minds of these people their experiences were unquestionably real and of momentous importance, and they want others to know about them. In fact they willingly dedicate their lives to telling any who will listen.

Cases of near-entry into what could be initial judgment are not uncommon. Meeting previously deceased friends and relatives seems to be a fairly common and pleasant experience. Determination of their type of existence in the spiritual world may conceivably lie beyond the obstacle many of them seem to encounter.

Only a few people seem to pass over the barrier and return to tell about it. Consider, for instance, the case of Betty Maltz who was in a coma for forty-four days following a ruptured appendix. During this time she could still hear everything spoken in the room. Though her physical senses seemed to have diminished, her spiritual senses seemed to have been sharpened.

While in the coma she had an experience of walking uphill in a splendid setting. She had no fatigue, only a feeling of ecstasy. An angel was walking with her, but she saw only the angel's feet. They came to a gate in a large marble wall, and she was invited to go on in and join in singing the beautiful hymns that were being sung. She was given the choice, however, of returning or continuing through the gate.

Then she surprised everyone by pushing off the sheets that had already been pulled over her face.[2]

All of the above cases indicate a separation of the spirit from the body as a very fundamental occurrence at death. Listen to the Scriptures as they indicate why our present bodies of flesh and blood cannot enter the kingdom of God:

> In the same way, our earthly bodies which die and decay are different from the bodies we shall have when we come back to life again, for they will never die. The bodies we have now embarrass us for they become sick and die; but they will be full of glory when we come back to life again. Yes, they are weak, dying bodies now, but when we live again they will be full of strength. They are just human bodies at death, but when they come back to life they will be superhuman bodies. For just as there are natural, human bodies, there are also supernatural, spiritual bodies.
>
> I tell you this my brothers: an earthly body made of flesh and blood cannot get into God's kingdom. These perishable bodies of ours are not the right kind to live forever. But I am telling you this strange and wonderful secret: we shall not all die, but we shall all be given new bodies! It will all happen in a moment, in the twinkling of an eye, when the last trumpet is blown.
>
> When this happens, then at last this Scripture will come true—"Death is swallowed up in victory." O death, where then your victory? Where then your sting? For sin— the sting that causes death—will all be gone; and the law, which reveals our sins, will no longer be our judge. How we thank God for all of this! It is he who makes us victorious through Jesus Christ our Lord! (1 Cor. 15:42-44a, 50-52a, 54-57, TLB)

In these last several paragraphs Dr. Rawlings has presented the Christian viewpoint. Let us now consider other viewpoints and their validity.

Notes

1. The following chapter is adapted by permission from Dr. Maurice Rawlings' fascinating book, *Beyond Death's Door* (Nashville: Thomas Nelson, 1978), pp. 79-101. It includes personal, real life experiences shared by Dr. Rawlings' patients.

2. Mrs. Carl Maltz, *The Texas Herald,* Austin, Sept. 1977, pp. 6-7.

CHAPTER THREE

Amazing Encounters with the Spirits

So far we have eased gently into the subject of what happens at death. Many of those who had "out of the body" or death experiences met other living beings, some apparently spirit beings, some identified as departed loved ones. Many have had these encounters apart from death. What is the evidence?

Victor Ernest, a friend of mine, is a former spiritualist medium. Years ago I spent a week with him in Baker, Oregon. Victor reveals some of his experiences as a medium in his book, *I Talked with Spirits*.

Victor told me how his parents were drawn into consulting a medium after the death of a beloved child. Their experience is not at all uncommon. They believed that they were able to assuage their grief by contacting their departed child. Then Victor and his sister were drawn slowly but inexorably into the occult. Victor recounted how he had seen his mother at a seance after she had died. To see her beautiful hair, "black as a crow's wing," and parted in the middle, particularly thrilled him. He progressed from seances to actually seeing and talking with spirits. He became a medium through whom the spirits spoke as they took possession of his body.

Dave Hunt cites the story of Joanna Melville in his book.[1] She had recently converted to Mormonism, and was saddened by the lack of an extraordinary testimony that Mormons believe demonstrates the "truth" of the Book of Mormon and identifies what the Mormon Church claims as the only true church. Her story follows:

> "One Saturday afternoon, about three months after joining the Mormon Church, preoccupied with my lack of a 'testimony,' I sat alone by a window and looked out on the beautiful summer day.
>
> Suddenly my attention was attracted to a distant speck of light. Spellbound, I watched as it rapidly came closer, grew larger, and materialized into the life-size figure of my great-grandmother, with whom I had been very close.
>
> She had been dead for nearly five years, yet there she was, as solid and real, so it seemed, as she had been in her lifetime.
>
> In the distinctive voice that I remembered so well, grandmother told me she had come to answer my need for a testimony. She assured me that Joseph Smith was a true prophet of God, that the Mormon Church was the one true church with the true gospel, and that I was to remain in it and become more active.
>
> Most of all, I was to begin doing my genealogical work, because she had accepted the Mormon gospel in the spirit world."

Skeptics might insist that Joanna's intense desire to have a "testimony" produced the hallucination of her great-grandmother. It makes little sense, however, to suggest that her longing for the traditional Mormon "burning in the bosom" would cause the appearance of a long-dead relative. The brief discussion of psychic research contained in Chapter 1 of this book *[The Cult Explosion]* should be sufficient to show that apparent visual and verbal encounters with spirit beings, such as experienced by Joanna Melville, can no longer be automatically dismissed as hallucination. Science itself is providing evidential backing for the validity of such psychospiritual experiences.[2]

Similarly, Dave Hunt records two accounts involving Ginnie Mason and Latter Day Saints President Wilford Woodruff.

> In her many years as a consultant at one of the largest Mormon genealogical libraries, Ginnie Mason discovered that the "spirits of the dead" were very active in helping Mormons. Only later did she become convinced that these were actually demons impersonating the dead. As Ginnie said in a recent interview:
>
> > "I began doing genealogical research even before I was baptized. From the very beginning, it was obvious that I had 'help' from somewhere. Books would literally call to me from the shelves, and upon opening them I would find evidence of family lines for which Mormon Temple work needed to be done. I began teaching genealogy classes my first year as a Mormon, and was soon recognized as an expert.
> >
> > Once I felt the presence of a dead grandmother with me in the temple, who I had not been able to believe would accept Mormonism even in the spirit world. Yet her presence was so real that I challenged her to help me locate her mother's records, which I had been unable to find. Two hours later in the genealogical library they 'turned up' miraculously.
> >
> > I knew others to whom dead relatives visibly appeared and spoke, telling of their conversion to Mormonism in the spirit world. One friend would see missing names written on her bedspread each night as she said her prayers. A voice once gave me a name that led me to records correcting false information I had accepted concerning an ancestor.

I submitted over 200 names of ancestors and performed most of the female Temple ordinances myself. Spiritist visitations and what would otherwise have been considered occultic manifestations were accepted in the name of the Church.

These supernatural experiences always came just when my testimony of the Church and Joseph Smith was wavering. For ten years I overlooked much that I knew was false and contradictory . . . convinced that if the spirits of dead ancestors were so anxious to have their genealogical work done, then the Mormon Church must be all that Joseph Smith had claimed.

In appearances to many Mormons, the spirits testify that the Mormon Church is the only true church, that they have accepted the 'restored' gospel of Mormonism in the spirit world, and urge the living to pursue genealogical work."

The Mormon Church takes these spirit appearances very seriously, and is rather proud of them in spite of the biblical prohibition against contact with demonic spirits. As to just how important these spirit contacts are to Mormons, consider the following excerpt from a letter written to an inquiring Mormon on April 1, 1976, by Larry C. Porter, Chairman of Church History and Doctrine at Brigham Young University:

> "Your letter regarding President Wilford Woodruff's experiences with visitors from the spirit world has been passed on to myself. . . .
> The enclosures . . . bespeak my personal belief that Wilford Woodruff actually entertained spirit visitors. . . . My colleagues here . . . all concur with my conclusion.
> I know, too, that long-standing tradition in the St. George Temple affirms the presence of spiritual visitors.
> Wilford Woodruff . . . also refers to visits with Joseph Smith, Brigham Young, Heber C. Kimball,

George A. Smith, Jedediah M. Grant, and others who
were dead. . . . There is no doubt that they appeared to
him in person. His experience with George Washington was a personal visitation . . . [he was also] visited
by Benjamin Franklin with a special request that he see
that his endowments be done in addition to baptism for
the dead. . . .

May the Lord ever bless you in your research of
these important events."[3]

Dave Hunt introduces a different scenario concerning
Eileen Garrett:

One of Eileen Garrett's most startling seances took
place in the London laboratory of Harry Price (famous for
his exposure of fraudulent mediums), who had the utmost
respect for Mrs. Garrett. On this occasion she had just gone
into a trance in an attempt to contact the spirit of Sir Arthur
Conan Doyle, who had died recently, when an agitated
male voice spoke rapidly through her, claiming to be the
flight officer in charge of a British experimental airship. He
had been killed three days before, when the dirigible had
crashed in France on its maiden flight to India. The voice
proceeded to give a lengthy and highly technical explanation of why the airship had gone down. Price was recording
everything spoken and delivered a copy to the British Air
Ministry, which had begun an investigation of the crash.

The official government investigation disclosed that
Mrs. Garrett's statements in trance were not only entirely
accurate, but included top secret information about the airship's fuel system and certain structural defects which she
could not possibly have known about. Mr. W. Charlton, an
officer of the Royal Airship Works at Bedford, where the
experimental craft had been built, carefully examined the
transcript of this seance. He called it "an astounding document" because of its mass of technical detail under-
standable only to an expert with firsthand knowledge of
this particular airship, containing over 40 references show-

ing knowledge that was both highly technical and secret. This evidence forced Charlton to the conclusion that the spirit of flight Lieutenant H. Carmichael Irwin, captain of the shattered craft, who had died in the crash, "did actually communicate with those present at the seance after his physical death." As a result, Charlton became an enthusiastic convert to Spiritualism.

This was exactly what the demons wanted. By overlooking the alternate possibility that an evil spirit could be impersonating the dead officer, Mr. Charlton made a costly mistake. Those who make this mistake generally do so out of prejudice against the biblical teaching that death is the result of sin and that Christ came to die in our place. This message is rejected by the majority, while the lie of spiritism gains ever-wider acceptance. The detailed story of Eileen Garrett's alleged communication with the dead airmen has recently been published by John G. Fuller. His book, *The Airmen Who Would Not Die*, is a best-seller and was condensed in the June 1979 *Reader's Digest*, even as Dr. Raymond A. Moody's *Life After Life*, with its similar message, had been condensed 14 months earlier.[4]

Josh McDowell and Don Stewart in their book, *Understanding the Occult*, cite the following account which speaks for itself.

Recently in the San Fernando Valley of California three husky clergymen tried to hold down a 120-pound girl who was possessed with multiple demons. She successfully resisted all three of them for a number of minutes, until she was finally subdued. However, she was still able to kick one man's shins until they were bloody, demonstrating tremendous supernatural power.

In Newport Beach, California, I encountered a case of demonic possession in which five persons, including myself, were involved. In this case the girl, who was about 5 feet 4 inches tall and weighed 120 pounds, attacked a 180-

pound man and with one arm flipped him 5 or 6 feet away. It took four of us, including her husband, to hold her body to a bed while we prayed in the name of Jesus Christ for the exorcism of the demons within her.

During the course of the exorcism we found out that she was possessed because she had worshipped Satan, and because of that worship he had come with his forces and taken control of her. She was a perfect "tare in the wheat field," as Jesus said (Matthew 13:24-30). She had married a Christian, was a daughter of a Christian minister, had taught Sunday school in a Christian church, and had appeared on the surface to be perfectly consistent with Christian theology. But the whole time she was laughing inwardly at the church and at Christ. It was not until her exorcism that she was delivered and received Jesus Christ as her Lord and Savior. Today she and her husband are on the mission field serving the Lord Jesus Christ.

I have a psychologist friend who was present with me at an exorcism in Newport Beach, California. Before we entered the room he said, "I want you to know I do not believe in demonic possession. This girl is mentally disturbed."

I said, "That may well be. We'll find out very soon."

As we went into the room and closed the door, the girl's supernatural strength was soon revealed. Suddenly from her body a totally foreign voice said quietly, with a smirk on the face (she was unconscious—the psychologist testified to that), "We will outlast you."

The psychologist looked at me and said, "What was that?"

"That is what you don't believe in," I said.

We spent about 3½ hours exorcising what the psychologist didn't believe in!

At the end of the exorcism he was not only a devout believer in the personality of the devil, but in demonic possession and biblical exorcism as well. He now knows that there are other-dimensional beings capable of penetrating this dimension and of controlling human beings![5]

McDowell and Stewart present yet another remarkable story by Allen Spraggett.

> Believe in ghosts? If not, how would you explain this true story?
>
> One winter night, in northern Ontario, Canada, during the early days of World War Two, a middle-aged widow awakened from a troubled sleep to see her younger brother standing at the foot of her bed.
>
> The eerie thing was that the woman knew her brother was in England serving with the Royal Canadian Air Force.
>
> Yet she saw him clearly, dressed in his pilot's flying suit, his face deathly pale and solemn beyond description. The effect was horrific. The woman screamed. Abruptly the strange phantasm vanished.
>
> When the woman's three teen-aged children rushed into the room, they found her sobbing, "He's dead, I know he's dead."
>
> The premonition proved to be correct. Sometime later, word came that the brother's Spitfire had been shot down over the English Channel on the same day—possibly at the same hour—that the woman saw the spectral figure in her room.
>
> This story was told to me by one of those intimately involved—the woman's son, who was a member of a church of which I was pastor.[6]

In her fascinating book, *The Beautiful Side of Evil,* Johanna Michaelsen gives more evidence of the reality of the spirit world.

> As much as I liked our group I never felt really comfortable with them, and I turned to the being in the theater for true companionship. I could sense his presence even

though there had not yet been any physical manifestation. I called him "Professor Koch" after the founder of Playmakers.

Then, late one night, the summons came. I was awakened by dark figures standing by my bed, whispering, murmuring, beckoning me to the theater. I rose, dressed quietly so as not to awaken Paula, my roommate, and ran through the arboretum and across the silent campus to the theater. I had managed to obtain my own key to Playmakers within weeks of arriving at Chapel Hill. I slipped into the dark hall, pulled the doors shut behind me, then ran up the few steps to the light switch. Soft lights filled the theater. I sat on the steps by the stage and waited, knowing I had been summoned, but still not certain why. Minutes passed, then I heard the inner swinging panels at the front entrance begin hitting against the locked doors. The sound stopped as abruptly as it had begun.

Then a two-dimensional, hazy figure of a man with thick grey hair and dressed in dark striped pants and a white shirt with an odd little tie appeared at the door. He paused and looked at me for a moment—then drifted towards me. He stopped halfway down the aisle, sat in a seat, and looked at me again. I said nothing. There was no need. I sensed he knew all I was thinking, all the expectation tinged with fear I was experiencing. A melody filled the theater—urgent, beautiful, a song of unrestrained longing and loneliness. The melody, in minor key like an old Hebrew desert song, rose and fell and spoke to me of the serenity of death. Then I realized my voice had become the instrument for that melody, that it was coming through my mouth, that it had become my own. When the song had run its course I stood, opened my eyes and looked again at Professor Koch. He smiled at me, then faded quietly from my sight. The gift of the song had been given. It was time to leave.[7]

Dr. Kurt Koch (not the professor mentioned above), a man who has counseled over 20,000 people, 10,000 or more of them involved in the occult, tells us of the case of Jochen.

Jochen's life revolved around drinking and girls. He used to drink on average about thirty pints of beer a day. He was seldom sober and if ever he could not get enough to drink, he used to roam around like a wounded animal. He had a temper as well, and at the slightest provocation he would lash out and smash anything within striking distance. On top of this he rejected completely both the idea of God and of the devil. To him it was all nonsense.

One day at the local public house a group was talking about the possibility of making a pact with the devil, and they were exchanging stories of this nature. Many of them laughed off the idea, Jochen being one of them. He went on to say that he was not afraid of meeting the devil, and so when someone challenged him, he agreed to attempt such a meeting for a bet of about £2 [2 pounds]. Thus one Friday night Jochen found himself at some crossroads outside the village. He drew a circle on the ground and repeated a charm that he had been told would summon Lucifer, and waited for the devil to appear. Nothing happened, and so he returned in triumph to receive his reward.

But his joy was short-lived. That night when he finally went to bed he suddenly saw a horrible face on the wall opposite his bed, and, frozen with fear, he watched as the face slowly advanced until it was less than a foot from his own face. He screamed, and his sister and her husband rushed to his door to see what the matter was. But when they reached the door they found that they could not enter. Something prevented them. The event recurred again and again, and on each occasion the others found it impossible to enter the room. Finally the experience became too much for Jochen and he went to consult his doctor. He was given a thorough examination but the doctor could discover nothing wrong with him. When asked if it could be the result of his drinking the doctors also replied to the negative. Jochen went on to describe in detail the face that had appeared to him, and also the background to the experience. The doctor was thoughtful, and then warned Jochen that if he really wanted to be healed he would have to do a right-about-turn and hand his life over to Christ. Unlike many of his profession, the doctor was a believing Christian and seriously believed in the power of Satan to rule people's lives through fear. Jochen accepted his advice and he began to seek God in earnest. In the end he experienced a complete deliverance not only from the apparitions but also from his addiction to alcohol and women. His life was entirely changed through his contact with the living Christ. Seventeen years have now passed by since that time, and Jochen is now an active worker in his church, having been elected to his own church council. The power of Christ has indeed delivered him from the power of darkness. He is now able to praise God with the same words as those of the early Christians, "Giving thanks to the Father who has qualified us to share in the inheritance of the saints in light. He has delivered us from the dominion of darkness and transferred us to the kingdom of his beloved Son" (Col. 1:12-13).[8]

Dr. Koch also relates the exploits of Uri Geller in another of his books. Scientists at the Stanford Research Institute had tested Geller under rigid conditions and were unable to detect any evidence of fraud. Uri Geller had said that he was the ambassador of advanced intelligences from the planet Hoova.

This young Israeli has roused great interest and controversy throughout the world by his experiments. On every continent there has been a conflict of views, ranging from believing acceptance to extreme rejection.
What is it all about? When Uri appears on the television or demonstrates his inexplicable abilities in a public hall, forks and spoons are bent. Old clocks which have not

worked for years begin to tick again.

Let us consider one well-documented example. On Sunday, January 9, 1975 a German television station broadcasted a program of entertainment.

During this show Uri Geller appeared, resting his finger on a fork. Without becoming hot, the fork slowly bent. Members of the audience examined the fork. It had become soft like plastic. Uri was asked what power it was that caused this. "Power from outside," he replied.

Uri also made the remarkable statement, "I should not be surprised if during this program, thousands of families find that their cutlery is bent."

That is exactly what happened. Professor Bender, who had been invited to take part in this show as an expert, has reported that after it nineteen thousand telephone calls were received. The *Bildzeitung* (a popular daily paper) received fourteen hundred and fifty letters from "victims." Professor Bender received nine hundred letters from Germany and three hundred from Switzerland.

One convincing example was mentioned in the course of the program. A Mrs. S. had had pieces of cutlery bent during and following Uri Geller's show. She called in her neighbor, and finally the police. Two officers examined the cutlery in her house. A spoon even bent in the presence of one of them. Cutlery in the open drawer kept bending, although no one went near it. There was no question of a trick or a secret source of power. One of the policemen said that he was ready to testify to the incident on oath.

After the people concerned had given their accounts of what happened, the panel were asked to give their opinions. The panel consisted of Professor Bender, a lawyer, and a journalist.

The lawyer said that in such a case he would have called in Professor Bender as an expert.

The journalist, 100 percent rationalist, threw doubt on the whole story.

Professor Bender answered this newsman, so convinced by his own skepticism, by citing an apt quotation from Freud, "He who regards himself as a skeptic should be honest enough to begin by doubting his own skepticism." In my opinion, Professor Bender should have described the journalist's attitude as the arrogance of ignorance.

I believe the most important thing in the program was Professor Bender's verdict. He spoke of the possibility of psychokinesis. This expression was coined by Professor Rhine of Duke University, USA. Other parapsychologists speak of telekinesis. Psychokinesis is a word which implies an explanation. Those who hold this view are of the opinion that these inexplicable phenomena are evidence of power in the psyche. This theory is in contradiction to other hypotheses according to which the mind can have a direct influence upon matter.

Those who hold either view agree that these powers come from the person himself, that it is an immanent rather than a transcendent factor which is responsible. The power is something within man, not something superhuman.

In common with thousands of mediums, Uri Geller has a different view. They attribute their gifts to power from outside. The animist and the spiritist explanations conflict on this point.

As far as Christian counseling is concerned, it does not matter which view is held. The counselor is concerned with the effect and the possibility of healing.

This is not all that must be said about the Uri Geller question. Since my first book on the occult appeared in 1952, I have counseled about twenty thousand people in conversations and by mail. More than ten thousand of these concerned occult experiences which had had negative effects. This large number of spontaneous cases enable one to form a truer overall impression than can be gained from experiments.

How does one explain the fact that during Uri Geller's

show thousands of viewers experienced similar effects? From one point of view, the problem is simpler than the parapsychologists think. There are hundreds of thousands of psychic people who are quite ignorant of the fact that they are psychic. Uri is a strong medium. Strong psychic powers like these appear when both sets of parents and grandparents have been psychic and have passed their psychic powers in dominance to their son and grandson, in this case Uri. There are also other ways in which such psychic powers can arise. Double or fourfold hereditary mediumship is extremely strong. It enables the medium to make contact with other people present who are psychic, or even with psychic people who are a great distance away.

All the people who found that their cutlery was bent during the Uri Geller show are either unconsciously or consciously psychic. Uri cannot bend a fork at distance of 500 kilometers (311 miles) unless there is in that place a psychic person whose mediumistic powers he can use. . . .[9]

Mike Warnke tells of one of a number of experiences he had in encounters with the spirit world in his book:

A night or two later, about midnight, I was sitting on the couch with a fat book on formulas and incantations when—*flash!*—this chick materialized in the middle of my living room. I knew my door was bolted! My book turned somersaults to the floor, and I sat there frozen as solid as ice, my jaw almost touching the floor. I *felt* like a block of ice.

"I have a message for you. Char says it's on for Saturday afternoon."

I did not recognize the chick, except that I knew she was for real. I was not high; I was not hallucinating or flashing back. I fervently wished I was.

I had read about astral travel and Eckankar and knew that they were part of the occult bag, but I had written it off as 99 percent wishful thinking and one percent supernatural phenomena. Now the living proof was standing in the middle of my living room. What in hell had I gotten into?

"Well?" the chick said.

"Yeah, yeah. Okay. I got the message," I replied.

She seemed satisfied. Then, zap!—she was gone, just like that. The chills returned to my scalp and trickled down my spine. I got up and poured myself half a glass of Scotch. As I started to gulp some down, I tasted blood mixed with it, and the glass fell to the floor. I ran to the bathroom, my hand over my mouth. A glance in the mirror revealed my nose was bleeding. An involuntary moan escaped me that frightened me as much as anything that had gone before.[10]

In *The Challenging Counterfeit,* Raphael Gasson relates his experience as a medium:

During this sort of seance the operating spirits make use of a substance which is drawn from the medium's own body. This substance is a semi-luminous thick vapor which oozes from the medium's mouth, ears, nose, eyes, or from the stomach and is dimly visible in the gloom. This mist which gradually becomes solid, as it eventually makes contact with the natural surroundings of the seance room, is called *ectoplasm* and is the basis of physical phenomena.

Ectoplasm being sensitive to light, necessitates the seance being conducted in darkness. Experiments have been made to produce ectoplasm in light with, however, only limited success. Nevertheless, photographs in darkness have been taken with special cameras and they present a very strange and repulsive sight, with the ectoplasm hanging down like icicles from the mouth, nose, etc., of the medium. When touched (only permissible by the controlling guide) it will move back into the body and if suddenly seized the medium will scream out or be caused to be violently sick. Such sudden graspings of ectoplasm have very often caused great bodily harm to the medium and could even result in loss of life. The reason for this being so dangerous is that the ectoplasm becomes solid through contact with the air and before it is able to enter back into the medium's body in the normal way, it has to dematerialize to its original state. If touched suddenly, without warning or permission, or unexpectedly contacted with light, the solid ectoplasmic mass will rush straight back to the body of the medium before having a chance to dissolve to its natural state. I have known of many mediums who have been crippled or blinded for life owing to the sudden impact of the solid ectoplasm which springs back with as much force as if it were connected to the medium by an excessively strong piece of elastic. I myself was blinded for nearly 24 hours after such an incident occurred. The force of the ectoplasm against the stomach caused a scar from side to side, which took many days to disappear.[11]

An Associated Press story claims the ghost of Abraham Lincoln has been seen in the White House:

> The elusive ghost of President Lincoln has another White House believer. "We've really seen it," reports Maureen Reagan. The president's daughter and her husband, Dennis Revell, often sleep in the Lincoln bedroom and an aura—sometimes red, sometimes orange— appears in the wee hours, reports *Newsweek* magazine. Nancy Reagan refuses to be spooked but reports family dog Rex often barks at the bedroom door but refuses to go in. Others who reportedly have seen the ghost: Winston Churchill and Princess Juliana of the Netherlands.

Literally thousands of episodes could be cited similar to these. Some contacts with the spirit world have been voluntary, some have been involuntary. The spirit world, and its spirits have been invoked, experienced, and approached via various media: spiritualism, table tipping, Ouija boards, hypnosis, fortune telling, phrenology, numerology, levitation, clairvoyance, colorology, water dowsing, pendulum healing, psychokinesis, automatic writing, clairaudience, materializations, voodoo, palmistry, fetishes, meditation, white and black magic, witchcraft, Satan worship, I Ching, tarot cards, telepathy, ESP, talismans, seances, astrology, reincarnation, psychic healing, astral-projection, thought transfer, Eastern religions, mind control, horoscopes, magic, acupuncture, and many others.

The next two chapters are particularly important, as we look at the evidence for the existence of spirits in a dimension we call the spirit world. Johanna Michaelsen takes us with her into that world.

Notes

1. Dave Hunt, *The Cult Explosion* (Irvine, CA: Harvest House, 1980).

2. Ibid., pp. 143-44.

3. Ibid., pp. 146-48.

4. Ibid., pp. 160-61.

5. Dr. Walter Martin, *Exorcism: Fact or Fable* (Santa Ana, CA: Vision House Publishers, 1975), pp. 17, 18, 21., quoted in Josh McDowell and Don Stewart, *Understanding the Occult*, pp. 52-53.

6. Allen Spragget, *The Unexplained* (New York: Signet Mystic Books, 1967), p. 13, quoted in McDowell and Stewart, *Understanding the Occult.*

7. Johanna Michaelsen, *The Beautiful Side of Evil* (Irvine, CA: Harvest House, 1982), pp. 44-45.

8. Dr. Kurt Koch, *Between Christ and Satan* (Grand Rapids: Kregel, 1972), pp. 169-71.

9. Dr. Kurt Koch, *Occult ABC* (Grand Rapids: Kregel, 1981), pp. 250-53.

10. Mike Warnke, *et al., The Satan Seller* (South Plainfield: Bridge, 1972), pp. 87-88.

11. Raphael Gasson, *The Challenging Counterfeit* (South Plainfield: Bridge, 1966), pp. 129-30.

CHAPTER FOUR

The Beautiful Side of Evil[1]

NOTE: Names marked with an asterisk (*) in this chapter are fictitious.

We were lost. The tension was almost unbearable as we searched through the dark streets of Mexico City. Using the light of a passing car, I peered at my watch. Almost eight o'clock. It was no use. We were too late to witness any of the operations scheduled for that night.

I felt a flash of anger as Tom* stopped the car again to analyze his directions. It probably didn't matter that much to him or Norah,* his secretary, whether we arrived at Pachita's on time. Both had been there before to see her work. In fact, Tom had an operation in which he claimed a rusty hunting knife had been plunged into his kneecap to repair an old football injury. No anesthesia or sophisticated antiseptic had been used. His knee was now fully healed.

I knew I could come again another time to see the medium work. But my sister, Kim, was leaving Mexico the next day. This was my last chance to make her understand.

"Well, there is nothing more I can do now," I thought. "It's in God's hand." I took a deep breath and relaxed my muscles.

"This is it! We're here!" Tom exclaimed as he slammed on the brakes. He jerked the car into a parking space in front of an old market. As I stepped out of the car, the pungent odor of rotting garbage in the gutter stung my nostrils. Even a lifetime in Mexico had not accustomed me to that smell.

We made our way across the dark street to a grimy white metal gate set into a long wall. The night was clear and still. As we stood there the sky suddenly filled with a host of unseen beings who swirled and spun around us with a sound like wind gusting through tall trees. My heart pounded in my throat. I was afraid. The others seemed oblivious to the motion all around them. I said nothing.

The metal gate swung open even as Tom knocked. We stepped into a narrow courtyard crowded with people, some obviously wealthy, others clothed in rags. But all were drawn together by a common bond—suffering which reached out into the unknown for the ray of hope and healing denied them by conventional medicine.

A loud angry voice broke through the hushed murmurings of the crowd. It belonged to a distinguished looking man with a mustache and greying hair. He was dressed in black slacks and a white shirt with sleeves rolled up to his elbows. Obviously he held a position of authority. I backed out of the way into a corner by the gate as he waved a fist at Tom.

"There you are!" he shouted angrily. "Come here. I want to talk to you!" His English was excellent, though heavily accented. "Do you know what happened here today? I will tell you. One of your Mind Control people showed up with motion picture cameras and *demanded* he be allowed to photograph Pachita during the operations. He said you sent him and refused to go when I told him this is not a circus act for curiosity seekers. He stuck a pin into

Pachita to see whether she was in a trance and then tried to strike me when I ordered him out."

"Dr. Carlos,* calm down!" Tom exclaimed. "I don't know anything about this. I didn't send him."

"I don't know whether you did or not. But I will tell you this—if you can't control your people and instill in them respect for the work that is done here, then not any of you will be welcome any longer in this place!" Dr. Carlos turned and disappeared into the crowd. Tom just shook his head and shrugged. After a few moments he followed in the direction the doctor had taken.

"Who was that?" I asked Norah, who had come up beside me.

"That," she said, "was Dr. Carlos. He's a surgeon—has his own practice in the area. He's been working as one of Pachita's main assistants for the last few months and is very protective of her. Come in. I'll take you in to meet her."

We made our way through the crowd and into a house, past a sink filled with dirty dishes, and then past a foul-smelling bathroom sheltered only by a flimsy plastic curtain. We were about to enter through a doorway when I heard a rustling sound above my head on the lintel. I looked straight up into a pair of beady little eyes that glinted at me over the top of a nasty looking beak.

"Oh, don't worry about *her*," Norah said softly. "That's Ursula, Pachita's pet falcon."

"How nice," I murmured to Ursula, in what I hoped was an ingratiating fashion.

We stepped into the darkness of a small waiting room. It was empty except for an old metal desk. Another plastic curtain shielded the entrance to the operating room. Norah held it aside for me.

Immediately I was overwhelmed by the smell in the room; dead musty roses and raw alcohol. The electric tingling I had felt after crossing the threshold of Pachita's home now intensified, as though this room was the source of the current. The Lord's Prayer, which I had quietly repeated since we had arrived, now screamed in my head. Unable to proceed, I stood in the doorway and looked around. A single bulb which dangled from the ceiling lit the small room. Eight or ten people, including Dr. Carlos, stood about talking quietly.

Against the bare cement wall on my right hung a medicine cabinet. Past it a rickety door opened onto the courtyard. To my left sat a small wooden table cluttered with rolls of cotton and bottles of alcohol. The focal point, however, was a large, tiered altar which filled the left hand corner of the room. Dozens of jars and vases with rotten roses covered it.

White candles surrounded a picture of Christ on the cross and a large wooden crucifix. Next to the crucifix, in the center of the altar, stood a bronze statue of Cuauhtemoc, the Aztec prince who had defiantly borne torture and death at the hands of Spanish conquistadores. At its feet lay a pair of surgical scissors and a rusty hunting knife.

My eyes turned to the right side of the room. There, on a cot, sat an old woman. A worn blanket was wrapped about her legs. She was smoking a cigarette as she talked to Tom, who sat before her. I watched as her stubby hands made frequent though tired gestures to emphasize a word or phrase. They moved often through her short grey-black hair, then over her face, which she now rubbed as though exhausted.

I stepped forward and looked closer, at first unable to

comprehend what I saw on her hands. They were covered to the wrist with dry, crusted blood.

Norah and Kim went forward to meet the old woman. "Where is Johanna?" Tom asked, as he looked around. "Come on," he urged me. "Pachita, this is Johanna, one of my best students."

I approached her and took her extended hand in my own as I looked down into a tired, stern-looking right eye. The left one was half-closed, perhaps from a mild stroke. Suddenly I felt naked as her eye focused on me. Her glare was as sharp and piercing as that of the falcon on her lintel. In a gruff voice she acknowledged my presence; then her eye turned again to Tom and I stepped back to the center of the room.

I turned to look again at the altar. Waves of soft light now seemed to be coming from the image of the warrior and the crucifix beside it. "Lord God," I whispered, "thank you for this place. After all the years of terror you have now brought me into a temple of light. Let me serve you here, Lord."

My prayer was interrupted by the voice of a sleek young man. "Tell me, what are you feeling," he asked. With an effort I looked away from the glowing altar.

"I'm not sure," I answered softly. "I feel I'm in the presence of my God."

The young man nodded. "Then you must touch the statue of Cuauhtemoc!" he exclaimed. "Go, place your fingers on the statue three times!" There was a sense of urgency in his tone. "Go!"

I hesitated, afraid for a moment of the still shining statue.

"Our Father, who art in heaven . . ." I reached out my

hand and with my fingertips lightly touched the image of the ancient Aztec warrior who was now Pachita's spirit guide, the one by whom the alleged miracles were performed. After the third touch a light shock ran through my fingers. My breath drew in sharply. I felt strangely light and detached. Even the Lord's Prayer, which had been repeating itself in my head, grew still and silent. A deep velvet peace enveloped me like a mantle on the shoulders of a priest.

The young man took me by the hand and led me to the old woman on the cot. "Pachita, you must talk with this girl!" The tired face turned to me and focused on my eyes, staring through me with frightening intensity. No one spoke a word for many seconds. Then a blood covered hand reached for one of mine and pulled me closer.

"You're very sensitive, very sensitive, aren't you?" she said softly. "Are you a medium?"

Her words startled me, and I hesitated.

"Well," she insisted, "are you a medium?"

"I . . . I'm not sure, Pachita," I answered. "Sometimes I think so."

"Well, my little one, you finish the studies in Mind Control you have begun with Tom and then return."

Then to herself she added, "We'll see. We'll see."

Notes

1. Johanna Michaelsen, a brilliant and attractive young woman, worked as an assistant to a very famous Mexican psychic healer. Chapters Four and Five of this book document her personal experiences with the spirit realm. The material in this chapter is adapted from her book *The Beautiful Side of Evil,* pp. 9-14.

CHAPTER FIVE

Assisting a Psychic Healer— Incredible Operations with a Rusty Knife![1]

NOTE: Names marked with an asterisk (*) in this chapter are fictitious.

The six days following my first meeting with Pachita I spent in deep mental and spiritual preparation. I sensed I was on the brink of my life's work and ultimate fulfillment in my search for God. I knew the years of fear were over; my spirit guides, Jesus and Mamacita, were with me, teaching me to overcome the lower spiritual entities. Now during the many hours I spent in meditation, waves of light and peace would flow over me and push away the darkness.

On the morning of the seventh day, 27 July 1971, I returned to see Pachita. Father Humberto and Peggie* asked to go with me. Padre Humberto, a Catholic priest and movie actor, had broken his leg in a car accident and was living at the Mind Control house in Cuernavaca while he recovered. I don't think he had yet met Pachita. He hoped Hermanito Cuauhtemoc (that is, "Little Brother," as the spirit who worked through Pachita was affectionately called) would heal his leg so he could return to his work with lepers in a colony near Tepoztlan.

51

Peggie, who was also living at the Mind Control house, had an operation at Pachita's about five weeks before. Hermanito had begun plugging the holes in her skull, which was decalcifying. He had also removed an inoperable brain tumor. The red scar was clearly visible on the back of her head when she pulled her hair apart to show me.

My father decided to join us that day. He was profoundly skeptical of the things he had heard about Pachita, but was wearing his "I'm-determined-to-be-open-minded-about-this" look. So I was hopeful he would eventually accept her.

We arrived at Pachita's around 11:30 A.M. People waiting to see Hermanito already crowded the courtyard. Many had been there since before dawn. Several women were organizing the crowd in preparation for Hermanito's arrival. First, she would see married women and their children, then the men, and last the unmarried women. Entrance coupons were sold for ten pesos each (about eighty American cents at the time). Young children and the very poor were not charged. Later I learned that Pachita's assistants recently devised this fee to help support her, since her failing health no longer allowed her to go out on the streets selling trinkets and lottery tickets. She herself had never charged for the healings.

Each person in line was instructed to have a fresh raw egg to present to Hermanito for the spiritual *limpia* ("cleansing"), which was performed on everyone during the morning consultation sessions. I had forgotten our eggs so I hurried out with several others to purchase them at the market across the street. I handed my father, Peggie, and Padre Humberto their eggs. Then I took my place in line to wait.

When my turn finally came, I entered the dark little outer room still guarded by the falcon and waited behind the plastic curtain with one of the assistants who monitored the flow of people into the altar room. I could feel powerful vibrations emanating from that room and started to pull the curtain aside to see what was happening, but an assistant quickly stopped me.

"No!" she whispered. "Keep it shut until the patient in there leaves! The curtain is here to keep any 'evil airs' that person may have brought with him from attacking you."

"I see," I mumbled apologetically.

"Is this your first consultation with Hermanito?" she said softly. I nodded.

"Then be sure you remember not to address him as 'Pachita.' It is her body you will see, but she is not in it."

I nodded again. Tom had explained that to me before. Pachita was always addressed in the masculine and as "Hermanito" when the spirit was present.

Minutes later the woman pulled aside the plastic curtain for me and I stepped in. Pachita was standing near the altar. She was wearing a short sleeved cotton dress covered by a dirty yellow satin garment that was tied in a knot at the shoulder. It was decorated with sparkles glued on in geometric designs and was worn by Pachita whenever Hermanito Cuauhtemoc was holding consultation sessions or operations. Pachita's eyes were tightly shut, one of the signs that Pachita's spirit was no longer there. Yet she seemed to see clearly, for later I watched her deftly thread a needle—with her eyes closed.

Three other assistants stood in the room—an old Mexican woman who stood to Pachita's right and held a plastic bottle filled with a sweet smelling balsam; a young man, an engineer and Yaqui Indian, who I later came to know as "Chalio," acted as secretary writing down any prescriptions or medications prescribed; a third person stood by the exit door to usher people out when their time with Hermanito ended.

I stood before Hermanito, still holding the egg in my hand. He placed both hands on my shoulders and, in a voice much deeper and gruffer than Pachita's own, commanded, *"A trabajar, m'hijita"* ("To work, my little daughter"). A strange shock ran through my body as his hands touched me.

"How do I begin, Hermanito?" I asked. He took the egg and began rubbing it briskly over my head and shoulders. Then he tossed the egg at the bucket that stood near him. It splattered on the floor. Hermanito nodded towards Memo, Pachita's oldest son, who was sitting on the cot.

"The son of my flesh will give you instructions." (Hermanito always spoke of Pachita in the third person calling her "mi carne" ["my flesh"].) He cupped his right hand towards the woman standing by him who filled it with the sweet smelling balsam. All who came before him were anointed with it. He rubbed it between his palms, then placed both hands firmly upon my head as he murmured something I could not understand. Then he brushed his hands down my front and back as though whisking lint off my clothing. Again his hands grasped my shoulders and the sightless eyes peered into my own. *"A trabajar!"*

Memo stepped outside with me as I left.

"What did Hermanito mean, Memo?" I asked him. Memo looked at me oddly.

"Hermanito said that you will work as a full trance medium—that you will one day heal as my mother does. You are to begin preparing immediately. Come back this Monday. Hermanito himself will tell you what you must do."

Padre Humberto had also been told to return on Monday. Hermanito had promised to give him a cure for leprosy. As for my father, his reception was cool. Hermanito seemed to have X-ray vision and could diagnose a person's exact disease or discomfort without having been given a clue. It was odd then that he should have asked my father what was the matter. Papa was not at all well at the time, but to test Hermanito had answered, "Oh, nothing. I'm fine."

"Why in that case," Hermanito said, with excessive politeness, "this house is at your service when required."

Several weeks later Padre Humberto and I waited in Pachita's living room for hours. We had been told to be there at noon. It was now six o'clock in the evening and Pachita was still not there. A small television set, a gift from a grateful American patient, had been blaring soap operas all afternoon. Pachita's daughter wanted to hear it from her bedroom. I spent the time recording in my diary the events of the last several weeks and feeding bits of meat to Ursula. It was beginning to get dark and thunderclouds were becoming thick and grey. "It's going to be pouring on the way home," I thought dismally as I walked back to the living room. The mountain pass between Mexico City and Cuernavaca could be treacherous anytime, but especially so in the rain.

At 6:15 P.M. Memo and Pachita arrived. Memo cast a dark look at me as he walked by. He nodded curtly but said nothing. Pachita went into the kitchen to have supper. As always, a group of people had gathered to see Hermanito.

One was a rather large girl who had a bandage wrapped around her neck. Her mother told me the girl had been the victim of a curse. She had become very ill about a year ago, but none of the many doctors she had seen had been able to give a diagnosis. Finally a friend led the girl and mother to Pachita. A week ago Hermanito had operated on her by materializing and removing a very large tarantula from her throat.

After her supper Pachita entered the altar room. We were told Hermanito would give only *consultas* (consultations) that night. There would be no operations.

"Oh, please, Hermanito told me last week he would operate on me tonight," a woman exclaimed. "My cataract operation at the hospital is scheduled in four days. Please let Hermanito operate on me tonight!"

"Well," said Pachita, shrugging her shoulders, "it is up to Hermanito. We will ask him during the *consultas* and see what he says."

Pachita lumbered across the courtyard and into the altar room with three of her associates. One by one the people who needed to see Hermanito filed in. I was about to go in myself when Pachita came out. She patted Rita* on the shoulder. "Prepare yourself. Hermanito will operate tonight after all."

Several minutes later Amado, a man who had been with Pachita for over eleven years, asked Rita to enter the altar room. "Only three other people will be allowed to enter to witness the operation," he announced. Rita's husband Alex* rushed immediately to her side. Padre Humberto went in as did another man who had been there several times before. Pachita looked at me as she walked by.

"You too, little daughter—Come along."

It began to rain. The sound was amplified as the large drops pelted the tin roof of the altar room. Water began to seep under the door and onto the coarse cement floor. Everything seemed drained of color, reflecting rather the flat grey of the thunderclouds above us. A candle was lit and placed upon the altar. The single naked light bulb was switched off. Pachita put on Hermanito's satin robe and sat on the straight-back wooden chair in front of the altar. She told us to gather around her and pray. The scrawny woman stood at Pachita's side holding the ever present bottle of protective holy balsam. She poured some into Pachita's hands and began a low chanting prayer. She muttered almost inaudibly as Pachita rubbed the balsam over her hands, into her hair, and down the front of her body. She closed her eyes, placed her hands straight and stiff on her spread knees, and began taking deep breaths. The atmosphere in the room seemed to thicken as a powerful unseen presence descended upon Pachita. Suddenly her body quivered violently. Her right hand raised in a sharp straight-armed salute and a deeper, stronger voice than hers announced *"Estoy con ustedes, hermanos queridos"* ("I am with you, beloved brothers"). Pachita had vacated the shell of her body to make way for Hermanito.

Hermanito arose and directed Rita to sit in the chair. Rita, obviously nervous, did so.

"Keep praying, my little ones," Hermanito said to us. "Only with God's help will we be able to heal this woman's eye." Chalio stood behind Rita on Hermanito's left side. He had cut large strips of cotton from the roll Alex had brought. Smaller patches were placed in a small bowl and alcohol was poured over them—Hermanito's one concession to physical antiseptics. Alex had been standing beside by his wife, but now he turned away and sat on the cot with his head in his hands. He had helped in a number of operations in the past but he chose to pray during this one. Hermanito called me to his side.

"Come, little daughter, you will help me." He instructed me to hold a large block of cotton under Rita's chin.

"Rita," Hermanito said, "I want you to sit very still now. Keep your eyes open and look up at the ceiling. Do you understand me, little one?"

"Is it going to hurt me, Hermanito?" she asked, her voice quivering as she spoke.

"No, little one, you are even now being anesthetized," Hermanito said reassuringly. He took the new bottle of alcohol I was holding, opened it, and poured it directly in her eye. I gasped, expecting the woman to cry out, but she just sat there. Then Hermanito sprinkled some of the balsam on the eye.

"Very well, little one, now hand me the cotton you have there." As I handed him the smaller cotton strips, he formed a square leaving the eye exposed in the center. Then he asked Amado for the scissors and the old knife that lay on the altar. Amado quickly wiped each with a square of cotton soaked in balsam and handed the scissors to him. Hermanito took the scissors and raised them in a salute toward the altar as he began a prayer in Nahuatl, the ancient Aztec language. His first words were audible, then diminished to a whisper. As he prayed, I saw that the area where we stood, and especially around Rita's head, became much brighter than the rest of the room, as though a soft spotlight were shining down on us. I could see clearly. I would witness this phenomenon at each of the several hundred operations in which I assisted in the coming months.

"Pray to God, little ones!" Hermanito pushed one point of the scissors into Rita's eye and began to cut. A pale reddish-white liquid trickled into a piece of cotton that fell off her face and onto her chest. I caught it and replaced it.

"Do you feel pain, little one?" he asked her.

"No, Hermanito," Rita answered. Her head began to turn as she spoke.

"Keep your eyes open—*open*," said Hermanito. He took the knife from Amado, raised it in a salute, and began peeling off a thin opaque scum from the center of the eye. The film broke. He placed the first piece on the cotton I held out. Then he gently lifted off the second part of the tissue and handed it to me. Again he poured alcohol into the eye. Then placed a clean pad of cotton over it.

"We have finished, dear brother," he said to Chalio. "You may bandage the eye now." The entire procedure had taken about fifteen minutes. Then he instructed two men to wrap Rita in a sheet and carry her across the courtyard to rest in the house. "Keep her lying down for one hour— head back. Then give her some red herb tea to drink. You'll find it in the kitchen." Alex was instructed to keep her quiet for three days, after which the bandage could be removed. A week later I learned that Rita's operation at the hospital had been cancelled. The doctors were astonished at the total disappearance of the cataract.

Chalio handed Hermanito a large piece of cotton soaked in balsam with which to cleanse his hands. Hermanito sat down on the chair—legs spread, hands on his knees. Padre Humberto approached him. I saw Hermanito take his hand and pat it warmly as he smiled. I had moved out of the way to the back of the room and couldn't hear what was said. Padre Humberto later told me Hermanito had instructed him to continue his mission to the lepers and gave him a recipe that would cure leprosy and certain forms of cancer. Then Padre turned to me and called me to them. Hermanito took my hand.

"This is the girl who will help you with your lepers. She is ready now to work as a full medium. In three weeks another spirit whom I have sent and even now is with her will begin to work through her." (I thought of Mamacita.) Hermanito then told us that for three weeks, either on a Thursday or on a Monday, Padre and I were to meet either at two o'clock in the afternoon or at eight o'clock in the evening.

"You are both to pray. You, my little daughter, watch me closely. You're to sit in a straight chair with your hands in your lap, thus, even as you saw my flesh earlier this evening. Relax and breathe deeply. Go down to level as you have learned. Then do this with your hands." (Here he showed a special circular movement of the hands.) "Then place your hands again on your lap and wait. Padre, when you see her hands begin to shake and rise from her lap, you are to place your hands over hers and say 'I give you the light of the Lord. May the light of the Lord be with you.' Pray continually that no evil overtake her. May the Lord go with you, little ones."

Padre Humberto and I met that Thursday as Hermanito had ordained.

"Almighty God," I prayed before we began, "You know I love You more than anything else and want to serve You. Help me now become an instrument of Your hand. I give myself to You, O Lord. Guide us now in this work. Help us discern between what is of You and what is false and of our imagination. Protect us from any evil being who would hinder this work that You have set before me. Let your perfect will be done, Holy God." I performed the motion with my hands, then breathed deeply and relaxed.

Almost immediately I saw myself encircled by a golden glow. My hands began to feel very light and detached from the rest of my body and began to rise. From far away I heard Padre's voice: "I give you the light of the Lord. May the light of the Lord be with you." A large number of people who stood in a circle surrounded me. Now the golden glow had expanded to touch these shadowy unknown figures. Pachita's spirit stood before me; Cuauhtemoc was just behind her; Mamacita, my Indian counselor, stood by Pachita. Then I saw Jesus, my counselor, translucent, shimmering with a glow brighter than all the rest. My spirit stood and I approached him with my hands outstretched. Again a flame of purification was in his hand. He poured the flames into my hands. They burned and yet were cold, and I was filled with joy and peace. It seemed that the Lord had heard my prayers and had sanctified my hands for his use.

During our session the second week the feeling was quite different. I saw two giant golden doors that slowly swung open—then shut again before I could pass through them. The figures that had surrounded me the week before stood on the other side beside a large book that lay open on an invisible stand. I knew that the mysteries of life were contained within its pages. Suddenly the doors swung open and did not shut. I walked through and stood before the book. A towering figure, like an angel in its flowing robes, stood behind it. He placed it in my hands, but I knew the

time had not yet come to read from it. I knew that many
sorrows and trials must be faced and overcome before I
would be worthy to read and understand it.

"Oh, God," my spirit prayed, "grant me the courage,
faith, and perseverance to obey Your will."

After the session with Padre Humberto, I drove into Mexico City as often as I could to be at Pachita's. That Monday
and Tuesday I was asked to stand at the curtain at the entrance to the altar room. Tom told me, however, to be at the
Mind Control house on Wednesday rather than at Pachita's.
Hermanito had promised to operate on a seventy-two-year-
old man who had flown in from Los Angeles to see him.

A large group of Mind Control people gathered to witness the event, but the hours dragged on and still Pachita
had not arrived. We assumed that perhaps Hermanito had
operated that night at her home after all, and that she would
arrive later, but by midnight still no word had come.
Pachita had no phone yet, so several of us decided to drive
to her house to see what had happened. There was a light
on when we arrived, so we knocked. Enrique, one of her
sons, opened the gate.

"Sorry you can't see her. Everyone just went to bed,"
he said.

"No, wait. I'm up," Pachita called from the living
room. "I'm sorry I couldn't come. The government people
have been here all day. Seems they think I'm practicing
medicine without a license." She smiled broadly. "What do
they know, the fools. Anyway, we raised enough to pay
them off. They won't be back for a while." She waved a
hand at me. "Come, little one. Help me get my things. I will
come with you," she said.

We walked into the altar room. She handed me various things to put into a large empty bag for her: Hermanito's cloak, the balsam, some hospital kidney bowls, a new bottle of alcohol, and a jar that contained two vertebrae.

"My friend in the morgue got these for me this morning—a poor man was run over last night." Then she handed me Hermanito's knife, which I also placed in the bag. (Human parts were not always used in the operations. It was not any more necessary than the use of anesthesia or antiseptics.)

When we returned to the house, Mr. Smith* and his wife were awakened and told to prepare. Pachita had a quick cup of coffee, and then went in to examine him. She prodded and pushed on his back, asking where it hurt. Then she took a small clean glass which I brought from the kitchen. At her request I lit a match and briefly held it to the mouth of the glass. A small exploding sound came within the glass as she quickly pressed the rim down into the small of his back. The skin began to bulge and rise, becoming a dark purple as it grew. Pachita nodded to herself.

"Move him to the floor now," she said. A large, clear plastic sheet had been made ready at the foot of the bed. Mr. Smith stretched face down upon it. A large candle was lit and placed on a bureau near him. Many people from the Mind Control group who had been present earlier that evening had reassembled. Now they crowded into the room to watch. This was a rare event, for usually only a few witnesses were allowed to watch. After a pair of scissors were located, Pachita had me cut strips of cotton from a new roll. Some of the strips were placed in the little kidney bowls and soaked with alcohol. Other strips were soaked in the balsam, while still others were kept dry.

Pachita put on her robe, rubbed the balsam over her hair and clothes, and sat in a straight chair to await Hermanito. After a few moments she shuddered and her arm raised in the now familiar salute.

"I am with you, my little ones," said Hermanito. Pachita's eyes were tightly shut. Hermanito motioned to me.

"Come, my daughter. You will assist me tonight." We knelt by Mr. Smith.

"Someone go and talk to the man during the operation and translate to him for me. Hold his hand . . . keep him talking . . . I don't want him to lose consciousness." One of the women knelt by Mr. Smith's head and began speaking softly to him. Hermanito had me pull up Mr. Smith's pajama top and fold his waistband down just enough to expose the lower back. I handed Hermanito a piece of alcohol-soaked cotton, which he rubbed briskly over the old man's back. Four large pieces of dry cotton were arranged in a square, leaving the spinal area where he would operate uncovered. He took the scissors in his hand and looked up at the intense faces in the room.

"Lift your thoughts to God, my little ones—pray!" he urged.

"Ask him if he is in pain." He wasn't. Hermanito plunged one end of the scissors into his back. Mr. Smith groaned as it penetrated his skin. I saw the scissors disappear into the back. I heard the flesh being cut. My hands on either side of the wound felt a warm thick liquid flow into the cotton. Mr. Smith groaned again.

"Keep him talking. Is he feeling pain? Ask him!" said Hermanito.

Yes, he felt some, but he could bear it. Hermanito

pulled the scissors out. He took his knife, raised it in supplication and pushed it into Mr. Smith's back. I felt a fresh surge of warm liquid flow out from the wound and over my fingers. Hermanito continued to cut for several minutes. Then he reached in and pulled out what appeared to be an odd-shaped bone covered with blood and bits of red flesh.

"This is one of the vertebrae, little one. It is badly damaged," explained Hermanito. Then he took a bone from the jar. As he did I looked down into the dark gaping wound in Mr. Smith's back and began to panic.

"My God, how will this ever close and be whole again!" I asked. But Hermanito turned and looked at me through those tightly-shut eyes and I felt a deep peace take the place of fear. God was with us. Hermanito placed the bone inside the hole, and then he hammered the bone into place with the knife's blunt side. I heard a dull squishing sound as it thudded against the wet raw flesh. Mr. Smith groaned. He was in pain.

"Keep him talking, little one!" Hermanito ordered the woman by Mr. Smith's side. "He must not pass out!" Hermanito's voice was urgent. He cut out a second piece of bone inside the back and repeated the process.

"Are you watching closely, little daughter?" Hermanito asked me softly. I nodded yes.

"This poor man. No wonder he has been in pain. He has a small tumor at the base of his spine," Hermanito said.

Again the knife entered the wound. Suddenly an incredible stench filled the room. Instinctively, I lifted my hand up to my face, but Hermanito grabbed it and placed it back inside the wound. "Hold the tissue firmly, little daughter. I must remove this tumor. It is cancerous." He cut something loose just above my fingers and pulled out a golf-ball size mass of flesh, which he wrapped in cotton and discarded. Hermanito took a large piece of cotton that I handed him and swept aside the bloody cotton. As he passed his hand over the wound, it closed.

We wrapped Mr. Smith with a piece of linen. In the confusion of the night no one had thought to bring a regular bandage. Hermanito supervised for a few minutes and then announced he was leaving. We lifted Mr. Smith onto a bed. His pre-operation pain was gone and his face showed new fresh color. Now he smiled and talked. Yes, he had felt Hermanito working inside his back; he had felt pain, but he was fine now.

Several of us went into the living room for coffee. Pachita watched me intently. Suddenly the look in her eyes changed. Flames seemed to leap out from her eyes at me. Then she leaned forward and spoke to me in an unknown tongue. It sounded like Nahuatl. Then as suddenly as the spirit had appeared, it was gone. Pachita took my hand and asked where my mother was. My mother had come into the city with me that day to witness—reluctantly—the operation. I introduced her to Pachita.

"You are a fortunate mother. Your daughter has a very special mission in life. One day she will be able to heal even as I do. You must begin preparing yourself to help her in case an emergency should arise. She will have great need of you." My mother was almost as stunned as I was.

Later that night I went back with Pachita to her home. Once there, she gave me a bottle of red herbal liquid and told me to be sure that Mr. Smith took doses of it for two days. He was to keep the bandage on for three days, rest in bed, and eat no pork during this time.

When we returned to the house, I gave Mr. Smith a

glass of the liquid. He was happy and excited. He got up and walked slowly to the bathroom and back. I saw that his new yellow pajamas were stained with blood in the back, as were his bandage and the bed sheets. His wife and I changed the sheets and his pajamas and put him back to bed. It was past 3:30 A.M.

I lay in bed thinking about the things I had seen. Was it possible it had all been a trick? Had it all been a fraud and sleight of hand? Had I been hypnotized? The replacement of the vertebrae was medically impossible. Yet I had seen the wounds with my own eyes. I myself had cut the strips of cotton and placed them on his skin. I had clearly viewed Pachita's working hands. And I had felt the warm blood pulse over my hands. My hands were *in* the wound—with blood smeared up to my wrists from it. What she had done was impossible![2]

That is true—for a human doctor. But the being who worked through Pachita was not human. It was supernatural—it was beyond the realm of physical laws. Its works were also supernatural and not bound by conventional rules.

The spiritists are right, I thought to myself. We are surrounded by the souls of those who have gone on. Some have reached a higher plane than others, some, perhaps even Hermanito, are closer to God, and therefore can produce wonderful miracles. Other souls were unquestionably evil and cruel. Many people whom these evil ones have successfully possessed have become incurably insane and are locked away in asylums. "That probably would have been my fate if not for Mind Control and Hermanito," I thought to myself. But those entities who choose to unite their disembodied spirits with a human body that acted as a medium for them could indeed perform wonders and miracles. This work of Pachita's was not satanic. How could it be? For years I had experienced the workings of those allied to Satan. Now I was experiencing the workings of God. The *feeling* between the two was so totally different. I could tell the difference. Wasn't there a crucifix on the altar and a picture of Jesus? I had seen nuns and priests there, sprinkling holy water throughout the room and reciting the rosary. All glory was given to "My Father and Lord"; we were constantly told to elevate our thoughts to God and to say the Lord's Prayer. Besides, what purpose would Satan have in healing and doing good works and in casting out "devils"? Dr. Carlos had told me that this had happened, and he was no credulous fool. He was a respected surgeon with his own practice and a large pharmaceutical company. For several months he had been working as one of Pachita's principal assistants, as I had done that night. He had assisted in dozens of operations and was in continual amazement at what he had seen Hermanito do. No, there was no question in my mind that what Pachita did was supernatural and found its ultimate source in God. Therefore I was determined that I should work there to learn and to serve as best as I could. I praised God again and again for having led me there.

Mom and I drove back to Cuernavaca the next morning. That night the Padre and I met for our last session. My sense of excitement and anticipation was high. I had seen awesome things and my mission had been confirmed. It was during this meeting that I would become a full trance medium as Hermanito had predicted.

The famliar procedures were followed. I went to level

and waited. Suddenly I felt myself sinking deeper and deeper. I felt something deep within me wrench away. My body seemed to fade. I looked down and could see my empty shell sitting straight in a chair—hands floating with palms up. I was aware of being in a new space far beyond where I had been before. I had passed through a deep darkness, but now a pure white light filled everything. Now I fully understood that my essence, my spirit, did *not* have to be tied down into a sack of flesh. My body had been given to me for a while to facilitate the work that lay ahead, to help fulfill my karma and to purify my spirit so it could rejoin God. But I, I was eternal, an inseparable part of the Living Force.

Thoughts like these had come to me before. But now, floating far above, I was *experiencing* it. I was filled with ecstasy. There was no time, no sorrow, no pain. I experienced only joy and light and peace beyond anything I had ever experienced. I looked down. A silent incandescent figure stood by my body waiting . . . waiting . . . yet not possessing me. Then from a great distance I heard an earthly voice calling to me. At first I couldn't understand the words, but they persisted.

"Johanna, Johanna. Come back. It's time to come back. It's time to rest." Oh, it was so hard to obey that voice. It was so beautiful where I was, and I wanted to go on. But I was drawn back. I felt my body again; it felt like lead and was drained of all energy. Padre Humberto touched my hands gently and they dropped like dead weight into my lap. I lay back in the chair, unable to move.

"Why did you call me back so soon? We've only just started. I wasn't ready to come back." But we had been working for over an hour.

After this I frequently experienced similar things during my meditations—a sudden detachment from my body, a sense of floating far off. I could see spirits hovering around my body, many of them evil who wanted to harm it; but I also saw other beings, benevolent and beautiful. I called them my guardian angels and knew that they were protecting me from the evil ones. I felt safe and unafraid.

My sensitivity and psychic awareness had increased greatly. Yet I knew for a fact I was not a full trance medium. I was deeply disappointed. Perhaps I had not developed far enough. Although Pachita treated me with great affection, I sensed a radical though subtle change in Hermanito's attitude towards me that hurt me deeply. What was it in me that impeded my progress? I did not discover the answer to that question until more than a year later when Hermanito gave me a clue during an operation in which I assisted. I was praying intensely as Hermanito cut open a women's abdomen when he suddenly looked up and pointed to me.

"Hurry, get her out of here! She is under attack from an evil one," he said to a woman in the group. "Brush her down with the carnations you'll find on the altar. Hurry!"

Then he added, "It is just a precaution; she has a most powerful spirit protecting her." He looked up at me as he said this, and for a moment I was paralyzed by the hatred I saw in his face. The look was gone in a flash and I never saw it again. Yet the impact remained with me.

___

Notes

1. The following chapter is adapted from *The Beautiful Side of Evil*, by Johanna Michaelsen, pp. 85-104.

2. In a phone conversation I had recently with Johanna concerning a book that was critical of the actual demon-possession of

Pachita by Hermanito, who controlled and empowered Pachita, especially during these "operations," she reaffirmed this whole experience. The authors felt that it was fakery, not a true case of demon-possessed healing. They demonstrated how a scratch could be made to look like the results of a bloody operation. However, for months Johanna sat or stood within a few inches of the famous lady healer. She had put her hands into the wounds, and had her hands and arms covered with the blood of those being operated on. She knew the facts.

As Johanna says, sometimes there is an "ostrich" syndrome. In her book *The Beautiful Side of Evil,* she says on page 172:

> Others, while believing in Jesus and the person of Satan, ascribe just about every form of occultism not to the "scientific" manifestations of parapsychology, or to "departed" spirits working through mediums, or, for that matter, to demonic intervention, but rather to sleight of hand or to some psychological aberration.
>
> It is unquestionably true that for every one hundred "occultic manifestations," most are fraudulent. Bogus palm readers, astrologers, psychics, mediums and occultists of every description certainly abound. Their "manifestations" can indeed frequently be duplicated by those proficient in *legerdemain.* These skilled magicians argue that, because they can reproduce much of the phenomena by sleight of hand and psychologically analyze the rest, *all* such phenomena are therefore unquestionably fraudulent. So, it is concluded, because these things don't exist, believers need not be in fear of them. In one sense, people who have taken this position are correct: We need have no fear whatever of the frauds.
>
> But unfortunately, because many occultists have been proven fraudulent does not automatically prove they all are. The existence of the counterfeit by definition must presuppose the existence of the original. Without it, a counterfeit is meaningless.

To this word by Johanna Michaelsen, we add this pungent comment on fallible logic by Dr. Robert Morey on page 74 of his book, *The New Atheism and the Erosion of Freedom.* "It is erroneous to assume that merely giving an alternate explanation for something automatically refutes any other interpretation."

CHAPTER SIX

The Metamorphosis of Johanna Michaelsen[1]

To my relief the jabbering hordes I had expected on my arrival at L'Abri never materialized. Well, that first night at dinner one girl did start visibly, exclaiming: "Don't you know that's of the devil!?" in response to my inadvertent revelation that I taught yoga. But I knew she was just a guest herself and not one of the staff, so I let it slide. At least I knew enough not to bring up Pachita, so I was allowed several days of relatively peaceful anonymity before I decided to talk to Os Guinness and Sheila Bird, a counselor with whom my sister Kim had suggested I spend some time.

Sunday morning, after chapel, I had someone point "Birdie" out to me. She was a small woman probably in her forties. I watched Birdie's face as she spoke with a young girl. Her eyes were stern but kind. As I moved closer, Birdie glanced over at me and stopped in mid-sentence, "You must be Kim's sister!" she exclaimed. I nodded.

"Kim called several days ago. Os and I have been expecting you. Why don't you come by my chalet after lunch today for a visit."

Birdie's chalet was perched at the end of a path that wound gently along the side of a mountain. Sections of the path closely bordered along the edge. It seemed a long way down to the bottom. My steps slowed as I neared her chalet. I was feeling a growing reluctance to talk with her and was tempted to go for a walk through the village instead. My upbringing got the better of me, however, and I arrived on time.

Birdie ushered me into a tiny, cozy room and finally, after much gentle coaxing, had me talking about the beings and manifestations that filled my life. I was telling her about my college days when Birdie said, "You know, if you had truly believed in Jesus and had known how to make use of the weapons He has provided, you wouldn't have had to go through all that."

"But I don't anymore, Birdie!" I exclaimed. "For the last year since I've been with Mind Control, yoga and Pachita I've gained control. If anything frightening appears, I just go deeper in meditation or call on Jesus or Hermanito and the evil ones disappear. I *am* learning to use God's weapons!"

Birdie just nodded. "Tell me about this Mind Control and Pachita."

She was silent for several minutes after I had finished.

"Well, Johanna, I can certainly see why you believe as you do, but something about what Pachita is doing makes me uncomfortable. Let's not talk about it just now, though. First I'd like you to spend the next day or so reading the Gospel of John and the First Epistle of John. It will help lay a foundation for our next meeting."

It seemed a reasonable request.

Back at my chalet that afternoon I settled down in a corner with a new Bible and opened to the Gospel of John.

"In the beginning was the Word, and the Word was

with God, and the Word was God. He was in the beginning with God. All things came into being through Him, and apart from Him. . . ."

Suddenly I was hit by a wave of exhaustion. I had been wide awake and willing to read minutes before, but now I was so tired I literally couldn't keep my eyes open. The words all seemed to fuse together. "I'll rest a while—I can read this later," I thought. I curled up and sank into a deep sleep for several hours until someone stopped by to call me for dinner. I spent all the next day in my room trying to read, but never got past a few words before an overwhelming desire to sleep pulled me under.

By Tuesday morning's meeting with Birdie I still hadn't read past the fourth verse of John.

"Actually I'm really not surprised," Birdie said cryptically when I told her. "Look—why don't you stay here today and read. There is a different spirit in this place. I don't think you'll have any trouble staying awake this time." She was right. I had read First John and the Gospels several times in the past, but the words never had the same impact on me they had now. The Jesus I was encountering on the pages of that Bible was not only alive and real, but was filled with awesome power and majesty. A mere spoken word of healing or deliverance was sufficient to bring it about. His claim to unique incarnate deity was unmistakable, despite what I still believed about it. Verse after verse asserted that apart from Him there was no forgiveness of sin.

I was shaken and confused by the time I finished the last verse in the Gospel of John. If what I had just read was true, then everything I believed about karma and the way to unity with God was wrong. It couldn't be both ways. The claims made by Jesus were too exclusive. And if I was wrong about what I believed about Jesus, then maybe I was wrong about the rest as well.

Despite a well-rehearsed serene exterior, I was in turmoil by the time I arrived at Os Guinness's home later that afternoon. Part of me wanted desperately to know the truth, another part of me still wanted to shut down and ignore the whole business. Os spoke to me about the irreconcilable dichotomy between the Eastern and biblical view of God, salvation, and Jesus. He said something about the physical and spiritual dangers of the occult and told me of how he and his wife, Jenny, had been frequently attacked by demonic forces while writing a chapter on the occult for a book he was putting together called *The Dust of Death.* I sat quietly and listened. I had arrived with so many questions to ask him but now my mind was blank. I couldn't say anything at all. I could hardly even focus on what he was saying.

My face probably looked as blank as I felt at that moment because Os looked at me rather curiously and said, "Ah, maybe it would be more helpful for you to listen to a couple of my tapes before we talk further. Play the one called "The East, No Exit" first, then listen to "Encircling Eyes." They're in the library. I'm going to be away for two days, but I'll be back Thursday night. If you have any questions, come by Friday morning, OK? Meanwhile be sure you keep in touch with Birdie."

"The East, no Exit"[2] was the first discussion concerning the philosophical dilemmas of Eastern philosophy versus the Christian alternative that actually made sense to me. I had always believed that Hinduism and Christianity were fully compatible. Swami Vivekenanda (1863-1902) had said, "We accept all religions as true." But Os emphasized that far from compatible the two philosophies were radically opposed to one another in their basic concepts of God, reality, morality, and personality. He pointed out that although several gurus taught that the teachings of "the Blessed Lord Jesus Christ" dovetailed perfectly with Hinduism, their claim lacked scholastic integrity. These gurus, Os continued, lifted phrases such as "The Kingdom of Heaven is within you" out of context and blatantly ignored other less pliable statements such as "I am the way, and the truth, and the life; no one comes to the Father, but by me" (John 14:6 RSV). This point especially caught my attention as this had been one of the sayings of Jesus with which I myself had long struggled and had sought to explain away. It was too intolerant a statement, too narrow-minded to possibly be anything other than a misinterpretation or mistranslation of the Bible. Yet the First Epistle and Gospel of John were filled with such statements:

> And the witness is this, that God has given us eternal life, and this life is in His Son. He who has the Son has the life; he who does not have the Son of God does not have the life (1 John 5:11, 12 NASB).

> And He [the Holy Spirit], when He comes, will convict the world concerning sin, and righteousness, and judgment; concerning sin, because they do not believe in Me (John 16:8, 9 NASB).

> For this is the will of My Father, that every one who beholds the Son, and believes in Him, may have eternal life; and I Myself will raise Him up on the last day (John 6:40 NASB).

> I said therefore to you, that you shall die in your sins; for

unless you believe that I am He, you shall die in your sins (John 8:24 NASB).

It was certainly evident that Jesus' contemporaries understood the exclusivity of His claims. "For this cause therefore the Jews were seeking all the more to kill Him, because He not only was breaking the Sabbath, but also was calling God His own Father, making Himself equal with God" (John 5:18 NASB).

Os summarized his discussion by saying: "It is quite plain that, if treated fairly on its own premises, Christianity excludes the full truth and final validity of other religions. If Christianity is true, Hinduism cannot be true in the sense it claims. Even though on the surface it appears that Hinduism is more tolerant, both finally demand an ultimate choice."[3]

Intellectually, Os's discussion made sense to me. Spiritually, however, I couldn't accept it.

It was as if there was a vast insurmountable barrier which was keeping me from taking hold. Suddenly, desperately, all I wanted to do was go home. It was too much. However much sense Os made in that tape or John in his Gospel, I simply couldn't accept it. I felt torn between two powerful relentless forces. The pressure finally drove me to my knees.

I again challenged God to once and for all show me the truth. Was Jesus the greatest avatar, the way-shower; or perhaps the greatest creation of Father God; or was He God uniquely incarnate in human flesh who died to take my sin, as the Gospel of John, Os, Birdie and Kim claimed? Was Pachita working in the power of God or was her source satanic?

"If you can, God, show me now. I'm willing to give up Pachita and yoga and all the rest if I'm wrong. But if not, then I'm putting all this nonsense aside and going on with it at Pachita's. Oh God, let me see the truth!" I had no idea how literally God would answer that prayer.

The night of November 15, 1972 was damp and cold as I walked alone on the slippery path to Birdie's chalet. It had been drizzling earlier that evening but the clouds were lifting now and I could see a few stars peeping through. Well, maybe with luck it would snow before I left, I thought with a smile. Yesterday I had just about decided to take the next train out of Switzerland, but had changed my mind that morning. I couldn't go until I had some answers. So, perhaps, there would still be time to see it snow after all.

I stopped. A dense black fog was forming all around me, blotting out the path. Within seconds I could see nothing. The dark mist was swirling, alive, filled with the presence of something more monstrous than anything I had ever before encountered. Voices began whispering, hissing incoherent words and laughter in my right ear. An ice-cold breath touched the back of my neck under my hair.

"Hermanito, help me!" I gasped. The voices shrieked in hideous laughter.

"We're going to kill you!"

I panicked and broke into a run. Something like a giant fist slammed into my back between my shoulders. I pitched forward in the thick darkness and instinctively reached out to break my fall. My fingers found the branch of a small bush and clung to it. I tried to scream out "Jesus!" but an iron hand closed upon my throat choking off the word. All I could do was scream in my mind "Jesus, Jesus, help me!"

"He can't help you," the voices shrieked. "He can't help you!"

But then suddenly the grip around my throat loosened—the blackness lifted. I could again see the light of Birdie's chalet at the end of the path.

Birdie's eyes widened a little as I burst into the room. "What on earth is the matter with you!" she exclaimed. "I don't know Birdie," I said, still shaking, "but I'm terrified."

Birdie hurried me into her little prayer room and closed the door. She took my hands in hers and began praying. I tried to focus on her words, but suddenly they sounded so far away. I felt dizzy. My eyes opened. The room seemed to have been taken up in a giant slow-motion whirlwind, spinning slowly around and around. The sound of voices began to build again. I turned my head towards the dark window on my left and froze. Outside I could see the faces of countless demons, contorted, twisted in indescribable rage.

"What is it, Johanna?" Birdie's voice was muffled as though it were coming across a vast distance.

"Can't you see them, Birdie," I gasped, "Can't you see their faces?"

"No," I heard her voice say, "but I know One who can. Satan, in the name of Jesus Christ of Nazareth, I command you to be gone! I forbid your presence here. I claim the protection of the blood of Jesus upon us. Go where Jesus sends you!"

Instantly the faces vanished. The room stopped spinning and was filled with a peace beyond all my understanding. They were gone.

I knew what had happened was a direct answer to my prayer. God had literally let me see the source behind my practices. Murderous demonic rage had been the spirits' reaction to my potential decision to accept Jesus Christ of Nazareth as He is, rather than as I had come to think He should be. The difference had been subtle, but vast nonetheless. There were still so many things I didn't understand, so many unanswered questions, but I knew beyond any doubt that I had been wrong about Jesus.

I wanted to pray right then to recommit my life to Him on His terms, but Birdie hesitated. She said I should wait until Os could be with us. Perhaps, understandably, she thought I was possessed and that she would need the presence of another strong Christian to help wage the war. There was no question I was severely oppressed, but the demons had never taken possession of me. ("There is a greater Spirit looking over you," Hermanito had said once. His bitter tone now made sense to me.)

I spent most of that night and the next day praying and reading the Bible. Tuesday night, however, the attack came again. I wanted to listen to Os's tape called "Encircling Eyes" before meeting with him and Birdie the next morning. The tape had run only a few minutes when the dense blackness filled the room and fear pressed in on me from all sides with frozen hands. Again my throat was taken in a vise as I tried to call on Jesus. I forced my body to stand and went into the next room, my eyes wide with terror yet unable to say a word to the girls who sat there. They urged me to call Birdie, but when she answered the phone all I could say was her name.

"They're back, aren't they," she said. "I have a terrible emergency here, a suicide threat, but I felt God wanted me to pray for you about twenty minutes ago. Claim the protection of the blood of Jesus, Johanna. Resist them. Is there anyone with you?"

"Yes"—the word came hard. The hand was still on my throat.

"Have them pray with you. I will call you again as soon as I can."

The girls prayed for me. After a while I was able to claim the Lord's protection for myself. By the time Birdie called back, the oppression had lifted.

That next morning, Friday, November 17, 1972, at 10 A.M. Os and Birdie supported me in prayer as I renounced my involvement with the occult and committed myself to Jesus Christ as my Lord and Savior. I would never again face the darkness alone.

Notes

1. Johanna Michaelsen was still searching for answers after her many experiences with the spirit world, with mind control, with spirit guides, and with the psychic healer Pachita, whom she assisted. Eventually she journeyed to L'Abri, Dr. Francis Schaeffer's spiritual retreat in Switzerland. In this chapter, adapted from her book *The Beautiful Side of Evil*, pp. 140-49, she resumes her story.

2. Os Guinness, *The Dust of Death* (Downers Grove: InterVarsity Press, 1973), p. 49.

3. Ibid., p. 50.

CHAPTER SEVEN

Another Look at the Spirit World "After Death"[1]

At last we turn to those reports that thus far have received little publicity. Some people, after returning from clinical death, describe themselves as having been in hell. Some of these include a few who apparently broke through the barrier or great divide separating the sorting grounds from what could be the place of judgment. Those who did not encounter the barrier seemed to leave the scene of death to enter a different type of sorting ground—one that was morose and dark, like a carnival's "spook house." In most cases, this place seems to be underground or within the earth in some way.

Hell

Thomas Welch, in his booklet *Oregon's Amazing Miracle,* describes a most unusual experience in which he saw a tremendous "lake of fire, the most awesome sight one could ever see this side of the final judgment."

While working as an engineer's helper for a lumber company thirty miles east of Portland, Oregon, Welch was required to walk across a trestle over a dam fifty-five feet above the water where the sawmill was located. He then gives this account:

I went out on the trestle to straighten out some timbers which were crossed and not moving on a conveyor. Suddenly I fell off the trestle and tumbled down between the timbers and into the pond, which was ten feet deep. An engineer sitting in the cab of his locomotive unloading logs into the pond saw me fall. I landed on my head on the first beam thirty feet down, and then tumbled from one beam to another until I fell into the water and disappeared from his view.

There were seventy men working in and around the mill at that time. The mill was shut down then and every available man was called to search for my body, according to the testimonies of these men. The search went on for forty-five minutes to one hour before I was finally found by M. J. H. Gunderson, who has written his own account of this to verify the facts of this testimony.

I was dead as far as this world is concerned. But I was alive in another world. There was no lost time. I learned more in that hour out of the body than I could ever learn while in this body. All I could remember is falling over the edge of the trestle. The locomotive engineer watched me go all the way down into the water.

The next thing I knew I was standing near a shoreline of a great ocean of fire. It happened to be what the Bible says it is in Revelation 21:8 ". . . the lake which burneth with fire and brimstone." This is the most awesome sight one could ever see this side of the final judgment.

I remember more clearly than any other thing that has ever happened to me in my lifetime every detail of every moment, what I saw and what happened during that hour I was gone from this world. I was standing some distance from this burning, turbulent, rolling mass of blue fire. As far as my eyes could see it was just the same. A lake of fire and brimstone. There was nobody in it. I was not in it. I saw other people whom I had known that had died when I was thirteen. Another was a boy I had gone to school with who had died from cancer of the jaw that had started with an infected tooth while he was just a young lad. He was two years older than I. We recognized each other, even though we did not speak. They, too, were looking and seemed to be perplexed and in deep thought, as though they could not believe what they saw. Their expressions were those of bewilderment and confusion.

The scene was so awesome that words simply fail. There is no way to describe it except to say we were eye witnesses now to the final judgment. There is no way to escape, no way out. You don't even try to look for one. This is the prison out of which no one can escape except by Divine intervention. I said to myself in an audible voice, "If I had known about this I would have done anything that was required of me to escape coming to a place like this." But I had not known.

As these thoughts were racing through my mind, I saw another man coming by in front of us. I knew immediately who He was. He had a strong, kind, compassionate face, composed and unafraid, Master of all He saw. It was Jesus Himself.

A great hope took hold of me and I knew the answer to my problem was this great and wonderful Person who was moving by me in this prison of lost, confused judgment-bound souls. I did not do anything to attract His attention. I said again to myself, "If He would only look my way and see me, He could rescue me from this place because He would know what to do." He passed on by and it seemed as though He would not look my way, but just before He passed out of sight He turned His head and looked directly at me. That is all it took. His look was enough.

In seconds I was back entering into my body again. It was like coming in through the door of a house. I could hear the Brockes (the people I was staying with) praying minutes before I could open my eyes or say anything. I could hear and I understood what was going on. Then suddenly life came into my body and I opened my eyes and spoke to them.

It's easy to talk about and describe something you have seen. I know there is a lake of fire because I have seen it. I know Jesus Christ is alive in eternity. I have seen Him. The Bible states in Revelation 1:9-11: "I, John . . . was in the spirit on the Lord's Day, and heard behind me a great voice, as of a trumpet, saying, I am Alpha and Omega, the first and the last, and, what thou seest, write in a book."

Among the many things John saw was the judgment, and he describes it in Revelation 20 as he saw it. In verse 10 he says: "And the devil that deceived them was cast into the *lake of fire. . . .*" Again in Revelation 21:8, John says he saw the *"lake which burneth with fire and brimstone."* This is the lake I saw, and I am certain of this one thing, that in the end of this age at the final judgment every corrupt thing in this universe will ultimately be cast into this lake and be forever destroyed.

I thank God for people who can pray. It was Mrs. Brocke I heard praying for me. She said, "Oh God, don't take Tom; he is not saved." Presently I opened my eyes and said to them, "What happened?" I had not lost any time; I had been gone somewhere and now I was back. Soon after this an ambulance arrived and I was taken to the Good Samaritan Hospital in Portland.

I arrived there just before six o'clock in the evening, was taken into surgery and my scalp was sewn with many stitches. I was put in the intensive care ward. There was really not much the doctors could do. It was simply a matter of wait and see.

During these four days and nights, I seemed to be in constant communication with the Holy Spirit. I relived the events of my past life and the things I had seen, such as the lake of fire, Jesus coming to me there, seeing my uncle and the boy I had been in school with, and the coming back to life again. The presence of God's Spirit was with me continually, and many times I spoke out loud to the Lord. Then I began to ask God what He wanted in my life, what His will was for me. . . . Then some time around nine o'clock the call of God came. The voice of the Spirit can be very real. He said to me, "I want you to tell the world what you saw, and how you came back to life."[2]

Another instance involves a patient dying with a heart attack. She attended church every Sunday and considered herself an average Christian.

I remember getting short of breath and then I must have blacked out. Then I saw that I was getting out of my body. The next thing I remember was entering this gloomy room where I saw in one of the windows this huge giant with a grotesque face that was watching me. Running around the windowsill were little imps or elves that seemed to be with the giant. The giant beckoned me to come with him. I didn't want to go, but I had to. Outside was darkness but I could hear people moaning all around me. I could feel things moving about my feet. As we moved on through this tunnel or cave, things were getting worse. I remember I was crying. Then, for some reason the giant turned me loose and sent me back. I felt I was being spared. I don't know why.

Then I remember finding myself back in the hospital bed. The doctor asked me if I had been taking drugs. My description must have sounded like the DTs. I told him I didn't have either of these habits and that the story was true. It has changed my whole life.

The variations in the being that takes people away or sends them back from the spirit world seems to vary considerably among those who have bad experiences. Among those who have good experiences this figure seems to be similar from case to case.

In his excellent book *Return From Tomorrow* George

Ritchie, M.D., describes his death from a lobar type of pneumonia. He describes how he unaccountably returned to life after nine minutes. During that time he experienced, however, a lifetime of adventure—some of it good, and some of it bad. He describes a journey with a glorious being of flooding light and power whom he identified as Christ and who took him through a series of "worlds." In this instance the world of the damned existed on a vast plain that seemed to be on the surface of the earth where depraved spirits were at constant warfare with one another.

In his pamphlet *My Testimony* Rev. Kenneth E. Hagin recounts experiences that changed his whole life. The experience caused him to enter the ministry to tell others and he relates the following:

> . . . On the twenty-first day of April, 1933, Saturday night, 7:30 o'clock, at McKinney, Texas, thirty-two miles north of Dallas, my heart stopped beating and the spiritual man that lives in my body departed from my body. . . . I went down, down, down, until the lights of the earth faded away. . . . The further down I went the blacker it became, until it was all blackness. I could not have seen my hand if it had been one inch in front of my eyes. The further down I went, the more stifling it was and the hotter it was.
>
> Finally, way down below me, I could see lights flickering on the walls of the caverns of the damned. They were caused by the fires of hell. The giant orb of flame, white crested, pulled me . . . drew me like a magnet draws metal unto itself. I did not want to go! I did not walk, but just as metal jumps to the magnet, my spirit was drawn to that place. I would not take my eyes off it. The heat beat me in the face. Many years have now gone by, and yet I can see it with my eyes just as I saw it then. It is just as fresh in my memory as though it happened last night. . . .

Upon reaching the bottom of the pit, I had become conscious of some kind of spirit-being by my side. I hadn't looked at him because I could not take my gaze off the fires of hell, but when I paused, that creature laid his hand on my arm half-way between my shoulder and my elbow to escort me in. At the same moment, a Voice spoke, away above the blackness, above the earth, above the heavens. It was the voice of God, though I did not see Him, and I do not know what He said, because He did not speak in English. He spoke some other tongue, and when He spoke, it reverberated throughout the region of the damned, shaking it like a leaf in the wind, causing that creature to loose his grip. I did not turn around, but there was a Power that pulled me, and I came back away from the fire, away from the heat, back into the shadows of the darkness. I began to ascend, until I came to the top of the pit and saw the light of the earth. I came back into that room just as real as at any other time. I entered in through the door, except my spirit needed no doors.

I slipped right back down into my body as a man slips into his trousers in the morning, the same way in which I went out, through my mouth. I began to talk to my grandmother. She said, "Son, I thought you were dead. I thought you were gone."

. . . I would that I had words to describe the place. People go through this life so self-complacent, and as though they will not have to face hell, but God's Word and my own personal experiences tell me differently. I know what it is to be unconscious, and it is black when you are unconscious, but I want to tell you that there is not blackness like the Outer Darkness.

Many other "hell" cases are accumulating rapidly but will not be mentioned here. One that I should mention, however, involves a regular church member who was surprised in death to find himself descending through a tunnel lined by fire in its lower half, which opened into a huge, fiery world of horror. He saw some of his old friends from the "good old days" who exhibited blank stares of apathy, who were burdened with useless loads, and who were continually going nowhere but never stopping for fear of "the main drivers" who, he said, were beyond description. Complete darkness outskirted the milieu of pointless activity. In some unknown miraculous way he escaped permanent captivity when he was summoned by God to come out. Since then he has followed a compulsive urge to warn others of the dangers of complacency and the need to take a definite stand in their faith.

Suicide

Many people attempt suicide to "end it all." According to the cases I've seen or heard about through other doctors, it may be only the "beginning of it all." I don't know of any "good" out-of-the-body experiences that have resulted from attempted suicide. Only a few who have attempted suicide, however, have had experiences they will talk about. One of my colleagues offers the following account:

> A fourteen-year-old girl became despondent over a report card from school. Communication with her parents usually centered upon her deficits, and recently upon her inadequacy to measure up to the grades of her sister, who was a couple of years older and seemed to be accomplished in nearly everything. Even "looks" were compared. She never seemed to receive any praise, and now she had to confront her parents with her report card. She went up to her room, and thinking of the best way to solve the problem, she took a bottle of aspirin from the bathroom. It probably had eighty tablets in it, and she had to take a lot of

water to get them down. Her parents found her a couple of hours later in a coma. She had vomited over her own face and onto the pillow. Fortunately, many of the aspirin had apparently not been absorbed and she recovered a couple of hours later in the hospital emergency room. . . . (She was fortunate it was aspirin she took and not Tylenol, because the latter causes less vomiting and results in delayed damage to the liver that is frequently fatal.)

During one of the vomiting episodes she inhaled some of the vomitus, developed spasm of the vocal chords, stopped breathing and then had a cardiac arrest. She recovered immediately with external heart massage and placement of a breathing tube down her throat into her windpipe. Her recollections during the recovery were poor, but at the time she kept saying, "Mama, help me! Make them let go of me! They're trying to hurt me!" The doctors tried to apologize for hurting her, but she said it wasn't the doctors, but "Them, those demons in hell . . . they wouldn't let go of me . . . they wanted me . . . I couldn't get back. . . . It was just awful!"

She slept for another day, and her mother hugged her most of that time. After the various tubes were removed, I asked her to recall what had happened. She remembered taking the aspirin, but absolutely nothing else! Somewhere in her mind the events may still be suppressed. Perhaps they could be reached with pentathol interview hypnosis. Frankly, I'm reticent to approach this area—it reminds me of demonology, a subject I respect but leave to others.

She subsequently became a missionary several years later. No despondency. I am told that everywhere she goes she brings exuberance—a contagious feeling.

The prevalence of depression, the prelude to suicide, is appalling. Suicide is the eleventh most common cause of death in the United States, accounting for approximately 25,000 deaths annually or a little less than 1.5 percent of all deaths. Next to automobile accidents, suicide is the most common cause of death among teenagers. For each suicide that results in death, there are probably several unsuccessful suicide attempts. The prevalence of suicidal thoughts, like bad experiences after death, tend not to be reported, much less discussed. They seem to be considered skeletons in one's life—something to hide and socially degrading. Ironically, therapy for this abnormal emotional life centers around release and discussion.

Due to emotional illness our pharmaceutical market for tranquilizer drugs and antidepressants has skyrocketed. Most people I see seem to be on something. Valium is now the best money-maker and most popular drug in the United States next to aspirin products.

The following case involved a fifty-four-year-old housewife with recurrent despondency:

> Nobody loved me. My husband and children used me as a servant. I was always cleaning up after them, but they acted as if I didn't even exist.
>
> One night I was crying and nobody listened. I took some Valium and told them I didn't want to live anymore. They still didn't listen, so I took a whole bottle of them—fifty of them.
>
> And then it was too late. I knew I had really done it. I was going to die! It was a sin—but so was living!
>
> As I got drowsy, I remember going down this black hole, round and round. Then I saw a glowing red-hot spot getting bigger and bigger until I was able to stand up. It was all red and hot and on fire. The earth was like slimy mud that sank over my feet, and it was hard to move. The heat was awful and made it hard to breathe. I cried "Oh, Lord give me another chance." I prayed and prayed. How I got back, I'll never know.

They said I was unconscious for two days and that they pumped my stomach. They said my experience in hell must have been a drug trip. But they don't really know. I've taken Valium many times before, but never had an experience with it.

Another despondent mother attempted suicide after her twenty-four-year-old daughter had committed suicide because of a negligent boyfriend. As soon as the daughter's funeral was over, she tried to take her own life with an overdose of Amytal, a barbiturate. She hoped to join her daughter. Instead of seeing her daughter, she found herself in what appeared to be hell, being jostled up and down on a blanket held between two satanic beings. The scene occurred in a huge foreboding cave. She said the beings had tails and slanted eyes, and looked horrible. After resuscitation and stomach washings she recovered and was told that her experience was probably due to drugs. Yet she remains unconvinced. She has received, however, a new purpose and insight by the experience. She now organizes clubs for the emotional support of family survivors of suicide victims.

Light That Is Darkness

Perhaps we should mention again the controversy over the significance of the "beam of light" that has been encountered by many who have had after-death experiences. The light appeared in the "good" experiences and seemed to represent acceptance for all people. According to some there was a sense of universal forgiveness—a general feeling of happiness and ecstasy, of indescribable peace and bliss.

Stephen Board takes issue with this observation. He expresses his belief that the benevolent beam of light described by others reveals an air of moral tolerance and the philosophy of "I'm okay, you're okay." To demonstrate that all cases do not involve an angel of light, Board reports an encounter with an "angel of death," as recorded by Dr. Phillip Swihart, clinical psychologist and director of Midwestern Colorado Mental Health Center, Montrose, Colorado:

> It was a Friday night, early in January 1967, when I was attacked, beaten, and kicked nearly to death. At the hospital the doctor decided to observe me the rest of the night and do exploratory surgery in the abdominal area in the morning. . . . While in the operating room awaiting surgery, I felt the presence of some thing or some power and I thought, "This is it." Next, blackness. Time became of no more importance.

> I had no idea how long I was without any sensation in that darkness. Then it was light. I awoke and I knew it was real. In front of me, I watched my whole life pass by. Every thought, word and every movement I had made in my life since the time I knew that Jesus was real. I was very young when I took Christ as my Savior. I saw things I had done which I had forgotten but remembered as I watched them pass before me. This experience was, to say the least, unbelievable. Every detail, right up to the present time. It all took place in what seemed just a fraction of a second, and yet it was all very vivid.

> All the time I was watching my life go by, I felt the presence of some sort of power, but I didn't see it. Next, I was drawn into total darkness. Then I stopped. It felt like a big hollow room. It seemed to be a very large space, and totally dark. I could see nothing, but felt the presence of this power.

I asked the power who I and who he or it was. Communication was not by talking but through a flow of energy. He answered that he was the Angel of Death. I believed him. The Angel went on to say that my life was not as it should be, that he could take me on but that I would be given a second chance, and that I was to go back. He promised me I would not die in 1967.

The next thing I remember I was in the recovery room, back in my body. I was so taken in by this experience that I did not notice what kind of body I had, nor how much time had elapsed, it was so real—I believed it.

Later in 1967, a car ran over my neck and shoulders. Still later in that year, I was in a car wreck in which both cars were totaled and in both accidents I came out almost completely unhurt. In neither accident was I at fault.

I did not tell many people about my experience; I did not want to be considered crazy. But the encounter was very real to me, and I still believe I was with the Angel of Death.[3]

Many theologians also take issue with the concept of universal forgiveness that is offered by the "angel of light." Many patients, regardless of their spiritual condition, have purportedly encountered this "angel" and its message. One must remember that Satan himself, who seldom appears in a bad light, is capable of appearing as an angel (see 2 Cor. 11:14-15).

Billy Graham reminds us that a life after death exists for all people. Those who have never accepted Christ as Lord and Savior, however, "will go away to eternal punishment, but the righteous to eternal life" (Matt. 25:46). Since all people will not be saved, some theologians remind us that Satan does not always appear evil but is a master of disguise, capable of the most clever deception. He can transform himself into an angel of light to convince the un-saved that they are already saved or to neutralize the neces-sity of the Christian gospel.[4]

Multiple Experiences

A few interviewed patients report multiple experiences from multiple deaths. These experiences may be bad at first, then good, but never in the reverse order. Some of them resemble the first case I described—the man who said he was in hell and then called for divine deliverance and subsequently had pleasant experiences.

I recall a similar case, one that I find difficult to ex-plain. It involved an active dedicated Christian who had ex-perienced three different episodes of heart attack, fibrilla-tion, successful resuscitation, and after-death experiences. The first episode was terrifying; the next two were quite pleasing—even euphoric.

> I don't remember the circumstances prior to the first time I passed out. They told me I had died, and when I woke up I found two red areas the size of small saucers, one over my left chest and one over the upper breastbone area. They said this was where the shock paddles were applied. I don't remember that either. I do remember you asking me, as soon as I woke up, what had happened. The only thing I remember was passing out into blackness and then I saw these red snakes crawling all over me. I couldn't get away from them. I would throw one of them off and then another one would get on me. It was horrible! Finally, I was dragged down to the ground by something and then other crawling things started getting on me. Some looked like red jelly. I screamed and cried out, but no one paid any atten-tion to me. I had the impression there were many other

people in the same fix all around me. It sounded like human voices and some of them were screaming. It was reddish black in there and hazy and hard to see, but I never did see any flames. There wasn't any devil, just these crawling things. Although my chest hurt real bad, I remember how glad I was to wake up and get out of that place. I was sure glad to see my family. I never want to go back there. I am convinced it was the entrance to hell.

Without any apparent reason, this patient's subsequent two experiences during other deaths were beautiful. He tried to describe one of them as follows:

I remember the nurse had come into the room to start oxygen through a tube in my nose because of the severe chest pains that were recurring. She said she was going to leave for a minute to get a shot for my pain. As she was saying that I remember that I must have fainted because she yelled to the other nurse on duty, "Come in her quick! Mr. Ledford has had a heart arrest!" That's all I remember. Everything was black. Then I remember seeing them working on me, and it seemed so strange because I felt perfectly fine. I had to move to one side to see my face to make sure it was my body. Just then about three or four more people came in. One of them was a boy in charge of oxygen, and the others seemed to be nurses from another unit. Then everything seemed to dim and go black again. As I was moving through this long corridor I noticed a small light that looked like a bird. Slowly it became larger and larger until it looked like a white dove that was flying. It kept getting bigger and bigger and brighter and brighter, expanding until the whole area was lit with this brilliant beautiful light. I have never seen anything like it. I found myself on a rolling green meadow that was slightly uphill. I saw my brother and he was alive, and yet I remember when he had died. He was so glad to see me. We put our arms around each other right there in the middle of the meadow. I had tears in my eyes and then we strolled arm in arm up the meadow. I remember that it was uphill a bit and then we came to a white fence that looked like a split rail, but I couldn't get over it. Some force seemed to keep me from getting over that fence. I didn't see anybody on the other side and there didn't seem to be any reason why I couldn't get over that fence!

The next thing I remember I was feeling a thud on my chest; somebody was pounding on me and pushing on me. I thought my ribs were breaking and I woke up looking up into your face! I remember I didn't want to come back. What I had seen was beautiful beyond expression.

This was his second experience. He was able to recall vivid details of the wonderful existence, but he couldn't recall details of the painfully unpleasant first experience, nor could he volunteer an explanation for its occurrence to a professing Christian.

His third experience was also pleasant and easily recalled:

I was floating and looking down over this beautiful city. It was the prettiest city I had ever seen. People were there. All in white. The whole sky was so lit up, brighter than sunshine. I was about to drift down and walk around in this city when I found myself back in my body, feeling the most terrible shock again as they put the paddles to me to revive my heart. Except for my wife's sake, I wish you hadn't brought me back.

This patient finally got his wish. A few months later he died a fourth time from cancer. This condition was entirely unrelated to the repeated heart attacks, which I was certain would be the ultimate cause of his death. I've often wondered what he's doing now.

Notes

1. This chapter is adapted from *Beyond Death's Door,* by Maurice Rawlings, M.D., pp. 102-120.

2. Thomas Welch, *Oregon's Amazing Miracle* (Dallas: Christ for the Nations, Inc., 1976), p. 8. (Used by permission.)

3. Reprinted with permission of Evangelical Ministries, from Stephen Board, "Light at the End of the Tunnel," *Eternity,* July 1977, pp. 13-17. Copyright © 1977.

4. Eric Wiggins, "A Glimpse of Eternity," *Moody Monthly,* October 1977. See also, Charles C. Ryrie, "To Be Absent From the Body," *Kindred Spirit,* Summer 1977, pp. 4-7.

CHAPTER EIGHT

Personal Experiences with the Spirit World

One of my first experiences in "hand-to-hand" combat with the demon world took place while I was holding evangelistic meetings in a large Canadian city. I met a charming young deacon named Brick. His pastor told me that while Brick was a faithful, willing worker, he had some serious problems. Although reluctant to discuss the specific nature of these problems he admitted that both he and a psychiatrist had been unable to help Brick solve them.

The pastor and I did much calling during the evangelistic campaign. Brick wanted to go with me when he could. On one occasion Brick cringed and cried out as a car drove by, "Mac, he zapped me . . . he zapped me . . . the guy driving that car zapped me!"

When I finally got Brick quieted down, I asked him what he was talking about. He told me that sometimes people, like the driver of the car, shot out hostile electrical impulses toward him that were threatening and painful. Gradually, other strange stories came to light.

When I returned to the pastor's study at church, I asked the pastor for more details. At this time he shared with me more fully his attempt, and the psychiatrist's attempt, to help Brick. But neither had any effect.

We called Brick into the study. We had been praying and thinking about what was wrong, and what to do. Suddenly, I said (almost as much of a surprise to me as it was to Brick), "Brick, do you think you may be demon possessed?" Brick's sandy head slowly sank. The ready smile left his friendly face.

"Yeah . . . I think I may be," he mumbled.

With prayer and considerable fear, I called out, "Demon, in the name of the Lord Jesus Christ, come out of Brick."

Brick fell from his chair. He began to writhe on the floor. Desperately I cried out to God to be covered and protected by the blood of the Lord Jesus Christ, and for Brick to be delivered in the name of Jesus. The room was filled with tension. Screams and groans came from his mouth. Finally, he was quiet. He seemed to come back slowly to *this* world. The pastor and I asked him if the demon had come out. He replied that he had actually felt the demon exit.

Brick still acted crestfallen. Remembering from Scripture that other demons might be present, I repeated the command. It did not work. The pastor took over. Both he and I questioned Brick about sin in his life. To the utter astonishment and dismay of the pastor, Brick confessed to leading a double life. He had been involved in adultery with another woman. The pastor then commanded in the name of Jesus that the demon of lust be cast out. Again Brick went down to the floor, his body contorting. Deep agonizing groans tore from his throat. That demon also left.

This wearing process seemed to continue endlessly, although I believe it actually took only several hours. Finally, Brick seemed to respond and be restored to something like his normal self.

In summary, I must add that great caution should be observed in considering demonology. Twin dangers exist—to overemphasize the influence, activity and authority of demons, or to ignore them entirely. Johanna Michaelsen and Kurt Koch, along with the authors of *The Fakers,* Danny Korem and Paul Meier, seem to agree on at least one thing—95 percent to 98 percent of so-called occult experiences, seances, spirit contacts, etc., are pure fakery, psychologically induced, imagination, or misunderstanding and superstition. There are other possibilities including physical and mental problems. As former spiritist mediums Ralph Gasson and Victor Earnest, now committed Christians, have pointed out, the conclusion that *all* spirit contacts, demon possessions, seances, etc., are false, is exceedingly foolish, naive, unrealistic, and unbiblical. The evidence is massive and the Bible is clear. Demons exist. As they say, Satan delights in counterfeiting the counterfeit to confuse the issue and continue his work unabated and unhindered. On the other hand, churches, pastors, and evangelists that deal heavily in exorcism can often become imbalanced. "The devil made me do it," becomes a convenient scapegoat. Ordinary sickness, mental or emotional illness, sins of the flesh . . . virtually everything is viewed through the cloudy, distorted lens of "demon possession." "And the seventy returned again with joy, saying, 'Lord, even the devils are subject unto us through thy name'. . . . 'Behold, I give unto you power to tread on serpents and scorpions, and over all the power of the enemy: and nothing shall by any means hurt you. Notwithstanding in this rejoice not, that the spirits are subject unto you; but rather rejoice, because your names are written in heaven'" (Luke 10:17, 19-20).

I believe in the authenticity of Johanna Michaelsen's encounter with the demon controlling the psychic healer, Hermanito, and other experiences listed in this book. Most certainly a world of spirit beings exists. Scripture and thousands of otherwise inexplicable experiences demonstrate this fact. It would be naive to deny that Satan and his demons would refuse inhabiting countless persons who personally invoke them to do so, and many others who live so that inhabitation is encouraged. (Some danger areas are mentioned later in this book.)

Satan does indeed counterfeit the counterfeit. Also, much fakery abounds in this confused world. Some people are even mistakenly identified as demon possessed. Nevertheless, it seems demon possessions still occur.

CHAPTER NINE

Face to Face with Spirit Entities

NOTE: Names marked with an asterisk (*) in this chapter are fictitious.

Carlotta* was a lovely young woman. Lustrous black hair framed her soft face and deep brown eyes. At first she was delighted when her husband became a Christian. After awhile, her joy seemed to fade. A haunting quality shadowed her eyes.

It was not long before her troubled husband shared with me that Carlotta often had "spells." The "spells" he described to me were chilling. A "spirit" talked to her and through her. Carlotta believed this "spirit" was a good spirit. Eventually we learned that Carlotta was a noted healer in her home country. Up to seven hundred people had been, or were, her followers. Carlotta was also a professing Christian. She believed that the power of God performed these healings. From her point of view the "good spirit" provided both power and comfort, and sometimes guidance.

We trained and counseled this couple in Christian basics. They were faithful and responsive. Nevertheless, as a lonely newcomer in this country, Carlotta was often depressed, even suicidal. One night in sheer desperation

Carlotta planned to commit suicide and drown her baby. Just as she was about to jump off the bridge with her baby, the "good spirit" came upon her and told her not to do this. She gained some semblance of sanity and refrained from this horrible deed. This provided one more bond to cement her relationship with the spirit and to convince her that he was a "good spirit."

Over a period of time, the evidence indicated that this was something beyond the ordinary. Though they loved each other dearly, Carlotta and her husband seemed to have increasing problems. These seemed to coincide quite often with the "spells" she experienced. After a "spell" Carlotta seemed "dragged out," drained. Apparently she could not control when and where she would have a "spell." Her husband counseled with me several times. He was puzzled. I was afraid. As time wore on, the problem worsened in spite of counsel and prayer. I dreaded what I feared was the answer.

April 27 was a beautiful spring day. Dr. DeHaven,* a mission executive and dear friend, was with me. Carlotta was sharing her story with us. Dr. DeHaven was politely interested. So was I.

Suddenly, a "spell" came on Carlotta. She began to hunch over like a very old woman. She shook violently. Her pretty face contorted. Her lips narrowed and turned inward until they looked as sharp as a razor blade. Her cheeks sucked in. The ugly old woman we saw was difficult to identify as Carlotta!

Than a deep, harsh, male-like voice spoke from Carlotta. It stunned Dr. DeHaven. Later he told me that he had never had an experience like this. Our "polite" interest grew intense.

It appeared evident that this was demon possession. Slowly and carefully we began to question the "spirit." We used standard questions such as the doctrine embodied in 1 John 4:1-6. We questioned the "spirit" about the blood of the Lord Jesus Christ shed on the cross for us, His bodily resurrection, and His deity. It was virtually impossible to pin the "spirit" down. He answered every question, although some answers evaded the truth here and there.

Like Carlotta, Dr. DeHaven was almost convinced that this was a "good" spirit. As we continued in prayer and questioning, I became increasingly suspicious. Apart from God, the unfallen angels of God are the only known category of good spirits—and they do not possess people. That left only one alternative—demon possession.

Satan does not always cause his subjects to do "bad" things. That would be a poor counterfeit of Jesus Christ and His good acts. Some people are attracted or enslaved by gross evil. While thinking they are following God, others are lured by good works from a bad source, deluded into following Satan and his cohorts. As 2 Corinthians 11:14, 15 truly states, "And no marvel; for Satan himself is transformed into an angel of light. Therefore it is no great thing if his ministers also be transformed as the ministers of righteousness; whose end shall be according to their works."

Despite the "good" things done by Carlotta's "good spirit," his presence had caused increasing trouble between she and her husband. Her experiences left her drained, morose, spiritless. Depression in her life had not lifted, but probably increased. 1 Corinthians 14:32 assures us that, ". . . the spirits of the prophets are subject to the prophets."

Carlotta did not control the spirit—the spirit controlled her. The spirit and his source confused Carlotta. The difference between what he said and what he did confused her. Her marriage was getting confused. Yet the Bible says that God is not "the author of confusion" (1 Cor. 14:33).

We prayed and asked for God's wisdom and power. As Dr. DeHaven prayed with me I cried out, "In the name of the Lord Jesus Christ, come out of Carlotta. I do not believe that you are a 'good spirit.' In the name of the Lord Jesus Christ, I command you to leave Carlotta alone!"

A titanic battle was obviously taking place. Satan's "good spirit" had been exposed. Tension filled the room. Slowly, slowly, God won the battle. The demon was cast out.

Carlotta recovered slowly. As the "spirit" left, so did the "male" voice and the contortions of face and body. Carlotta became herself again. She still did not know for certain what had happened to her. From word she has sent me, I know that she has become a growing Christian, witnessing and sharing Christ with others. Much of the stress caused by her "spells" has left the marriage. Gradually, she has realized the actual source and nature of this "good" spirit. To my knowledge, she has been bothered by the spirit only once in all the years since. She has had no more "spells" of demon possession. Glory to God!

It is not unusual for demons, even "benevolent" ones, to reveal their true spirit once they have been exposed and cast out. Victor Earnest, my friend and former spiritualist medium, told me that for a long time after his deliverance, spirits tried to choke and kill him. At times he had to call in utter desperation for fellow Christians to gather around him and pray. They pled the blood of Christ over him and the power of the resurrected Lord to deliver him from these unbearable attacks until he was finally free.

Playing with demonism can be dangerous, even fatal. Even concentrating our attention on them in excess can have its perils. One late night Pastor Si Foster and I were praying in his study for revival in our churches in Anchorage. After prayer we sat quietly while discussing demons and demon possession. Out of the corner of my eye, I saw a blur of movement. Instantly I moved sideways. (I had boxed a bit in the Navy, once fighting the National Golden Glove champion, and the instinctive movement saved me at least a headache, or much worse.) A huge book wedged in the shelf above me had fallen directly at my head!

Both Si and I were considerably shaken. We examined the place from where the book had fallen. Si explained to me that it was impossible for the book to have fallen of its own accord. Impossible, that is, from any *natural* cause. He showed me how the big volume had been placed securely on the shelf.

Near my home in the Pacific Northwest lives J. Z Knight, a lady who claims that when she is "possessed" she speaks with the voice of "Ramtha," a prophet who lived 35,000 years ago. "Ramtha" uses her as a channeler. As he possesses her, her voice changes and deepens. Supposedly, she can also heal and prophesy. Many people have moved into the area to be near her. It has become very profitable for her, and she has acquired a ranch, a mansion, and a fabulous Arabian horse. J. Z. Knight has received national attention. Yet her story is not unique. Today there are actually more than one thousand channelers in California alone who claim to be channeling spirit entities.

Another interesting event took place in my home area. On 15 February 1987, on ABC, KOMO Channel 4 TV's

Town Meeting with Ken Schram featured a young lady in her twenties. She claimed to be a "channeler" used by a spirit named Mafu. Her religious background was Catholic. She said that when Mafu possessed her she left her own body and could look down upon it. At these times she experienced great love and came back only reluctantly into her body. Mafu, a male entity, took over her female body. He claimed to have lived seventeen lifetimes on this planet.

Penny Torres, the young lady, asked for twenty or thirty seconds of silence. Penny seemed to be a rather quiet, shy girl. She sat quietly while her lips moved, apparently invoking Mafu to take over. Her body slumped, her head lowered. Deep breathing and moans began to issue from her. Dramatically, she stiffened. Her head snapped up. Now her personality seemed to transform from shy to brash, even brazen boldness. She seemed confident. Her voice deepened, strengthened. She now spoke in somewhat of a British accent. Mafu had taken over her body.

Mafu responded to questions from Ken, members of the panel and audience, and especially Constance Cumbey, lawyer, Christian, scholar, and expert on the New Age Movement and the occult. Mafu said he had come "from the Father within you to bring peace and love to you."

A Mr. Larry Woodin said that though the New Age Movement was much more than channeling, it was, nevertheless, a major focus of the New Age Movement. He stressed the importance of feeling, not necessarily knowing with the mind. He claimed that the entities possessing and channeling through human beings know these human beings thoroughly, in this life and past lives.

One of several reasons Mafu gave for coming in the

body of a woman was that if he had come as a man he might have been murdered and a religion started from that murder. (Obviously a veiled allusion to, and total misunderstanding of, the purpose of the crucifixion of Christ!)

When Mafu was asked what kind of entity he was, Mafu replied that he was a "wondrous entity!" Mafu professed great love for everyone. He claimed not to be offended by skeptics or Christians who asked penetrating questions damaging to his claims. However, when someone accused him of "running a scam," he showed obvious agitation. He responded with considerable scorn that the "greatest scam was the Jehovah of the Old Testament who made people murder and eat their children and eat of their own dung."

Constance Cumbey picked up on this quickly. She noted that Mafu had been professing his unbounding love for everyone. Yet, he had in fact just shown extreme hatred for Jehovah God. He had blasphemed the God of the Christians and the Jews!

Under close questioning, Mafu said that he had no conflict with fundamental Christian beliefs. He also said he had no conflict with Jesus. Constance asked him if Jesus Christ was *the* Lord God. Suavely, he replied, "Jesus is Lord God . . . but so are you, lady!"

Any true Christian recognizes this instantly as a denial of the deity of the Lord Jesus Christ, and therefore blasphemy! Jesus said of Satan, ". . . When he speaketh a lie, he speaketh of his own: for he is a liar, and the father of it" (John 8:44b). Many today have re-defined deity. Some believe we *all* are deity. The unique claim of Jesus is that He was God in the flesh (1 Tim. 3:16) and that there is only *one God* (Mk. 12:29-34).

Mafu went on to say that Jesus came to teach us "love of self and the whole of humanity!" Notice Luke 9:23: "If any man will come after me, let him deny himself, and take up his cross daily, and follow me." Notice also 2 Timothy 3:1-5: "This know also, that in the last days perilous times shall come. For men shall be lovers of their own selves, covetous, boasters, proud, blasphemers, disobedient to parents, unthankful, unholy, without natural affection, trucebreakers, false accusers, incontinent, fierce, despisers of those that are good, traitors, heady, highminded, lovers of pleasures more than lovers of God; having a form of godliness, but denying the power thereof: from such turn away."

Quite antithetical to Mafu's statement of "why Jesus came" is Jesus' own statement in Matthew 10:34, 35: "Think not that I am come to send peace on earth: I came not to send peace, but a sword. For I am come to set a man at variance against his father, and the daughter against her mother, and the daughter-in-law against her mother-in-law." This is a reference to the inevitable conflict between those who accept Him, and those who do not.

Jesus said He came "to seek and to save that which was lost" (Luke 19:10). Those who accept Him, on His terms, become children of God. We are to love them, whatever their denomination, as fellow heirs of the grace of God, brothers and sisters now and forever. We are to love also those who refuse Jesus, unless they force us to make a choice between them and Him. Then we are to "speak the truth to them in love," as we are admonished. We are not to pretend, however, that they are OK apart from a personal relationship with Christ, when every moment of every day they are one breath away from eternal judgment. The present-day love proclaimed by the secular world, cults, and others is a perfumed poison rising from the miasmic swamps of deceit.

After about forty-five minutes Mafu sat down with Penny's body. Then as Mafu left we heard groans, and deep breathing, and saw slight agitation of the body. Penny came back to consciousness. She seemed very subdued, especially in contrast to Mafu. Once again she was the same diffident young lady. She said she was not aware of what had taken place, but claimed to be a bit dizzy. She said she has questioned Mafu closely and everything he had told her was love. He has met with medical men, a scientist, and an under secretary of State. A few more questions and answers revealed that Penny charged money for people to hear Mafu speak. At this point Ken Schram closed the Town Meeting.

Those who do not or will not come to Christ often take one of two paths. Either they deny that Jesus Christ is God and deserves their total trust, submission, and obedience, or they say that he is God, even as they are a part of God, or "sons of God." The former makes us the God of our own life, subject only to our "inward consciousness." The latter, which is more subtle, denies Jesus while professing to believe in Him, and denigrates His deity. Jesus clearly said that He was "the way, the truth, and the life" (John 14:6), that no one could come to the Father apart from Him. This is a claim to total exclusiveness, made not by Christians, but by Christ! Similarly, Acts 4:12, speaking of Jesus, absolutely affirms, "Neither is there salvation in any other; for there is no other name under heaven given among men, whereby we must be saved."

The truth is, *no* "good spirits" possess or channel through people. All of this is gross deception. Sometimes it is humanly induced. Sometimes it is satanically or demonically induced. The only benevolent "possession" occurs when people surrender to Jesus Christ. He then makes them children of God and indwells them by the Holy Spirit. "But as many as received him, to them gave he power to become the sons of God, even to them that believe on his name" (John 1:12).

In his book *People of the Lie,* M. Scott Peck recounts a revealing story about a brilliant woman named Charlene. Charlene had formerly taught Christian doctrine for two years. She claimed to "love" everyone. Yet she was bisexual, manipulative, deceptive, a liar, unable to hold a job, a law unto herself, immoral, and involved in various cults. Peck hinted that he suspected demon possession. In a rare moment of honesty while under severe questioning, Charlene admitted that according to the Christian doctrine she had once taught, human beings existed to glorify God. For the first time in years of therapy, Charlene nearly cried and her voice began to quiver. Then she exclaimed that she did not want to live for God. She felt that would be the death of her. She declared she wanted to live only for herself, for "me."

Basically, that is the heart of the problem. "All we like sheep have gone astray; we have turned every one to his *own way,* and the Lord hath laid on him [Jesus Christ] the iniquity of us all" (Isa. 53:6). As natural men we rebel against God in favor of our own selfishness. This behavior is categorized as sin, from which we need a savior. "Going our own way," being in effect our own god, being self-centered instead of God-centered, is at the heart of rebellion against God. Is it harmless to believe Mafu? To be our own god? What are the eternal consequences? The Bible tells Christians that to be absent from the body is to be present with the Lord (2 Cor. 5:8). If people are *not* Christians, Jesus describes in detail what happens to them. They go to the hell that they have chosen (see Luke 16:19-31). Later they are resurrected and cast into the lake of fire (Rev. 20:11-15).

If there is no hell, certainly there is no heaven. Jesus firmly taught the existence of both. Everything predicted by the Bible has come true. God does not and cannot lie. Jesus, who is God, does not and cannot lie. If all He said comes true, then what He said about hell will come true also, whether or not one believes it.

Dr. Robert Morey in his book *Death and the Afterlife* states that:

> . . . merely to assert that God's love excludes eternal punishment but guarantees salvation does not prove anything. Where is this ever stated in Scripture? Nowhere. Is this revealed in nature? Hardly. The results of God's punishment for man's sin are visible on every hand.
>
> The attempt to base man's salvation solely upon God's attributes, such as His love or goodness, is unscriptural, for the Bible never speaks of God's love except in the context of Christ's vicarious atonement (John 3:16; Romans 5:8). Thus God's love, in and of itself, cannot save anyone, much less all of humanity. None of God's attributes, in and of themselves, can save anyone. Because this is everywhere assumed in Scripture, Christ's atonement was viewed as being absolutely necessary. After all, it is the manifestation of God's love in Christ that saves sinners, not "love" as mere sentiment.[1]

God's love in Christ is the most positive, powerful, life-changing force on earth as millions of people can testify! Contact with the occult world, which the Bible forbids, attempts to get answers about God and us apart from

God's revelation about Himself and us. The consequences are the same whether or not one professes to believe the Bible. Whatever "good" one may experience, whatever "visions" or "ecstatic experiences" one may enjoy in search of "God," or whatever "answers" one may get to life itself, they will be elusive, delusive, temporary, and eventually damning. The Bible pictures Satan as being an angel of light, powerful, and intelligent. Satan is perfectly willing to use or misuse the Bible. He is deceptive beyond belief, and overwhelmingly convincing to non-Christians, and even to some Christians who are unestablished in the Word of God, and unwilling to obey it.

God gives no protection or revelation of Himself to those who disregard His Word and seek Him by any means apart from His Word. He sends them a powerful delusion so that they are utterly and possibly forever convinced of the lie they chose to believe. God sends this delusion on them because they chose to reject the truth and believe a lie. "The coming of the lawless one will be in accordance with the work of Satan displayed in all kinds of counterfeit miracles, signs and wonders, and in every sort of evil that deceives those who are perishing. They perish because they refused to love the truth and so be saved. For this reason God sends them a powerful delusion so that they will believe the lie and so that all will be condemned who have not believed the truth but have delighted in wickedness." (2 Thess. 2:9-12, NIV).

Interestingly, these "entities" seldom reveal that man is a sinner. Jesus is never given the place of *the* God of the Universe. Hell is absolutely denied, or reinterpreted so as to lose its character of eternal torment apart from God and all hope. The need of a Savior, of Christ's redemption and atonement, is ignored or rationalized. In its place we are taught the Law of Karma and of reincarnation. Here we are falsely told that we are accountable to no one but ourselves, that we have no need for a savior, but pay for our own bad behavior in succeeding lives. The biblical teaching of the resurrection of all men, some unto eternal life and some unto eternal judgment, is denied. What is the source of these doctrines?

In spite of Shirley MacLaine's alleged experiences, described in part in her books *Dancing In The Light* and *Out On A Limb,* F. LaGard Smith rightly took her to task in his book *Out On A Broken Limb.* Christ declares that He and He alone, is *the* Light of the World. All other "light" comes from Satan, the "angel of light." Satan attempts to counterfeit the light of Christ, and so lure men away from Jesus, the true Light (2 Cor. 11:14, 15).

Jesus is the high and holy one who "inhabits eternity." He reveals God to us. He knows all about heaven for it is His home. He knows the way, the *only* way, to get there. He alone reveals to us all the facts we need to know at this time about the afterlife. No other source of information is reliable or necessary.

In our study of death it is necessary that we closely evaluate the teachings of reincarnation. Scripturally, it is certainly not supported. ". . . man is destined to die *once,* and after that to face judgment" (Heb. 9:27, NIV). Can reincarnation stand, however, after being tested by its *own* merits? For help with this question we again look to Dr. Robert A. Morey.[2]

> The present popular Western concepts of reincarnation are actually refinements of the ancient theory of transmigration. This theory states that all human "souls" are involved

in a cyclic series of rebirths in which the soul is eventually purged of evil by suffering, administered through the Law of Karma.

In the Indian *Vedas,* the word "Karma" originally meant "a sacrifice" or "a ritual act." In the *Upanishads* it evolved into the concept that any act in this life will have an effect on one's next life. Finally, in the *Bhagavad Gita,* Karma is viewed as a punishment in this life for evils done in the past life, with a prospect of purification for future lives.

According to the Law of Karma, one's soul can be reborn into an insect, animal, or human body. For example, a gluttonous man could be reborn into a pig's body as punishment.

The Law of Karma is the immutable law that a person pays for evil he does in this life by suffering for it in the next life. If he is reborn as a worm or as a blind girl, this is his Karma. No one can pay his Karmic debt for him. All the suffering he experiences in this life is his own fault. The Law of Karma will always catch up with him. There is no escape.

A person's soul, according to this doctrine, is eternal and is part of the "world soul" or "ultimate being" (sometimes called "God"). A person emanates out of this "cosmic energy" and passes through multiple cycles of rebirths until he is finally absorbed back into unconscious reality. One is "fallen" now because he is under the illusion of self-consciousness (I-am) and of subject-object relationships to the world (I-Thou and I-it). Through cyclic rebirths he will return to an impersonal nonconscious fusion with "ultimate reality." In other words, the person was *nothing,* is now in trouble because he *thinks* he is *something,* but will return to being *nothing* through Karmic cyclic rebirth.

The theory of Karmic transmigration has been modified to suit the Western Christian mentality. Since a "Christian" would not accept rebirth into a bug or animal, the concept was redefined so that rebirth always took place in a human body. This westernized form of transmigration was first expounded by occult groups such as Theosophy, and later by many of the Indian Hindu gurus who came to the United States. It was eventually adopted by such psychics as Jeane Dixon and Edgar Cayce.

The arguments for reincarnation which are based on alleged recall point out a major defect in the theory of reincarnation: since the vast majority of people never recall any past life, or lives, they don't know *why* they are being punished with Karmic suffering in this life. This raises several crucial questions.

1. How is justice served if people have no knowledge of *why* they are being punished?

2. Since people don't know why they are being punished, how can they avoid the same evil which originally caused the Karmic suffering?

3. If they don't know the evil which led to their suffering, are they not bound to *repeat* the evil?

4. Must people, therefore, keep making the same mistake life-after-life-after-life? How can they break out of this cycle if they do not *know* what evil to avoid?

5. Without any knowledge of the past, how is progress made or measured? Does it not seem that one is like a rabbit slowly turning on the spit of reincarnation while roasting in the fires of Karma?

It is doubtful that reincarnationists can satisfactorily answer the above questions. People's ignorance of "past lives" short-circuits any knowledge of or hope for the process of purification by Karmic cycles of rebirth.

There are also other problems. First, since virtually no one knows of his past lives, how can one know if this is his "last" life? If it is, should one "live it up" or deny himself in his last life?

Second, since one is involved in a cycle of rebirths and will be eventually absorbed back into "being," is there any real ethical pressure to live righteously in one's present life, seeing one always has another life to live?

Third, all the recall experiences we have examined omit any reference to anyone remembering when he was an orthodox Christian in a past life. This is astounding, as well as being an important observation.

If the theory of reincarnation is true, and its recall experiences are valid, then we should expect that when people are regressed into past lives through hypnosis or when they spontaneously remember a past life, they would recall all religious beliefs, regardless of their present beliefs. We should see cases of present-day reincarnationists who, when hypnotically regressed into past lives, remember being evangelical Christians. Thus we should find "readings" which proclaim that Jesus is the Christ, that He is God manifested in the flesh, that Christ arose bodily from the dead, that the Creator is distinct from the creation, that reincarnation is a doctrine of demons, etc. Where are these Christian recalls? Where are the evangelical readings?

Suspicion is justifiable when *all* recalls and *all* readings espouse the same theological and philosophical beliefs. It is absurd to believe that all past lives recalled are only those of Eastern reincarnational belief! Why is there only one theology arising out of these occult experiences of recall?

The Christian knows why only one theology arises. Satan, the father of lies, began to espouse such beliefs in the Garden of Eden when he told Adam and Eve that they could become "like God" (Gen. 3:5). Throughout history, Satan has continually baited people with this vain doctrine of the divinity of man. He is the antichrist who forever denies that Jesus is the Christ, the Son of God, the second person of the Trinity.

Inadequacies of the Law of Karma

Several other clear reasons demonstrate that the so-called "Law of Karma" itself is a myth. It simply does not exist except in the minds of reincarnationists. And it is not even a *good* myth, but rather a pernicious, evil concept which has caused untold human suffering and misery.

1. It has no scientific evidence to support it.

2. It has no analogy in nature. There is no illustration or example of it in the world in which we live.

3. Its infinite regression to past lives in order to explain everything which happens in the present robs history of any meaning. It assumes a cyclic view of history which denies that unique and final events take place in history. Everything is repeated endlessly with no final meaning. There is no beginning or climax to history.

4. It does not satisfy man's moral sensitivity or sense of justice.

5. It does not provide any absolute standards of right and wrong. Thus, its administration of suffering must be arbitrary and capricious.

6. It teaches that suffering is the only real purpose in life. Man has an innate aversion to such a theory.

7. Since it views each individual life as having no purpose outside of its own suffering, there is no concept of living for the glory of God or for the good of others. Hence, the Law of Karma is intrinsically selfish and self-centered.

8. It cripples the unity of humanity, since each soul is trapped in a cycle of rebirths which benefits only that individual soul.

9. It produces despair, fatalism, pessimism, etc.

10. It cannot apply any ethical pressure to live a good life *now* as opposed to waiting until a later life.

11. It teaches that suffering is one's own fault, and that it can never ultimately come from the world or other people. It is a psychologically devastating concept.

12. It causes people to ignore the suffering of others.

13. It does not encourage people to alleviate human suffering.

14. It produces pride among the rich and healthy, and

shame within the poor and sick.

15. It destroys all self-identity. Since "you" are "you" only in this life and "you" have actually been an endless number of people, and "you" will never know any or all of your past lives, "you" are a faceless nonperson with no self-identity. This is psychologically harmful.

16. It allows no place for forgiveness, since Karma can neither give nor recognize forgiveness. It gives no grace, exercises no mercy, displays no love. How can the Law of Karma be just, yet supposedly solve the problem of evil if it does not have grace, mercy, love, or forgiveness as an essential part of its nature or administration? The Law of Karma is cruel.

17. It does not answer the question, "If I sin as an *adult* in this life, how is it just to punish me as an *infant* in a future life?"

18. It makes unnecessary any repentance or restitution in this life for evil done in this life. According to some reincarnationists, the Law of Karma does not even allow expiation in this life for evil done in this life. Since you will have to pay your Karmic debt in a a future life, nothing need be done. How can the Law of Karma be *just* if it makes repentance useless?

19. It does not demonstrate why it is not possible for someone else to suffer vicariously in your place and to pay off your Karmic debt for you.

20. Those who believe in the Law of Karma assume that all punishments for evil will be *finite*. They assume that there are no evils so great that the punishment for them will be infinite in duration and intensity.

Social Problems and Reincarnation

The theory of Karmic reincarnation is politically reactionary. It is a convenient tool of the rich upper classes for oppressing and exploiting the lower classes. It teaches the oppressed majority to accept their poverty and deprivation as punishment for past evils. The rich deserve the "good life" while the poor deserve their suffering. A consistent re-incarnationist would never seek the overthrow of corrupt governments. The plight of the Untouchables in India reveals the political impact of the theory of reincarnation.

The theory of transmigration also leads to financial and ecological ruin. Because insects and animals may be Karmic rebirths of human souls, no attempt is made to destroy insects and rodents which eat food supplies. Thus, by allowing these marauders to eat tons of food, people are forced to die of starvation! Also, nothing is done to stop the spread of disease by insect infestation. Is it any wonder that disease as well as famine is a common experience in cultures where the theory of transmigration is accepted? It leads to human misery on a massive scale.

The Western world should take a long and probing look at the Eastern world and its human misery because such misery is a direct result of the embracing of Karmic reincarnation. Too many Westerners have embraced Eastern theology without accepting the life-style that the theory entails.

The caste system of India which locks an individual into a certain class and prohibits any movement from one caste to another is the sociological fruit of the theory of Karmic reincarnation. Just as Christianity produced Western democracy and compassionate capitalism, Karmic reincarnation produces the oppression of India's caste system.

Why, then, do Westerners assume that they can embrace the *root* of Karmic reincarnation and, at the same time, escape from experiencing the economical, sociological, and political *fruit* of Karmic reincarnation? To the Eastern mind it must seem that Westerners "play" with reincarnation and do not seriously practice it as it should be. The Westerners want to live off the fruit of *Christianity* but embrace the root of Karmic reincarnation. Their attempt to "have their cake and eat it too" will only end in spiritual ruin.

Conclusion

Serious doubts arise concerning the intellectual integrity and scientific validity of the theory of Karmic reincarnation. It does not explain the world in which we live. It is devastating to every level of human existence. Its arguments have been examined and found to be invalid. The life-style which arises out of a reincarnational world and life view leads to political, economic, and sociological disaster. It is rooted in the world of the occult which is clearly denounced in the Scriptures.

It cannot, therefore, be accepted as a valid theology, philosophy, or life-style. Only the Christian world and life view can provide a credible, consistent perspective of life in the here and now as well as life beyond the grave.

Dr. Morey also points out other contradictions within the theory of reincarnation. The theory holds that souls are eternal and no new souls are being generated. Therefore, the number of souls available to inhabit bodies on earth is decreasing as they are being absorbed back into the "one." We find, however, a population explosion so great that more than half of all people who have ever lived on earth are alive today.

Reincarnation teaches that through its process our moral condition will improve. There should be some trace of this improvement throughout mankind in the world scene today. Unfortunately the opposite is clearly seen. One might also ask, If all is God, all is one, and all is good, as reincarnation and the New Age Movement teach, where did the thought that *we are not one,* and that *there is evil* come from? Also, why is there a need to get back to what we already are?

Finally, what is there to look forward to under the

teaching of reincarnation? Supposedly we eventually "melt" into an impersonal existence of oneness of being. As a drop of rain is absorbed into the ocean and loses its identity to the whole, so our soul becomes absorbed into the oneness of nature. What a morbid future that would offer.

To conclude this chapter, please read and observe several clear scriptural warnings and promises.

"Keep on, then, with your magic spells and with your many sorceries, which you have labored at since childhood. Perhaps you will succeed, perhaps you will cause terror. All the counsel you have received has only worn you out! Let your astrologers come forward, those stargazers who make predictions month by month, let them save you from what is coming upon you. Surely they are like stubble; the fire will burn them up. They cannot even save themselves from the power of the flame. Here are no coals to warm anyone; here is no fire to sit by. That is all they can do for you—these you have labored with and trafficked with since childhood. Each of them goes on in his error; there is not one that can save you" (Isa. 47:12-15, NIV).

Leviticus 19:31 (NIV) warns, "Do not turn to mediums or seek out spiritists, for you will be defiled by them. I am the Lord your God."

Leviticus 20:6 (NIV) further warns, "I will set my face against the person who turns to mediums and spiritists to prostitute himself by following them, and I will cut him off from his people."

". . . I have the same hope in God as these men, that there will be a resurrection of both the righteous and the wicked. So I strive always to keep my conscience clear before God and man" (Acts 24:15, NIV).

"For my Father's will is that everyone who looks to the Son and believes in him shall have eternal life, and I will raise him up at the last day" (John 6:40, NIV).

"Jesus said to her, 'I am the resurrection and the life. He who believes in me will live, even though he dies; and whoever lives and believes in me will never die. Do you believe this?' 'Yes, Lord,' she told him, 'I believe that you are the Christ, the Son of God, who was to come into the world.'" (John 11:25, 26, NIV).

We are now ready to see how all of the preceding information about the occult, after death experiences, spirit entities, inner power, etc. fit together.

Dave Hunt, world famous author and researcher, begins to pull back the curtain in the next chapter, "The Force and the Master Plan."

Notes

1. Dr. Robert A. Morey, *Death and Afterlife* (Minneapolis: Bethany House Publishers, 1984), p. 233.

2. Dr. Robert A. Morey, *Reincarnation and Christianity* (Minneapolis, MN: Bethany House Publishers, 1980). Portions used with permission.

CHAPTER TEN

The Force and the Master Plan[1]

One of the most remarkable occurrences of the past decade has been the worldwide resurgence of religion. This has continued to accelerate in spite of the adverse reactions that were predicted after the mass suicide-murder of cult members in Jonestown, Guyana. Iran is a prime example. Who would have imagined that an exiled religious leader would force the ouster of the shah, whose armed forces were among the strongest and whose rule the most stable in the Middle East? Yet Iran is now under the absolute control of a religious fanatic, whose contempt for international law and whose vow to "exterminate without mercy" all non-Islamic governments make Jim Jones seem mild in comparison.

Following Ayatollah Khomeini's takeover of Iran—effected not with military power but by religious fervor—Islam is experiencing a fresh revival around the world. Yet this is also true of religion in general. Islam is very similar to Mormonism, which is spreading rapidly around the world—to say nothing of the worldwide explosion of other religious cults of every conceivable variety. What happened in Iran is not so much the *cause* of Islam's revival as it is the *result* of it, along with a general resurgence of religious faith worldwide. Everything points toward a much larger role in world affairs to be played by religion and religious leaders in the future. The 1980s could become known as the decade of religious revival (the last thing the experts would have predicted for the space age).

Having proclaimed himself "the guardian of Shi'ah Islam," Mohammed Reza Shah Pahlavi took every possible step to control and secularize the Muslim religion in Iran.[2] Yet Islam proved to be beyond government control. In the end the *ulema* (clergy) conquered their secular "guardian." It is a mistake to explain the Iranian revolution as due to the reaction of a backward people who rejected modernization and Westernization of their culture. It was the Shah's *religious* reforms that led to his downfall. The same surprising vitality of religion in an age where science is supposed to be the new god has won out against secularization in many other countries in spite of seemingly impossible odds.

Russia and China are two astonishing examples. After more than six decades of totalitarian determination to stamp out every vestige of religious faith, atheism is on the wane and far more people admit—though many of them only secretly to close friends—to religious faith in the Soviet Union today than ever before in its history. Even in Red China, where every church had been closed and millions of believers of all religions murdered, churches are now being reopened in what can only be interpreted as an admission by Peking that its program to destroy religion has failed.

An Astonishing Prophecy

Shortly before His crucifixion, Jesus Christ predicted a number of specific conditions that would characterize the world in the last days. These signs would indicate that His Second Coming is near. Numerous books, such as Hal Lindsey's *The Late Great Planet Earth,* have dealt in detail with various prophesied signs of Christ's return: wars and rumors of wars . . . nation will rise against nation, kingdom against kingdom . . . famines and earthquakes in various places . . . the increase of wickedness . . . great distress, never equaled again (Matt. 24:6-8, 21).

Jesus gave another sign, however, that has received little attention by writers and preachers. When His disciples asked him, "What will be the sign of your coming?" the first words of His reply were, "Watch out that no one deceives you!" (Matt. 24:4). He then went on to explain that His Second Coming would be preceded by a period of *religious revival that would be characterized by great deception.*[3] Specifically, Jesus declared that false messiahs and false prophets would arise in large numbers and succeed in deceiving multitudes into following them through the display of "great signs and wonders" (Matt. 24:24). These counterfeit miracles will be Satan's way of getting the world to accept the Antichrist, who will unite the entire world *under one religion.*

Did Christ and His apostles have psychic phenomena in mind when they warned of great signs and wonders that would deceive many people in the last days? Is the present cultic and occultic explosion a sign that Christ's Second Coming is near? What part will psychic power play in the Antichrist's new world religion?

Psychic Powers

In early February, 1979, major news media featured stories about psychic M. Kathlyn Rhea. Called in to help locate two missing persons whom the authorities had been searching for without success, Ms. Rhea announced that both were dead, and she described with uncanny accuracy where their widely separated bodies could be found. She correctly stated that the eight-year-old girl, Victoria DeSantiago, had been murdered by heavy blows to the head, and that the 78-year-old man, Russell T. Drummond, had died naturally. Calaveras County sheriffs confirmed that Ms. Rhea had told them exactly where to find Drummond's body, and doubted that they would ever have located it without her help.[4]

These two cases immediately brought national prominence to Ms. Rhea, who directs the Parapsychology Education and Awareness Center in Los Altos, California. Following the publicity, a private detective asked Ms. Rhea to help locate Richard Ogden, 48, who had disappeared twenty months before. While holding a photo of the missing man, Ms. Rhea had a vision of a blood-spattered blue workshirt. Hiking into a hilly area that Ms. Rhea had described to him, Richard's brother, Harry Ogden, soon found a blood-stained workshirt, which he immediately recognized as his missing brother's—almost exactly where the psychic has "seen" it!

Such uncanny powers were rare only a few years ago. Today they are becoming commonplace. Some psychics have revealed so many unpublished details of crimes under investigation that police have arrested them as suspects. Could there be "vibrations" in a photograph that provide information about events that happened to the person months or even years after the photo was taken ? Are psychic powers proof that we are all part of a Universal Mind and thus potentially know everything and can do anything through turning into the Force? Or are there other minds out there channeling paranormal information and power through psychics in order to deceive us about the nature of reality? If so, why?

Changing Attitudes

Until very recently, most church leaders classified clairvoyance, psychokinesis, out-of-body experiences, and other psychic phenomena as occult. That attitude is changing rapidly. In 1977, Morton Kelsey, a prominent Episcopal priest who taught at Notre Dame University, came out openly in favor of cultivating psychic experiences. In his book *The Christian and the Supernatural,* Kelsey described Jesus as comparable to a shaman (psychic) and encouraged Christians to develop psychic powers such as clairvoyance, precognition, and telepathy. While acknowledging that there are some dangers, Kelsey believes that development of ESP within the Christian church would help to validate the miracles claimed in the Bible.

Many other Christian leaders, however, would still reject any attempt to equate psychic phenomena with miracles, attributing the former to Satan and the latter to God. Unquestionably there are many passages in Scripture that explicitly forbid any involvement in the occult.[5] There is considerable disagreement among Christians, however, as to whether all psychic phenomena are necessarily occultic in origin. Could certain kinds of ESP, for example, be natural abilities? But if so, why do they evidence themselves so seldom?

Contrary to general expectations that the advance of science would cause religion to die out, science itself is turning to religion and is accepting the supernatural in the form of psychic phenomena. Various kinds of apparently supernatural manifestations are an integral part of the current cult explosion and are also gaining an increasing acceptance within established churches. Will the Christian church now turn to Eastern mysticism, as Western science and society are doing? Is there a difference between psychic phenomena and miracles, and if so, what is it? How is it possible to distinguish one from the other? We will face these questions, and others equally important, in the following pages.

Modern Science and the Occult

In the summer of 1974, twenty-one of the top scientists in the Western world gathered in Toronto to participate in a series of seminars and tests of three leading psychics. The results were staggering, including the possibility of storing the peculiar brain waves of psychics in computer memory banks to be fed later into the brains of nonpsychics and to thereby develop their ESP. One of the participating researchers, Cambridge Professor Brian Josephson, winner of the 1973 Nobel prize in physics, made this statement at the conclusion of the tests:

> We are on the verge of discoveries which [involve] . . .
> a new kind of energy. . . .
>
> In times past, "respectable" scientists would have

nothing to do with psychic phenomena . . . the "respect-able" scientists may find they have missed the boat.[6]

Shoshone Indian medicine man Rolling Thunder has predicted, "Scientists will eventually discover what savages have always known."[7] This is happening today. Paganism is basically primitive "mind science." Neopaganism and other forms of occultism are experiencing explosive growth worldwide. According to recent reports reaching the West, witchcraft is having a revival even in Red China, where "Fortune tellers and soothsayers . . . [have] openly offered their services in the streets of many cities . . . for the first time in decades."[8] The connection between UFOs, psychic phenomena, paganism, occultism, and the present cult explosion will become clear in the following pages.

One of the most interesting facets of the current psychic explosion is the manner in which it is moving science and religion together, thus reversing centuries of mutual animosity and suspicion. Bam Price, an associate of former astronaut and now psychic researcher Edgar Mitchell, recently said: "The powers described by the mystics through the ages are now being described by scientists, proof that underlying the material world is a vast nonsubstantial world. The priests of old were also the scientists. Today the priest and the scientist are coming back together again."[9] It has taken a hundred years to catch up with Mary Baker Eddy, the founder of Christian Science, whose writings were an early attempt to move Christianity in the very direction that science is now turning—to the East.

Through various occultic devices and techniques such as the I Ching, tarot cards, Ouija boards, astrology, dows-ing rods, hypnosis, biofeedback, psychedelic drugs, yoga, and other forms of Eastern mysticism (such as TM), modern man is seeking to tune into a mysterious Force that many scientists suspect is the primary element in the universe. In the process, we are discovering that consciousness may involve "higher states" where hidden powers of the mind lie awaiting discovery. The nonphysical dimension long recognized by pagan religions is more than mere superstition after all. In fact, it is the world both of the cults and the occult, as we will see.

Psychic research conducted in scientific laboratories in recent years has verified the existence of nonphysical forces that have always been associated with the occult. Many mysterious powers that were once the trademark of witchcraft and sorcery are being demonstrated under strict laboratory controls by today's psychics and accepted in the name of science. There is an accelerating merger between science and Eastern mysticism. This surprising partnership seems logically necessary if biblical prophecies about the last days are to be fulfilled. Is the world even now being prepared to welcome the Antichrist? What role will cults play?

Transcendental Meditation

In many ways, Joan Harrison was typical of an entire generation of young people who rebelled against the establishment in the 1960s and began a search for spiritual reality to fill the void left by the failure of materialism. This inner emptiness fueled Joan's desire to find her "real Self." She was attracted to a form of yoga that promised it would help her to realize her full potential through tapping secret powers that apparently lay dormant within her own mysterious being. The cult that Joan Harrison joined made seemingly unique claims. Yet beneath the surface it was remarkably similar to a growing number of cults that are still trapping millions of others like herself.

The path she followed was a familiar one. But let Joan tell her own story:

> I was a seeker looking for ultimate answers. My search began . . . in psychoanalysis . . . encounter groups and . . . psychedelic drugs.
>
> I was particularly impressed by Timothy Leary's book *The Psychedelic Experience*, which showed the relationship between LSD and mystical experiences of Tibetan Buddhist monks. That led me into Eastern mysticism.
>
> I became interested in TM in 1967. It was very big in Berkeley, and many of my friends were getting into it. There were posters all over town advertising TM as a way to bliss consciousness, relaxation, and one's full potential.
>
> I was looking for . . . answers to life. That was the main reason why I got into TM. And I did experience superficial results right away—relaxation and a euphoric feeling that would come and go.
>
> Eventually I stopped taking pot, because in TM I experienced a "high" that was greater than on drugs. It wasn't that TM "cured" me of drugs—it was the next logical step for which drugs had prepared me.
>
> I became a TM teacher and had many supernatural experiences. Definitely it wasn't just in my mind, because I didn't even believe such things were possible until I experienced them.[10]

Although Transcendental Meditation had been offered to her as a scientific method of relaxation that had nothing to do with religion, Joan eventually discovered that Maharishi Mahesh Yogi was cleverly leading Westerners into Hinduism by calling it a science—and that she had joined a Hindu cult. Joan became a willing accomplice in Maharishi's deliberate deception. She credits TM and Maharishi with numbing her conscience:

> Although people are led to believe that TM is a scientific relaxation technique, it really comes from the Hindu scriptures and is a form of yoga. The initiation everyone must go through is a Hindu worship ceremony honoring the Hindu gods and Ascended Masters, including Maharishi's own dead guru Dev.
>
> As a teacher of TM, I was told to . . . lie. We were taught that the state of consciousness of the general public was so low that to tell them the truth about TM would only confuse them.
>
> We were told to tell them that the mantra we gave them was a meaningless sound, the repetition of which would help them to relax—whereas it was really the name of a Hindu deity with tremendous occult powers behind it.
>
> For those who really got into it, TM was like taking a rocket ship into another state of consciousness, where their whole view of reality and of God would be changed.
>
> So many people came into TM as Christians or Jews or whatever—and in a year or two of meditation they had become Hindus without even realizing it.
>
> They would eventually believe that through the progressively higher levels of consciousness TM led them into they could become God.
>
> This is not a Christian belief, but a Hindu belief.[11]

TM's scientific mask is worn more loosely in India. Recent visitors to Maharishi's "university" at Rishikesh on the banks of the Ganges River found no evidence of academia, but "a real guru center with lingam worship . . . [and] a new TM order of monks."[12] The brand of "science" being practiced in the TM ashram seems hardly distinguishable from the Hinduism being practiced in the numerous ashrams of the many other Hindu gurus in this "holy city" at the base of the Himalayas. It is from his Swiss headquarters, however, that Maharishi directs his program to take over the world—and he intends to do it!

The Twilight of Rationalism

The youth rebellion of the 1960s had powerful religious undertones that few people recognized at the time. It spawned both the Jesus Movement and the even larger Satan Movement. The counterculture of drugs and mysticism that grew out of the radical revolution brought a "new consciousness" to millions in the West. Fundamental to the consciousness revolution is the ancient teaching of shamanism, or witchcraft—that there is something infinitely more powerful than atomic power, a mystical Force that pervades the universe and which can be activated by the minds of those initiated into its secrets. Those who learn to control this Force become gods, to whom all things are possible.

To those who understood, the movie *Star Wars* was not so much about future science and space escapades as it was about witchcraft's Force. In the final analysis, the stock in trade of witch doctors and voodoo priests proved to be greater than the most advanced technology. That was the secret weapon wielded by those two master magicians, Darth Vader and Obi-wan Kenobi—one using this "old religion" for "good," and the other for "evil," in a colossal battle that the film implied is far from over, and in which there can be no ultimate victor. After all, if it is the same all-pervading Force, why should either the "dark side" or the "light side" prevail over the other?

The effect of the consciousness revolution upon an entire generation in the last few years can be seen clearly in the making of the well-known "American folk guru," Bab Ram Dass. Dr. Richard Alpert's magical metamorphosis into Ram Dass[13] reveals a pattern that has become all too familiar. In their search to "find themselves," millions of others have been led along the same path from psychotherapy and drugs into Eastern mysticism. During the past two decades, an unprecedented transformation of consciousness has occurred throughout the Western world that will have an enormous impact in the years immediately ahead.

The Mystic Trip

For Richard Alpert, first came materialistic and academic success, with a Ph.D. and a teaching position at Harvard. The accompanying sports cars, sailboat, airplane, social prominence, and parties did not forestall the disillusionment, frustration, personal insecurity, and neurosis that followed. Psychoanalysis during five years at a cost of $26,000 left Alpert at least as neurotic, if not more so, than before—"Too sick to leave analysis," in the words of his therapist, though Alpert was himself "treating" others as a psychotherapist and was teaching at Harvard.

Next came the whole drug trip (in association with fellow Harvard professor Timothy Leary), beginning with pot and moving into psychedelics in an effort to find a permanent "high." Eastern mysticism (in many cases the next step after drugs) followed naturally. Alpert surrendered himself to a guru in India, who led him down the yoga path of "Self-realization" (recognizing his own divinity), to become a guru himself. Finally, he became involved in spiritism, which was always at the core of pagan religions and retains this position in most pseudo-Christian and neopagan cults even today. Baba Ram Dass now claims to be in touch with various spirits of famous persons who are guiding him, including a fourteenth-century cabalist, a great Buddhist, Ramakrishna, Jesus, and his own guru (who is now dead), Baba Sant-ji Maharaj.

Modern society is being increasingly bombarded by the same influences that turned Dr. Richard Alpert into Baba Ram Dass. No careful student of the Bible could fail to recognize the deep significance of this fact. With an alarming and accelerating momentum, today's world is being conditioned to look to psychic miracles and Eastern mysticism for its ultimate salvation. One has the distinct impression of a Pied Piper gathering in his wake countless millions, who imagine that they are being led into a New Age made possible through "higher states of consciousness." Is the stage even now being set to act out the "last days" scenario written thousands of years ahead of time by biblical apostles and prophets?

Through the increasing influence exerted by drugs and Eastern mysticism upon every level of today's society, the Western worldview has changed dramatically within the past twenty years, from the Christian belief in a Creator who is separate from creation, to the Hindu belief in an impersonal Force that is everything. This consciousness revolution, which grew out of the youth rebellion of the 1960s, has brought us from skeptical rationalism to an open acceptance of the supernatural. The spirit realm and strange psychic occurrences that had been written off as mere superstitions are once again being taken seriously not only by the man in the street but also by scientists.

The Death of Materialism

Modern laboratory research has provided a scientific basis for seriously evaluating mystical experiences such as those of Joan Harrison and Richard Alpert. Investigation of psychic phenomena has verified the reality of a spirit dimension and has led to significant findings with regard to the spiritual nature of man himself. Laboratory experiments reveal that man is more than a conglomeration of protein molecules wired with nerves. He is a spirit being alive within a physical body. Moreover, there is substantial evidence that other spirits—without bodies of their own and perhaps capable of "possessing" human bodies—also exist.

The discovery and verification of ESP, psychokinesis, clairvoyance, telepathy, precognition, psychometry, and other forms of psychic power have produced evidence that the human mind exists separate from the brain in a nonphysical dimension beyond space, time, and matter. The late Dr. J. B. Rhine, father of American parapsychology, declared:

> The evidence of PK along with that of ESP established the case for the reality of mind . . . in spite of the fact that a couple of generations of psychologists had been trying to discourage the idea and supplant it with a model of mechanistic behaviorism.
>
> The man in the pulpit . . . was right in preaching that the human spirit is something more than the material of his body and brain.[14]

In his special address to the 1975 Annual Para-Psychological Association Convention, Stanford University Professor Willis W. Harman said:[15]

. . . the paramount fact that has emerged is the duality of his [man's] experience. He is found to be both physical and spiritual, both aspects being "real" and neither fully describable in terms of the other. "Scientific" and "religious" metaphors are complementary; renowned psychic investigator Dr. Milan Ryzl (formerly of the Czechoslovakian Academy of Science) has summed up the implications of recent laboratory discoveries in these words:

> "Apparently we are heading toward the finding that our 'physical' universe is only a part of a more extensive reality . . . [where] the former contradictions between 'matter' and 'spirit' disappear. . . .
>
> We can further assume . . . parts of the human personality that exist outside the material universe . . . [which] could survive even after the material part has been destroyed by death.
>
> There are indications that what we know as the 'material world of physics' is only a part of a far wide reality. . . ."[16]

Unfortunately, in deriving such evidence, science has moved into the spirit dimension, where it is ill-equipped to venture. In spite of increasingly sophisticated scientific instruments and computers, scientists are no less vulnerable to spiritual deception than anyone else. Parapsychologists may well emerge as the new high priests of the coming world religion. Through blindly following the latest discoveries of science, the entire world could be swept up in a psycho-spiritual deception that will compel humanity to follow the Antichrist.

The Spirits in Action

There is no good reason to conclude that human minds are the only intelligences in the universe, or that higher beings, if they exist, would necessarily be benevolent. Nor can we assume that extraterrestrial minds must occupy physical bodies and live on other planets like ourselves. It is entirely possible that other intelligences could function in a spirit dimension without ever being connected with bodies of their own. Under the appropriate state of consciousness, they may well be able to "possess" human bodies for their own purposes, much as a hypnotist controls his subject.

There is considerable scientific evidence indicating that spirit beings provide the intelligent direction behind psychic phenomena. It would be diverging too much to include that evidence here. However, there are interesting analogies in physics that support the reasonableness of parapsychology's evidence that nonphysical entities do exist. It is sufficiently important to give one example—the neutrino. Oddly enough, this intriguing particle behaves very much like a spirit.

The neutrino has virtually no physical properties, and is unaffected either by gravitation or electromagnetic fields. A neutrino zooming in from intergalactic space at the speed of light would pass right through the entire earth as though it didn't exist, just as spirits are presumed to pass through solid walls. The great astronomer V. A. Firsoff said:

> The universe as seen by a neutrino eye would wear a very unfamiliar look. Our earth and other planets simply would not be there. . . .
>
> A neutrino brain might suspect our existence from certain secondary effects, but would find it very difficult to prove, as we would elude the neutrino instruments at his disposal.[17]

We would laugh at the naivete of neutrino-bodied

beings—if such existed—who refused to admit the existence of humans simply because they could not "see" us with their neutrino eyes. But is it any less naive for materialists to deny the existence of nonphysical beings simply because they are not visible to human eyes? Spirits can no longer be dismissed for lack of a physical explanation of their existence. To do so would be very unscientific.

We have taken time for this brief scientific apologetic on the existence of nonphysical beings because spirits play a large part in the entire cult-occult world. Like Baba Ram Dass, most cult leaders claim to be in contact with various spirit entities. Such claims cannot be automatically dismissed as fraud or hallucinations, nor should they be gullibly accepted without investigation. Although recipients of visions or other supernatural experiences may be seduced or deceived, there is considerable evidence to indicate that something real is going on in at least some instances. The mystical experiences of the members of a wide variety of cults are too similar to be explained as coincidence. We cannot just dismiss the fact that cultists who are widely scattered around the world have independently received very similar "revelations" from apparent spirit beings.

Extensive investigation in many countries reveals similar supernatural occurrences in the lives of people who have never met one another. This common pattern argues very strongly for the probability that a single Mastermind behind the scenes is orchestrating the current cult-occult explosion. The Bible calls Satan the "god of this age" (2 Cor. 4:4) Does this imply that he is the author of every false religion, the real genius behind the cult explosion? We will consider this possibility later.

If nonphysical entities, such as demons, do exist in a spirit dimension, they would be undetectable by even our most sophisticated physical instruments. But if human consciousness exists at a juncture of the physical and spiritual, then under the right conditions these nonphysical beings could make sight or sound or other seemingly sensory contact with us, *and even manipulate the neurons in our brains!* Altered states of consciousness induced by drugs, Eastern meditation, hypnosis, mediumistic trances, and clinical death appear to open the door for such contact and manipulation. So does the surrender of reason to follow blindly a cult leader.

Scientology

Hal Richards was another dropout who moved into Haight-Ashbury and turned onto drugs at about the time Joan Harrison was finding that she could have psychedelic experiences in TM and was abandoning pot and LSD. Hal, too, had tried to find himself through psychology, which he began to study at Princeton University in order to better understand his LSD experiences. Hal hoped to become a psychotherapist, if only he could conquer his own depression and learn how to relate properly to others. After being introduced to Scientology, Hal thought he had found the answer to his psychological problems. With deep roots in psychology and Eastern mysticism, Scientology claimed to go far beyond psychotherapy. Looking back, Hal recalls:

> A good friend of mine in Los Angeles, who was a drug dealer, introduced me to Scientology. I was skeptical at first, but after going to a few lectures and seeing some films, my eyes began to open to the fact that there was su-

pernatural power available. L. Ron Hubbard [founder of Scientology] was clearly a man who had this Force in his life, and I wanted it too.

I had always been interested in the occult. Fascinated from the very first lecture, within two or three weeks I was so impressed with Scientology that I left Princeton University to become a full-time worker in an eastern office of the organization.

Several years later I was transferred to the international headquarters of this powerful organization. There I reached one of the ultimate states of consciousness in Scientology, which is called going "clear." You could equate this state with Nirvana of Buddhism or Self-realization of Hinduism—or Unity-consciousness under the influence of drugs.

In this state I was supposed to have risen beyond my psychological problems. I certainly had developed a certain amount of seemingly supernatural power that I had never known before . . . but I still had problems and was still searching for answers, still very much aware that something vital was missing in my life.[18]

Hal didn't know what a religious cult was, and much less did he suspect that he had joined one. He was eventually to learn, however, that he was trapped in a group that was determined never to let him escape its control. Though at first he seemed to find in Scientology what he had been searching for, Hal gradually became disillusioned. In desperation, he turned at last to Jesus Christ for forgiveness of sins. Excited by the inner transformation that Christ had worked in his life, Hal began to share the good news. To his surprise, friends in the organization reacted in anger when he told them that Jesus Christ had died for their sins and risen from the dead, and was now seeking an entrance into their lives. They were convinced that Hal was suffering from a delusion caused by the surfacing of detrimental "engrams" he had picked up in prior lives. (Reincarnation is a central doctrine of Scientology, as it is for many other cults.)

Seeing that his closest friends were becoming increasingly hostile toward him, Hal decided to leave Scientology. He made the mistake of announcing this decision. One of the marks of a cult is the belief that it alone has the truth and that there is no salvation outside the group. Scientology is no exception. It was devastating for Hal to find himself made a prisoner in the very offices where he had worked for so long. Those he had trusted as his close friends were now threatening him with bodily harm if he tried to escape. Arrangements were made to put him aboard the Scientology ship, where his thoughts were to be "restructured" to bring them back into agreement with the cult. Hal was able to escape only by pretending to recover his loyalty to Scientology.

The Cult Explosion

The broad interest in psychic phenomena is of relatively recent origin. Who had heard of Scientology or TM two decades ago? The few religious groups in America that were labeled cults by the established churches were nearly all offshoots of Christianity: Jehovah's Witnesses, Mormons, the Worldwide Church of God, Christian Science, Science of Mind, Religious Science, Unity, and Spiritualism. While there has always been a heavy Hindu and Buddhist influence in Spiritualism and the Mind Science religions, the newer cults are more blatant in their embrace of Eastern mysticism. This coincides with the consciousness revolution currently sweeping the West, which has popularized vegetarianism, reincarnation, karma, yoga, the martial arts, holistic health, occult devices such as I Ching and tarot cards, and psychedelic drugs. Beneath this diversity lies an intriguing unity.

Today it is estimated that there are more than 5,000 religious and pseudoreligious cults in the United States. Not a passing fad (as some have thought and many hoped), this unprecedented cult explosion is accelerating in spite of the horrible fate that overtook the followers of Jim Jones. Each cult is headed by a self-proclaimed "prophet" or "prophetess," who generally claims to have new and unique revelations. Hundreds and probably thousands of today's new wave of prophets literally profess to be God incarnate, and most wield absolute authority over cult members. They are taken seriously by millions of followers, who consider them to be modern messiahs, fresh reincarnations of the "Christ spirit."

In a book of this size it would be impossible to deal with thousands of cults. Instead, we will cover a few basic beliefs and practices that nearly all cult groups have in common. Strange as it may seem, most cults are about the same. Even apparent differences are generally only skin deep. Could there be a common source of inspiration for most, if not all, cult-occult beliefs and experiences? Could there even be a common purpose?

Such a possibility inevitably confronts any investigator of the cult-occult explosion. At first the thought seems too sensational, too preposterous—and one reacts with skepticism. But the deeper one digs, the more evidence there is of a single Mastermind at work. Even investigators of UFO phenomena are eventually led to a cult-occult connection.

As Dr. Jacques Vallee, astrophysicist, computer scientist, and one of the world's most credible ufologists, has said:

> A few investigators—notably Ray Palmer, John Keel, and Savatore Freixedo—have suggested both in public statements and in private conversations with me that there may be a link between UFO events and "occult" phenomena.
>
> At first view, the very suggestion of such a link is disturbing to a scientist. However . . . the phenomena reported by [UFO] witnesses involve poltergeist effects, levitation, psychic control, healing and out-of-body experiences . . . familiar [themes] . . . [of] occult literature . . . found in the teachings of the Rosicrucian Order, [etc.]. . . .
>
> . . . which have inspired not only the witchcraft revival, but also . . . "psychic" writers and . . . "scientific parapsychologists."
>
> Furthermore, there is a connection between UFOs and occult themes in their social effects. . . .[19]

After eighteen years of careful investigation of UFOs, Dr. Vallee comes to some startling conclusions in his sixth book on the subject, *Messengers of Deception:* 1) UFOs are real but probably not physical; 2) they are part of some evil scheme for the victimization of earthlings; and 3) one of their major purposes is to manipulate human consciousness and to program us psychologically for some ultimate deception. Commenting further on the evidence of some unified plan behind the entire UFO-cult-occult scene, Brad Steiger has said:

> Nearly every observer of the contemporary spiritual scene seems to agree that there is some kind of new Pentecost going on at this time, some kind of spiritual awakening process at work.
>
> And a good many of these observers feel that this

growing mystical consciousness may have something to do with the Last Days.[20]

The Thread of Deception

Whether we are actually in the last days remains a matter of individual opinion. We propose to trace the common thread of deception that links the entire cult-occult scene. An explanation must be found for this underlying unity among cults that otherwise appear to be at odds with one another. Part of that explanation appears in the next chapter by Dave Hunt.

Notes

1. The following chapter is adapted from *The Cult Explosion*, by Dave Hunt, pp. 5-20.

2. George W. Braswell, Jr., "Civil Religion in Contemporary Iran," *Journal of Church and State*, vol. 21, no. 2 (Spring 1979) (Waco, Texas: Baylor University), pp. 223-46.

3. Matthew 24:4, 5, 11, 24; see also 1 Timothy 4:1, 2; 2 Thessalonians 2:10, 11.

4. *Los Angeles Times*, 11 February 1979, Part I, pp. 3, 22, 23.

5. Leviticus 19:31; 20:6, 27; Deuteronomy 18:9-14; Isaiah 8:19, 20.

6. Matthew Manning, *The Link* (New York, 1974), p. 16.

7. Stanley Krippner, *Song of the Siren* (New York, 1975), p. 244.

8. *Los Angeles Times*, 30 November 1979, Part I, p. 14; 17 October 1979, Part IV, pp. 1-3.

9. Ibid., 28 July 1975, Part I, p. 25.

10. Personal interview with Joan Harrison.

11. Ibid.

12. *Up-Date*, July 1979, pp. 47-52. Published by Dialogue Center, Katrinebjergvej 52, DK-8200, Aarhus N., Denmark.

13. Baba Ram Dass, "The Transformation: Dr. Richard Alpert, Ph.D., into Baba Ram Dass," *The Inward Journey*, ed. by Joseph F.

Doherty and William C. Stephenson (New York, 1973), pp. 287-320.

14. Lousia E. Rhine, *Mind Over Matter: Psychokinesis* (New York, 1970), pp. 389-90.

15. *Research in Parapsychology 1975,* Annual Report of the Parapsychological Association, p. 234.

16. Milan Ryzl, *Parapsychology: A Scientific Approach* (New York, 1970), pp. 190-91.

17. Arthur Koestler, *The Roots of Coincidence* (New York, 1972), p. 62.

18. Personal interview with Hal Richards.

19. Jacques Vallee, *Messengers of Deception* (Berkeley, 1979), pp. 204-5.

20. Brad Steiger, *Gods of Aquarius* (New York, 1976), p. 222.

CHAPTER ELEVEN

The Universal Master Plan for Inner and Outer Unity, Power, and Peace[1]

> . . . who opposes and exalts himself above every so-called god or object of worship, so that he takes his seat in the temple of God, displaying himself as being God (2 Thess. 2:4 NASB).

> And all who dwell on the earth will worship him (Rev. 13:8 NASB).

Many people think of prophecy as an intriguing subject that involves the latest rumors concerning an alleged Trilateralist plot, the newest developments in the Middle East, or recent maneuvers by the Soviets and Arabs in their continuing campaign against Israel. Interesting as that may be, there is something far more important. Whether one has a year's supply of food in case of famine or a suitable shelter for surviving a nuclear attack may be important, but it affects one's temporal condition only. To be deluded into believing "the lie," however, will seduce the entire world into accepting the Antichrist and will affect one's eternal destiny (2 Thess. 2:11, 12).

We have been in the midst of a cult/occult explosion for the last twenty-five years—an explosion that began with the drug movement and turned into a mystical trip mainly oriented to Hindu/Buddhist practices. The counter-culture that began as a largely political movement protesting the Vietnam War and evils of a materialistic society became a *spiritual* movement through the influence of drugs and Eastern mysticism. The failure of materialistic science to answer ultimate questions (but instead to bring us to the brink of a nuclear holocaust and ecological collapse) has caused modern society to turn to the realm of the spirit for the answers it seeks. This is preparing humanity for the coming world religion of Antichrist, and the prophetic warnings in the Bible concerning it deserve to be taken seriously.

The Cashless Controlled Society

Biblical prophecies also have a good deal to say about political, military, and economic developments in the last days. As "negative" as it sounds, Antichrist will rule the earth. The Bible declares in unequivocal language:

> And he causes all, the small and the great, and the rich and the poor . . . to be given a mark on their right hand, or on their forehead, and he provides that no one should be able to buy or to sell, except the one who has the mark (Rev. 13:16, 17 NASB).

In our modern world, 1900 years after the words above were written by John under the inspiration of the Holy Spirit, they at last make sense. Today's credit card system has brought the fulfillment of this ancient prophecy closer than almost anyone would have guessed fifty years ago. Nor is it any secret that we are heading for a completely cashless society, which will be one more step toward this prophecy's fulfillment. There are about 600 million credit cards now in use in the United States alone. In 1983 the reported fraudulent credit card transactions were about 200 million dollars. The possibility of counterfeiting cards is being eliminated by new devises such as those developed by Light Signatures, Inc., of Los Angeles.[2] However, this does not solve the problem of lost or stolen cards. The only real solution is to do away entirely with cards as well as with cash.

The logical manner for accomplishing this is exactly what the Bible prophesied 1900 years ago: every person on the planet will eventually have an irremovable identification number on their hand or forehead. We now have the technology not just to impregnate a *number* but to implant a *micro chip* with considerable data that would be invisible except to electronic scanning devices. This is the next logical step for banking and commerce, but it could also allow surveillance from satellite of the movements of every person on earth.

This may be why "the mark of the beast" will only be put into operation by Antichrist himself. Speculation about what that mark will be and the meaning of "666" has filled volumes. The most important thing to realize is that receiving it will be an act of submission to Antichrist, causing all who take this mark to forfeit the possibility of salvation. Those who do not accept it will lose the privilege of buying or selling. The choice will be between time and eternity.

The Coming World Government

It is no longer a question of *whether* but *when* humanity will be united both economically and politically under a one-world government. Lists of the many top leaders and organizations working openly toward this goal can be obtained by anyone who is interested. Books on the subject are legion, from James P. Warburg's *The West In Crisis* ("We are living in a perilous period of transition from the era of the fully sovereign nation-state to the era of world government")[3] to *Between Two Ages,* by Assistant to the President for National Security Affairs Zbigniew Brezinski, in which he openly advocates a one-world government as a necessity. The United States has officially made statements favorable of a new world order, such as the following addressed to the Secretary-General of the United Nations: "[It] would be hard to imagine that the American people would not respond very positively to an agreed and safeguarded program to substitute an international rule of law and order. . . ."[4] Of the Carter administration, the *Washington Post* said:

> If you like conspiracy theories about secret plots to take over the world, you are going to love the administration of President-elect Jimmy Carter. At last count 13 Trilateralists had gone into top positions . . . extraordinary when you consider that the Trilateral Commission only has about 65 American members. . . .[5]

The coming world government has been dealt with in countless books and sermons. Yet the most important part of what the Bible tells us about the Antichrist is seldom mentioned.

It would be fruitless to speculate further about global conspiracy theories involving the Trilateralists, Masons, Illuminati, or New Age networks. These organizations are only pawns in the real game. No one is going to take over the world by conspiring to do so. Far more important than knowing the individuals and groups involved is understanding the common lie that deceives them all. The mastermind behind the scenes is Satan himself, and the world takeover is his move. Even so, that can only come when God allows it, and it will be made possible through some startling developments. Regardless of how it is going to come about, however, the Bible declares that it *will* happen:

> And the whole earth was amazed and followed after the beast [Antichrist]; . . . saying, "Who is like the beast, and who is able to wage war with him?" . . . and authority over every tribe and people and tongue and nation was given to him (Rev. 13:3, 4, 7 NASB).

In attempting to understand these prophecies, we must not forget that Antichrist will be far more than a military/political dictator. He will also be the revered and *worshiped* head of an unprecedented official world religion. The world's loyalty to him will be of a *religious* nature. His takeover of the world is above all a *spiritual* event toward which Satan has plotted since the Garden of Eden. Those who overlook that fact miss the real significance of Antichrist and are more likely to fall prey to the deception by which the world will be seduced into worshiping him. When we finally see prophecy in its religious context, it takes on new meaning and urgency.

What Secret to His Power?

In language that cannot be misinterpreted, the Bible foretells that Antichrist will declare himself to be God and that the whole world—Marxists, Maoists, Muslims, Hindus, Buddhists, atheists, professing Christians, *everyone*—will believe this astonishing claim and *worship* him. This seems so fantastic that many sincere Christians have tried to interpret this prophecy to mean that only Western Europe (the revived Roman Empire) and possibly the remainder of the Western world will be under the Antichrist's dominion, whether political or religious; but the descriptions are unequivocal: "the whole earth," "every tribe and people and tongue and nation," "all who dwell on the earth," and "the earth and those who dwell in it."

There can be no doubt as to the meaning intended: the entire human race (except for those few who will resist and pay for it with their lives) will *worship* a mere man as God. Earth's inhabitants at that time will not recognize this claim as the outrageous lie of a diabolical counterfeit. It will seem to be the sincere revelation of truth from the very Savior the world desperately needs. Here is what the Bible says:

> And for this reason God will send upon them a deluding influence so that they might believe what is false (2 Thess. 2:11 NASB).

> And the whole earth . . . worshiped the dragon, because he gave his authority to the beast; and they worshiped the beast. . . . And all who dwell on the earth will worship him, every one whose name has not been written . . . in the book of life of the Lamb who has been slain (Rev. 13:3, 4, 8 NASB).

Surely the Soviets, Chinese, Arabs, Western Europeans, Americans, and *everyone* upon planet Earth would never surrender absolute control to Antichrist without fighting to the finish, if he were merely an aspiring world dictator. Even assuming that he had conquered or blackmailed the world through some secret superweapon, it would certainly be necessary for him to disarm the Soviets, Chinese, and all those he had conquered in order to keep them in subject. Yet the Bible indicates that at Armageddon the armies of all nations will gather against Jerusalem, which means they will still have their weapons.

The logical secret to Antichrist's mysterious power over humanity lies in the astonishing fact that the entire world will *worship* him as *God*. Worship brings reverence and obedience. Military power is hardly necessary to force the members of a religion to obey the "God" they worship. His bold claim that he is God, however, is not made by Antichrist as a ploy to gain control. There is something much deeper behind it.

The new world religion of Antichrist will be thought of as scientific. This new religious science will promise to lead humanity into the experience of its own divinity, that each of us is "God." This basic lie of the serpent in the Garden of Eden will seem to be validated by the godlike psychic powers the Antichrist will manifest and the whole world will pursue. It will be a religion of self-love and self-worship, centered in man himself and oriented to human beings' personal success rather than to the glory of the true God.

It is already clear that we are heading rapidly in this very direction. The evidence is there for all to see in the New Age movement, which is a blend of science and Eastern religions.

The New "Spiritual" Science

Another name for the New Age movement is the Holistic movement, about which we will have much more to say later. Under this influence, science, medicine, psychology, sociology, and education have all taken a sharp turn to the "spiritual," but not in a biblical sense. Instead, they have turned to the occult, and Christians need to be aware of the seduction that they face in every area of today's society. Parents especially need to awaken to the fact that their children are being seduced by occultism taught now as science in our public schools under the move to "Holistic education." The world is being conditioned to accept the coming satanic religion of Antichrist as a scientific mind-technology.

The turn to a new "religious science" has been apparent for some years in the field of psychology, but is now accelerating. Both humanistic and transpersonal psychologies are heavily involved in what they call "spiritual" therapies and concerns, which are simply a revival of occultism under psychological labels, as we will document later. Past president of the Association for Humanistic Psychology, Jean Houston, is called the "Prophet of the Possible"[6] (upon whom Margaret Mead's mantle has presumably fallen). Known as "a dazzling visionary, scholar, and teacher in the human potential movement"[7] and a leading spokesperson for the coming "transformation into the New Age," Houston declared in an interview:

> I predict that in our lifetime we will see the rise of essentially a New World Religion . . . I believe a new spiritual system will emerge. . . .[8]

Increasing numbers of influential world leaders are expressing in New Age terms the growing belief that the predicted world government must be founded upon a new world religion. Five months before his death in Los An-

geles, Buckminster Fuller, designer of the geodesic dome
and the world's most honored architect, declared that
man's future on "Spaceship Earth depends entirely" upon
his cooperation with the "Divine Mind always present in
each individual."[9] The belief that we can tune into this
inner "Divine Mind" to experience "peace through [East-
ern] meditation [Yoga]"[10] was the major premise of a recent prestigious "Universal Peace Conference." The conference was held in India at the World Spiritual University,
headquarters of the Brahma Kumris Raja Yoga society, a
United Nations affiliate. Among the three thousand delegates from forty-two countries were such notables as
Tibet's Dalai Lama, Stanford University professor and SRI
scientist Willis Harmon, and United Nations Assistant
Secretary-General Robert Muller. In his keynote speech to
the delegates, Muller said:

> The time has come to obtain peace on this planet . . .
> the United Nations Charter has to be supplemented by a
> charter of spiritual laws. . . .
> I think that what is wrong . . . we have forgotten that
> . . . we have a cosmic evolution and [spiritual]
> destiny. . . .[11]

Gurus and Godhood

The prophecy quoted at the beginning of this chapter that
"he takes his seat in the temple of God, displaying himself
as being God" (2 Thess. 2:4) will have its primary fulfillment in a particular man, Antichrist, and the temple yet to
be rebuilt in Jerusalem. There is an obvious secondary application. The human body is supposed to be the temple of
God. God intends that we should open our hearts to receive

Jesus Christ as Savior and Lord and be indwelt by His Spirit. Paul wrote to the Christians at Corinth: ". . . you are a temple of God . . . the Spirit of God dwells in you" (1 Cor. 3:16). The teaching of Eastern religions, however, is that the *self* is God, but we just don't realize it. The spirit of Antichrist causes humans to look within themselves in that temple of the heart where the spirit of God ought to dwell, and to declare their own divinity.

The goal of Yoga is "self-realization"—to look deeply within what ought to be the temple of the one true God and there to discover the alleged "true Self" or "higher Self" and declare self to be God. This is the religion of Antichrist; and for the first time in history, it is being widely practiced throughout the Western world as Transcendental Meditation and other forms of Yoga. These are now taught in nearly every YWCA or YMCA, in public and private schools from kindergarten to graduate level, and in many churches. Humanity is being conditioned to accept a coming world ruler who will have psychic powers from Satan to "prove" that he has indeed "realized" his own "godhood."

The many gurus who have invaded the West are actively converting millions to this satanic religion of Antichrist with a missionary zeal and success that is a new phenomenon for Eastern religions. Each claiming to be God himself, the gurus have opened the Western world to the belief and practice of worshiping a man as God, and to the idea that each person can realize his own godhood through following his guru. It will not seem strange, therefore, when Antichrist claims to be God; and the millions who have been worshiping gurus such as Rajneesh and Muktananda will easily worship Antichrist.

The hundreds of Eastern gurus are preparing us for the ultimate Guru; the many false Christs are paving the way for the Antichrist. San Diego psychiatrist Samuel H. Sandweiss is one example of the millions of Westerners who have been converted by one guru or another. The following are excerpts from a letter he wrote to his wife in May 1972 from India, where he had gone to investigate a miracle-working guru known as Sai Baba, who has about 20 million devoted followers:

> There is no doubt in my mind that Sai Baba is divine. I astound myself . . . a rational, scientific man, to say such a thing.
> I believe Baba to be an incarnation of God. . . . How strange, when just a few days ago I was such a skeptic. Yesterday I experienced more miracles. . . . Baba is allowing me to see this wonderful power close-up. . . .
> I am witnessing in live color and in the flesh an experience a million times more astonishing than the fairy-tale stories I have been telling my four sweet children . . . after witnessing Baba's greatness, I can do nothing but accept fully what he says.
> Yesterday . . . a very well known nuclear physicist with an international reputation came here. . . . I saw this man lie face-down at Baba's feet. . . .[12]

The Seductive Appeal of Self-deification

People join cults for a variety of reasons: to find love, security, community, their own identity, or God. However, the goal of "cosmic evolution" and the "destiny" of humanity to realize its inherent godhood referred to by the U.N.'s Robert Muller is the predominant theme running through most of the cults now popular in the West. For example,

Joseph Smith's Mormonism, Ernest Holmes' Church of Religious Science, and Herbert W. Armstrong's Worldwide Church of God all teach it. Raised a fundamentalist and now one of the most influential New Age leaders, David Spangler lays it all out, including cosmic evolution of the self to godhood and the key role played by Lucifer (Satan):

> When man entered upon the pathway of self, he entered into a great creative adventure . . . of learning the meaning of divinity by accepting to himself the responsibility of a microcosmic world unto whom he is the god. . . . There he can say, "I have fully and absolutely accepted the responsibility of who and what I am. . . ."
>
> The being that helps man to reach this point is Lucifer . . . the angel of man's evolution . . . the spirit of light in the microcosmic world.[13]

Werner Erhard, founder of est (Erhard Seminars Training), declares, "You're god in your universe."[14] Benjamin Creme's Maitreya states, "Man is an emerging God. . . . My plan and My Duty is to reveal to you a new way . . . which will permit the divine in man to shine forth."[15] Maharishi Mahesh Yogi, founder of the TM cult, perverts the Bible by saying, "Be still and know that you are God. . . ."[16] Sun Myung Moon has written, "God and man are one. Man is incarnate God."[17] Echoing the same lie from Eden's serpent, Ernest Holmes, founder of the Church of Religious Science, declared, "All men are spiritually evolving until . . . each will fully express his divinity. . . ."[18] As the Master who traveled the astral plane to communicate in an audible voice to Napoleon Hill declared (concerning the person who fully followed the teachings of the Temple of Wisdom):

> He will not only understand the true purpose of life,

but also he will have at his command the power to fulfill that purpose *without having to experience another incarnation on this earthly plane* [emphasis in original].

And the Masters of the Great School, on this earthly plane and all other planes, will rejoice at his triumph and will bid him godspeed toward his own Mastership.[19]

That this message of self-deification is gaining credibility and acceptability at an accelerating rate around the world is another convincing sign that the coming of Christ must be drawing near. This belief will undoubtedly play a major role in causing the world to accept the Antichrist and his world religion, as the Bible foretells. It comes as no surprise that the world would follow such teachings. The close relatedness of self-deification to the entire Human Potential movement, this movement's penetration of the evangelical church, and the movement's subtle seduction of overwhelming numbers of Christians should cause alarm. "Self" is the predominant theme of a large percentage of Christian books and sermons. Zen Buddhist Master Alan Watts, a former Episcopal priest, is a good example of where this seduction leads a "Christian" who succumbs to it. Watts declared:

> The appeal of Zen, as of other forms of Eastern philosophy, is that it unveils . . . a vast region . . . where at last the self is indistinguishable from God.[20]

Man-God

The world will be convinced that this godhood that the cults and gurus offer has apparently been realized by Antichrist. Satan will give him supernatural powers to back up his claim that he is the first human to have achieved the full potential of our alleged inherent godhood. This amazing world ruler will "prove" through the demonstration of supernatural powers that seemingly rival the biblical miracles of Jesus Christ that he is a self-realized Master in the fullest sense of Eastern tradition. This will give credence to the hope that everyone else in the world can also reach the goal of "self-realization." It will seem to be the exciting dawning of a New Age for humanity and planet Earth!

It is important to understand that Antichrist will not claim to be God in the classical biblical sense, but *a man who has achieved godhood*. In fact Antichrist will deny the existence of God as a personal being who has created all that exists out of nothing. John Denver exemplified the respectability and broad popularity that this belief has achieved. Like Marsha Mason and many other popular celebrities, Denver was a follower of Swami Muktananda before the latter's death.

Muktananda's advice to his disciples was: "Kneel to your own self. Honor and worship your own being. God dwells within you as You." Of Werner Erhard and Muktananda, Denver declared, "They're gods and they know it . . . they're running the universe."[21] Inspired by this insight, Denver expressed the goal that millions of Westerners now hold as the result of the influence of the gurus: "One of these days I'll be so complete I won't be a human. I'll be a god."[22] This concept that seemed so incredible to almost every Westerner just a few years ago is now accepted as a liberating new truth by those who have *experienced* it. Increasing numbers of celebrities, such as Shirley MacLaine, are testifying to the transforming power of mystical experiences. In her best-seller *Out On a Limb*, MacLaine explains that she now accepts what she once considered "science fiction or . . . the occult" because "it happened to me."[23]

The power of mystical experience (a form of *initiation*) is expressed eloquently by Gerald Jampolsky, a famous psychiatrist and best-selling author/lecturer. He tells of his meeting with Swami Muktananda:

> He touched me with peacock feathers. I began to have the impression that our minds were joined. He touched me again on the head with his hand.
>
> After this, beautiful colors appeared all around me, and it seemed as though I had stepped out of my body and was looking down on it. I saw colors whose depth and brilliance were beyond anything I had ever imagined.
>
> I began to talk in tongues. A beautiful beam of light came into the room and I decided at that moment to stop evaluating what was happening and simply be one with the experience, to join it completely. . . . For the next three months, my energy level was heightened and I required very little sleep. I was filled with an awareness of love unlike anything I had known before.[24]

Within this context the otherwise incredible Antichrist prophecies become believable. It is no longer difficult to imagine that *everyone will worship him*. If initiation by gurus such as Muktananda has such a transforming power, what will it be like to be initiated into Antichrist's New Age kingdom? Moreover, Antichrist will symbolize the godhood they all hope to achieve. It is important to remember that everyone will know that they are not worshiping the God of the Bible. They would not worship the true God, because to acknowledge His existence would be to admit their own inferiority and total dependence upon Him. To acknowledge Antichrist as God, however, is to reaffirm their own claim to godhood. He has simply "realized"

ahead of others what all hope to achieve; and the fact that
he has reached this goal is proof that all can reach it. Everyone will want to sit at his feet and submit to his power in
order to learn his acquired secret.

The Luciferic Initiation

Whatever the exact nature of the "mark" that the Antichrist
will require on everyone's hand or forehead, it will have
more than political/economic significance. Not only will it
give the possessor the right to buy and sell, but it will identify those who are in Antichrist's kingdom—his loyal followers who worship him as God. Thus the presence of this
mark will be an initiation into the official world religion.
This will involve the entire world in Satan worship: "The
whole earth . . . worshiped the dragon [Satan]" (Rev. 13:3,
4).

This seems impossible to believe, because most people
think of Satan-worshipers as weird fanatics performing bi-
zarre rituals under a full moon at midnight in a cemetery.
On the contrary, this will all be very scientific and respect-
able. Few if any will be aware that they are worshiping
Satan. Those who are aware, like David Spangler, will call
him Lucifer, who is allegedly "an agent of God's love acting through evolution."[25] Spangler is not alone in honoring
Lucifer; and such ideas repeated often enough exert a subtle influence even upon Christians. This is especially true
of children and teenagers. Christians had better awaken to
what is happening to their children.

Consider, for example, the recent popular movie *2010.*
In the film a new sun suddenly appeared in the sky and
brought peace to earth just as the Americans and Soviets

were about to engage in nuclear war. What the film failed to explain was elucidated by Arthur C. Clarke in his book: the sun was named *Lucifer,* no doubt in honor of the power that brought it into existence. Spangler further explained the relationship of Antichrist to Lucifer and why Lucifer will be worshiped:

> Christ is the same force as Lucifer. . . . Lucifer prepares man for the experience of Christhood . . . [he is] the great initiator. . . . Lucifer works within each of us to bring us to wholeness, and as we move into a new age . . . each of us in some way is brought to that point which I term the Luciferic initiation . . . that many people now, and in the days ahead, will be facing, for it is an initiation into the New Age.[26]

The Great Delusion

So the world will undergo a Luciferic initiation into Satan worship, and it will be considered the latest advance of science. This would have seemed impossible even fifty years ago, but today it is right in line with growing trends. Already we can see the beginning stages of what the Bible prophesies. An incredible worldwide delusion is gathering momentum. Every person on earth during these days prior to Christ's return must face it and choose God's truth or Satan's lie. So compelling will be the seduction that Jesus warned that "even the elect" would be deceived "if it were possible." Such language ought to put all Christians on their guard.

What is most important for us to understand is that the glue that will hold Antichrist's empire together is the universal acceptance of what the Bible calls "the lie," i.e., human beings are God. The consequences ought to be obvious: If we claim that we are God, we have demeaned the very concept of God, and have dragged God down to our level.

If everything is God, as Hinduism teaches, then nothing is God because the very word "God" has lost its meaning. Thus the declaration that human beings are God is religious atheism. That kind of heavy delusion doesn't happen in a moment; it requires considerable preparation. That it will indeed happen, however, is clearly stated. This is not pessimism but realism. It should not cause us to become fatalistic, but to work even more diligently to rescue as many people as we possibly can before it is too late.

The Bible plainly declares that Christ died for the entire world (Jn. 3:16), and that God "desires all men to be saved and to come to the knowledge of the truth" (1 Tim. 2:4 NASB). Therefore, in spite of prophecies about coming delusion and the Antichrist's takeover, we must attempt to convert all people for Christ. That is a worthy goal, and the love of Christ would compel us, for God is not willing that any should perish. However, there must be genuine repentance and conversion. The Bible repeatedly makes it clear that the issue is *truth,* and Paul warns that all those who "did not receive the love of the truth so as to be saved" would be given from God Himself "a deluding influence so that they might believe what is false" (2 Thess. 2:10, 11 NASB).

In the next chapter, we will begin to consider the evidence for the Source Book that provides the ultimate answer.

Notes

1. The following chapter is adapted from *The Seduction of*

Christianity, by Dave Hunt and T. A. McMahon (Eugene: Harvest House, 1986), pp. 47-61.

2. *Los Angeles Times,* 28 October 1984, part VI, p. 4.

3. James P. Warburg, *The West in Crisis* (Doubleday, 1959), p. 30.

4. *The Economic and Social Consequences of Disarmament: U.S. Reply to the Inquiry of the Secretary-General of the United Nations* (Washington, D.C.: USGPO, June 1964), pp. 8-9.

5. *Washington Post,* 16 January 1977.

6. *Whole Life Times* October/November 1984, Cover Story, p. 24.

7. Ibid., p. 5.

8. "Jean Houston: The New World Religion," *The Tarrytown Letter,* June/July 1983, p. 5.

9. Buckminster Fuller, "Human Integrity," *Spectrum,* November-December 1984, p. 7.

10. *India-West,* 14 January 1983, p. 22.

11. Ibid.; *The Movement Newspaper,* January 1983.

12. Samuel H. Sandweiss, *Sai Baba, The Holy Man . . . and the Psychiatrist* (San Diego, 1975), pp. 79-82.

13. David Spangler, *Reflections on the Christ* (Findhorn-Thale, Scotland, 1977), pp. 36-37.

14. Werner Erhard, *If God Had Meant Man to Fly, He Would Have Given Him Wings,* p. 11.

15. Benjamin Creme, *The Reappearance of the Christ and the Masters of Wisdom* (London: The Tara Press, 1980), Message No. 81, Sept. 12, 1979, p. 246.

16. *Meditations of Maharishi Mahesh Yogi* (New York: Bantam Books, 1975), p. 178.

17. Sun Myung Moon, *Christianity In Crisis* (New York: HSA Publications, n.d.), p. 5.

18. Ernest Holmes, *What Religious Science Teaches* (Los Angeles: Science of Mind Publications, n.d.), p. 21.

19. Napolean Hill, *Grow Rich with Peace of Mind,* (New York: Fawcett Book Group, 1983), p. 164.

20. Alan Watts, *This Is It* (New York: Random House, 1972), p. 90.

21. Author, "Article," *Newsweek,* December 20, 1976, p. 66.

22. Ibid., p. 68.

23. Shirley MacLaine, *Out On A Limb* (New York: Bantam Books, 1983), Introduction inside front cover.

24. *Teach Only Love*, quoted in Phil Friedman, "Interview with Gerald Jampolsky, M.D.," *Orange County Resources*, p. 3.

25. Spangler, *Reflections*, op. cit., p. 41.

26. Ibid., pp. 40-41, 44-45.

CHAPTER TWELVE

Compelling Evidence

Charles Wesley cogently stated, "The Bible must be the invention of either good men or angels, bad men or devils, or of God. (1) It could not be the invention of good men or angels, for they neither would or could make a book, and tell lies all the time they were writing it, saying, "Thus saith the Lord," when it was their own invention. (2) It could not be the invention of bad men or devils, for they would not make a book which commands all duty, forbids all sin, and condemns their souls to hell for all eternity. (3) Therefore I draw this conclusion, that the Bible must be given by divine inspiration."

All of us, I believe, have a deep hunger to know the truth. Our hearts ache to find out why we are here, where we came from, what happens to us when we die, where we are going. We long to know the real purpose for our existence.

I suspect all of us have a "Bible" by which we live, whether we are aware of it or not. The "Bible" I personally lived by was a mishmash of my own wisdom and that of others. These sources—books, sometimes famous scientists, psychologists, professors and my own conclusions—often were uncertain, prone to error, and speculative. All of the sources for my "Bible" were cluttered with mistakes and full of naked opinions. My "Bible" was unsure about the origin and purpose of life and life's destiny. If this is true of others also, my heart cries out for my fellow travellers on the road of life. In the love of one who is now my Saviour, I ask, "Is this true of your 'Bible'? Have the sources you may be depending on ever made mistakes? Have they final and absolute knowledge? Have you? Will you risk your life, your eternal destiny, on wishful thinking or opinions?" Dear reader, you and I *know* this is not the measure of truth.

In contrast, the Bible of the Christian is God's Word—certain, infallible and tested.

The Bible claims to be the Word of God. About 3,800 times, phrases including "Thus saith the Lord," "The Word of the Lord came to me," and others express these claims. 2 Timothy 3:16, for example, tells us that, "All scripture is given by inspiration of God, and is profitable for doctrine, for reproof, for correction, for instruction in righteousness."

Unity

Imagine forty men, separated in time by centuries, coming from many different cultures, towns, cities, and backgrounds. Imagine that they are working independently on a statue of Jesus. Each has a particular part of the statue to carve: one, a toe; one, an ear; another, the neck; another, the chin; another, a leg; yet another, a shoulder blade; and so on. After hundreds of years, all of these carvings are brought to one place and put together. Incredibly, they all fit together perfectly, and form a beautiful statue of Jesus. Impossible, by chance. Possible only by the superintending act of a supervising God.

Yet this corresponds to what we have in the writing of the Bible. Some forty to fifty authors, working over a period of 1,500 to 1,600 years, writing sixty-six books, came up with a perfectly unified book portraying one perfect person—the Lord Jesus Christ!

Archaeology and the Bible

As Paul E. Little pointed out in his book, *Know Why You Believe,* "more than 25,000 sites showing some connection with the Old Testament period have been located in Bible lands."[1] This does not even include the well-known sites and cities mentioned in the New Testament. Even the Jewish archaeologist Nelson Glueck has said, "It may be stated categorically that no archaeological discovery has ever controverted a biblical reference."

Biblical accuracy is illustrated in the case of the Hittites. Skeptics had ridiculed the Bible, saying that such a city-state never existed. Yet in 1906, excavations made at Boghazköy, 90 miles east of Ankara, Turkey, uncovered the capital of the ancient Hittite empire! (The Hittites were mentioned forty-six times in the Bible, and, as in hundreds of similar cases, the Bible was right and the critics wrong.) At one time people disbelieved the existence of Ur of the Chaldees, Abraham's former home—but archaeologists excavated it, also. As archaeologists have dug into the ruins of Egypt, Palestine, Babylonia, and Assyria, the historicity and accuracy of the Bible has been repeatedly confirmed. The grandeur of Solomon's reign and wealth was questioned until excavations at Megiddo and discoveries elsewhere confirmed the biblical accounts.

Scholars once argued that Luke had erred in the account of the events surrounding the birth of Jesus. According to them, no census was conducted, Quirinius was not governor of Syria at that time, and people did not have to return to their ancestral home. Again, archaeological discoveries proved every one of Luke's statements to be true. Quirinius was governor according to an inscription found in Antioch. The Romans did have a regular enrollment of taxpayers. A papyrus found in Egypt gives directions for conducting a census, including the return of people to their ancestral home. Archaeology has proven again the Bible's historicity and accuracy, a fact that also lends credibility to its inspiration and preservation.

Fantastic for a book thousands of years old! Since we can trust the Bible in the things we can see, we know we can trust it in the things we cannot see.

Science

S. Maxwell Coder and George F. Howe contend in their book, *The Bible, Science and Creation*, "The Bible is the only ancient book that is accurate in all scientific details. Other ancient holy books from the East include legends and errors too childish for consideration. Even comparatively modern books like the Koran abound in historical and chronological blunders."[2] For instance, Plato thought the world to be a living soul, a vast and visible animal, and that earthquakes resulted when the creature shook itself! The Greeks believed that Atlas, a giant, stood under the earth and held the broad heavens with his head and arms; thus we call a book of maps an atlas.

Although skeptics have claimed that the Bible contains scientific errors, none of the allegations have been proven.

This is true of no other ancient religious book. Many times in fact, science has been proven wrong and the Bible right. Science textbooks are changed frequently and often hopelessly contradict one another after a few years. The Bible never has to be changed. It is accurate where it touches on science.

The Jews

Deuteronomy 28:25, 26 tells us of the coming suffering and scattering of the Jews, and Deuteronomy 30:1-6 adds to this prophecy, which had indicated that the Jews would be scattered among all nations, but would someday be regathered to their own land. These prophecies were given centuries before the full fulfillment. Yet God had given certain very literal prophecies concerning the inheritance of the land of Palestine to Abraham and to the Jews. Leviticus 26:31-33, given in 1491 B.C. adds to this prophecy, as does Ezekiel 36:33-35 and Ezekiel 37. Luke 21:23, 24 reasserts these prophecies. It was also predicted that Jerusalem would be trodden underfoot of the Gentiles until the time of the Gentiles is fulfilled.

From these and other Scriptures let us give a brief summary of what God's Word says the future held for the Jews. (1) Scattering, worldwide among all nations. (2) Intense persecution, suffering. (3) Other, mightier nations around them would be destroyed, but they would never lose their identity as Jews, and a remnant would always survive. (4) They would someday return to their own land and reestablish their own nation. (Though we will not deal with it here, they will also rebuild their temple and Anti-Christ will sign a pact with the nation of Israel for "peace" just after the coming of the Lord Jesus Christ for His people.)

Now consider these well known facts. Surrounding the Jews were formidable and warlike people, some of them more numerous and more powerful at times than the Jews. Hittites, Canaanites, Philistines, Edomites, etc. Dear Friend, when is the last time you met a Hittite? A Philistine? They have long since passed off the scene. Yet the Jews remain! They were persecuted horribly, six million dying in Hitler's horrendous Holocaust. For nearly 2,500 years they had no nation, no country of their own. They were scattered worldwide, but they were not assimilated like the Anglos, Saxons, and Jutes, or the Goths or Visigoths. Neither were they exterminated like countless others, and miraculously they retain their identity! In Hungary, there are Hungarian Jews, and there are American Jews, Soviet Jews, English Jews, Polish Jews, etc. No totally wiped out, dispossessed nation ever returned to life even after a few hundred years, but God said the Jews would! They did, proving the Bible to be God's Word!

Men like Increase Mather saw this truth in the Bible and preached that the Jews would return to Palestine and reestablish their own nation again . . . and he preached it in 1669, as reported by Hal Lindsey in *The Late Great Planet Earth*. This is no "after the fact" application of some vague generalities to a historical event, but a precise fulfillment of prophecy men of God had been expecting for centuries. Suddenly, it happened! After, and during World War II, (at one time the Jewish population of Palestine had shrunk to about 10,000!) the Jews returned, feeling persecution in Germany, Europe and Russia. True, but many wealthy

Jews around the world, some from America, also returned to Palestine! Imagine that! Why? This inexplicable urge of many to return to a "homeland" after 2,500 years was not because they believed in the Bible. However, the return of the Jews to Palestine fulfilled exactly what God said would happen. The British, in charge of Palestine at the time, put their gleaming warships in the way, but did not know what to do with unarmed men, women and children in merchant ships. Finally, the Jews were allowed in. Miracle of miracles, they declared themselves a nation on May 14, 1948! With heavy odds against them, they were attacked a week later by neighboring forces. Some say they were outnumbered 100 to 1, but they survived and conquered. They survived again when they were attacked in 1967 and in the 1970s. The Arabs had controlled Jerusalem, but now that city too is under Jewish control. (See Luke 21:24.) God's Word continues to be fulfilled and will be!

Consider this powerful presentation of proof by Fred John Meldau in his book, *Messiah In Both Testaments*, pp. 6-9:

"PROPHECY" IS GOD'S OWN METHOD OF PROVING HIS TRUTH

The teachings of the Bible are so peculiar and different from all other religions, and so important—telling us that man's eternal destiny, for weal or woe, depends on his acceptance of the Christ of the Bible—that we have the right to *know* whether the Bible is or is not a Heavenly Decree, the absolute and final Word of God, whether its message is fully authorized by the Almighty. If God *has* given a revelation of His will in the Bible, there can be no doubt that in some unmistakable way He will show men that the Bible is indeed His revealed will and the way He has chosen to show men that the Bible is His Word in a way that all men of average intelligence can understand; and that way is through the giving and through the fulfillment of specific, detailed prophecies. It is the Divine seal, letting all men know that He has spoken. This seal can never be counterfeited, affixed to the Truth which it attests—for His foreknowledge of the actions of free and intelligent agents, men, is one of the most "incomprehensible attributes of Deity and is exclusively a Divine perfection."[3]

In challenging the false gods of Isaiah's time, the true God said:

> "Produce your cause . . . bring forth your strong reasons . . . show us what shall happen . . . declare us things for to come. Show the things that are to come hereafter, that we may know that ye are gods" (Isa. 41:21-23).

There are false faiths like Mohammedism and Buddhism that have tried to prop up their claims on pretended miracles, but neither these, nor any other religion in the history of the world, except the Bible, have ever ventured to frame prophecies.

It is the peculiar "glory" of the Almighty, the all-knowing God, who is "the Lord, the Creator" (Isa. 40:28) to "declare new things before they spring forth" (Isa. 42:8-9) and *that* glory He will not share with another (Isa. 42:8). The true God alone foreknows and foretells the future. And He has chosen to confine his foretelling to the pages of Scripture.[4] Though there are many other subjects of Divine Prophecy in the Bible—such as the Jews, the Gentile nations that surrounded Israel, ancient cities, the Church, the last days, etc., the divine perfections of foreknowledge and fulfillment can be seen better in the realm of prophecies concerning Christ than in any other sphere.

Here is the clear statement that God alone, in the Bible alone, gave true prophecies:

> "I am God, and there is none else; I am God, and
> there is none like Me, DECLARING THE END
> FROM THE BEGINNING, and from ancient times the
> things that are not yet done, saying, MY COUNSEL
> SHALL STAND AND I WILL DO ALL MY
> PLEASURE" (Isa. 45:9, 10).

(The appeal by God that He alone can give and fulfill
prophecy, and that it is to be found alone in the Bible, is
found in many places in the Bible. See 2 Timothy 3:16;
2 Peter 1:19-21; Deuteronomy 18:21, 22; Isaiah 41:21-23;
Jeremiah 28:9; John 13:19, etc.).

Sensing the tremendous force of this fact, Justin Martyr said, "To declare a thing shall come to pass long before
it is in being, and to bring it to pass, this or nothing is the
work of God."

[AUTHOR'S NOTE]: Some may disagree with Meldau's
claim that there is not true prophecy outside the Bible.
Justin Martyr makes an equally strong statement. God does
say in Deuteronomy 13:1-5, that a false prophet or a
dreamer might indeed give a sign or a wonder that comes
to pass. The passage then declares that if the prophet or
dreamer leads away to other gods, this reveals that he is a
false prophet used to prove the love of God's true people.
Occasionally some prognosticator or medium does have a
prediction, sign, or wonder come to pass. Read Meldau's
claims carefully. Also read Keith Pierson's, Danny
Korem's and Paul Meier's claims about prophecy which
follow. Prophecy given in meticulous detail, consistently
fulfilled without failure, is given only in the Bible! We are
not talking about random predictions, devoid of many
specific details, which *by chance* may occasionally come
true. Satan's false prophets and the occult world may also
have partial knowledge of the future but never complete

and perfect knowledge. This is revealed in their prophecies when a number of prophecies are given or meticulous detail is attempted. Some always fail, revealing the true source (Deut. 18:20-22).

"CHANCE FULFILLMENT" OF PROPHECY IS RULED OUT

Desperate atheists and other unbelievers, seeking a way to circumvent the fact of fulfilled prophecy and its connotations, have argued that the fulfillments were "accidental," "chance," or "coincidental." But when a number of details are given the "chance" fulfillment of prophecy is ruled out. One writer says,

"It is conceivable that a prediction, uttered at a venture, and expressing what in a general way may happen to result, may seem like a genuine prophecy. But only let the prophecy give several DETAILS of time, place and accompanying incidents and it is evident that the possibility of a chance fulfillment, by a 'fortuitous concurrence of events,' will become extremely desperate—yea, altogether impossible. Hence the prophecies of heathen antiquity always took good care to confine their predictions to one or two particulars and to express them in the most general ambiguous terms. Therefore, in the whole range of history, except the prophecies of Scriptures, *there is not a single instance of a prediction, expressed in unequivocal language, and descending to any minuteness, which bears the slightest claim to fulfillment.* Suppose, that there were only 50 prophecies in the Old Testament (instead of 333) concerning the first advent of Christ, giving details of the coming Messiah and all meet in the person of Jesus . . . the probability of chance fulfillment as calculated by mathematicians according to the theory of probabilities, is less than one in 1,125,000,000,000,000. Now add only two more elements to these 50 prophecies, and fix the TIME and the PLACE at which they must happen and the *immense improbability that they will take place by chance exceeds all the power of numbers to express (or the mind of man to grasp). This is enough, one would think, to silence forever all pleas for chance* as furnishing an unbeliever the least opportunity of escape from the evidence of prophecy. (Gregory Letters)[5]

Let it be further observed that many of the prophecies about Messiah are of such a nature that only God *could* fulfill them, such as His virgin birth, His sinless and holy character, His resurrection and His ascension. Only GOD could cause Jesus "to be born of a virgin or be raised from the dead" (David Baron).

CHRIST'S COMING IS THE CENTRAL THEME OF THE BIBLE

The Coming of Christ, promised in the Old Testament and fulfilled in the New—His birth, character, work, teachings, His sufferings, death and resurrection—are the grand, central themes of the Bible. Christ is the bond that ties the two Testaments together. The Old Testament is in the New revealed, the New Testament is in the Old concealed.

It is a well known fact that over 300 prophecies were fulfilled about the birth, life, death, and resurrection of the Lord Jesus Christ. This would be an incomprehensible mathematical impossibility by chance alone. Thirty-three prophecies were fulfilled on the day He was crucified, many of them given seven centuries before he was born in Bethlehem, as was also prophesied. The Bible is demonstrably God's Word, as it claims to be. It would take a lot more faith to believe that this all happened by chance, than to believe that God gave us His Word, the Bible.

The Predictions

Consider carefully the following excellent presentation of prophecy by Danny Korem and Paul Meier in their book, *The Fakers*. (Reprinted by permission.)

"For the better part of two thousand years prior to the birth of Jesus of Nazareth, the Jews looked for and anticipated the physical coming of the Messiah or Savior. The Old Testament is laced with over 60 major prophecies and 270 ramifications of how the Messiah would be born, live, and die, even the implications surrounding his life and death. It is common knowledge that when a Jewish prophet recorded a prophecy, he believed in a literal, historical fulfillment of that prediction. What follows are eight predictions made by the Old Testament prophets hundreds of years before the birth of Christ.

Prophecy #1

> "Behold, the days are coming," declares the Lord,
> "When I shall raise up for David a righteous Branch;
> And He will reign as king and act wisely
> And do justice and righteousness in the land. . . .
> And this is His name by which He will be called,
> 'The Lord our righteousness.'"

> Jeremiah 23:5, 6 NAS

RELEVANCE: Jeremiah, as did all the prophets, looked towards the coming of the Messiah. Jeremiah and other prophets made many prophecies concerning who the Messiah would be so that when He lived on earth men would know who He was through the revelation of the Lord's message rather than just one claiming to be the Messiah with no evidence to back his story. Here Jeremiah makes reference to the fact that the Messiah would be born out of the lineage of King David.

This is significant because it eliminates eleven of the twelve tribes of Israel. David was a member of the tribe of Judah. So what Jeremiah is stating is that the Messiah would come from the tribe of Judah and specifically from the royal line of David. These events were foretold so that the Messiah could be recognized. There have been thousands who have claimed to be the Messiah, but none have fulfilled the prophecies except Jesus.

FULFILLMENT: Jesus was born out of the family line of David. Luke details the exact family lineage in Luke 3:23-28. Considering Luke's meticulous attention to details as earlier demonstrated and the fact that the family lineage has never been credibly contested, we may assume—based upon the historical proofs earlier applied—that Jesus was from the family lineage of King David.

Prophecy #2

"But as for you, Bethlehem Ephrathah,
Too little to be among the clans of Judah,
From you One will go forth for Me to be ruler in Israel.
His goings forth are from long ago,
From the days of eternity."

Micah 5:2 NAS

RELEVANCE: Here the Prophet Micah tells of the birthplace of the Messiah. Notice that it is not just any king but one "whose goings forth are from long ago, from the days of eternity."

FULFILLMENT: Luke accounts for the location of Jesus' birth in Luke 2:4, 5 and 7 NAS.

And Joseph also went up from Galilee, from the city of Nazareth, to Judea, to the city of David, which is called Bethlehem, because he was of the house and family of David, in order to register, along with Mary, who was engaged to him, and was with child. . . . And she gave birth to her first-born son. . . .

Prophecy #3

"Behold, I am going to send My messenger, and he will clear the way before Me, And the Lord, whom you seek, will suddenly come to His temple; and the messenger of the covenant, in whom you delight, behold, He is coming," says the Lord of Hosts.

Malachi 3:1 NAS

RELEVANCE: Here the Prophet Malachi states there will be a forerunner who will precede the Messiah, one who will announce and prepare the people for His coming.

FULFILLMENT: John the Baptist was, of course, the one who prepared the way for Christ.

Now in those days John the Baptist came, preaching in the wilderness of Judea, saying, "Repent, for the kingdom of heaven is at hand."

Matthew 3:1, 2 NAS

Prophecy #4

Even my close friend, in whom I trusted,
Who ate my bread,
Has liften up his heel against me.

Psalm 41:9 NAS

RELEVANCE: King David is referring to the time when the Messiah would be betrayed by a close friend. History would later record his name as Judas Iscariot.

FULFILLMENT:

While He was still speaking, behold, a multitude came, and the one called Judas, one of the twelve, was preceding them, and he approached Jesus to kiss Him. But Jesus said to him, "Judas, are you betraying the Son of Man with a kiss?"

Luke 22:47, 48 NAS

Prophecy #5

And I said to them, "If it is good in your sight, give me my wages; but if not, never mind!" So they weighed but thirty shekels of silver as my wages.

Zechariah 11:12 NAS

RELEVANCE: Zechariah states that the price to be paid for the betrayal of the Messiah would be thirty pieces of silver.

FULFILLMENT:

And said unto them, What will ye give me, and I will deliver him unto you? And they covenanted with him for thirty pieces of silver.

Matthew 26:15

Here Matthew recounts that Judas was paid thirty pieces of silver to betray Jesus. Zechariah 11:13 further states two other incidents that would surround the betrayal. ". . . So I took the thirty shekels of silver and threw them to the potter in the house of the Lord." Matthew reports in Matthew 27:5-7 that Judas took and threw the money into the sanctuary and that the money was then picked up by the chief priests and was used to buy a potter's field. This was done because it was unlawful to take "blood money" and place it in the treasury. This gives us seven ramifications that were fulfilled around these two prophecies.

1. Betrayal
2. By a friend
3. For 30 pieces (not 29)
4. Silver
5. Thrown down (not placed)
6. In the House of the Lord
7. Money used to buy potter's field

Prophecy #6

> I can count all my bones. They look, they stare at me;
> They divide my garments among them,
> And for my clothing they cast lots.

Psalm 22:17-18 NAS

RELEVANCE: King David refers to how the Messiah would have his clothing divided among the Roman soldiers, who cast lots for them.

FULFILLMENT:

> And when they had crucified Him, they divided up His garments among themselves, casting lots; and sitting down, they began to keep watch over Him there.

Matthew 27:35-36 NAS

In verse 17 of Psalm 22 reference is made to the Messiah's bones: "I can count all my bones." In Psalm 34:20 there is a similar reference: "He keeps all his bones; not one of them is broken." These passages are significant because the Romans would often break the legs of the person being crucified in order to speed his death. The Messiah would not have his bones broken, thus fulfilling the prophecy of Psalm 22:17 and 24:30.

Prophecy #7

> His grave was assigned to be with wicked men, Yet with a rich man in His death. . . .

> Isaiah 53:9 NAS

RELEVANCE: Isaiah plainly states that the Messiah would be buried in a rich man's tomb.

FULFILLMENT:

> . . . there came a rich man from Arimathea, named Joseph . . . and asked for the body of Jesus. . . . And Joseph took the body and wrapped it in a clean linen cloth, and laid it in his own new tomb. . . .

> Matthew 27:57-60 NAS

Luke detailed the same account of the burial of Jesus in Luke 23:50-53.

Prophecy #8

> . . . They pierced my hands and my feet.

> Psalms 22:16

> And I will pour upon the house of David, and upon the inhabitants of Jerusalem, the spirit of grace and of supplications; and they shall look upon me whom they have pierced, and they shall mourn for him, as one mourneth for his only son, and shall be in bitterness for him, as one that is in bitterness for his firstborn.

> Zechariah 12:10

> And one shall say unto him, What are these wounds in thine hands? Then he shall answer, "Those with which I was wounded in the house of my friends."

> Zechariah 13:6

RELEVANCE: This is perhaps the most stunning of all prophecies. Death for the Messiah is clearly delineated through the piercing of the hands and feet as stated by King David roughly eight or nine hundred years before the birth of Jesus and the prophecy of Zechariah dates approximately 450 years before the birth of Christ. What is remarkable is that both men were describing the penalty of death by crucifixion. Crucifixion wasn't even in existence at the time either David or Zechariah made their prophecies! The first time crucifixion was used in Israel was approximately sixty years before Jesus was born."

The Probability Factors

One might argue that the prophecies stated have been fulfilled in other men. Maybe one or two of the prophecies have, but not the eight just detailed. Peter Stoner wrote a treatise called *Science Speaks*. In it he illustrates the mathematical probability for the eight prophecies to be fulfilled in one man's life. The manuscript was then sent to H. Harold Hartzler of the American Scientific Affiliation. Mr. Hartzler states in the foreword to *Science Speaks*:

> The manuscript for *Science Speaks* has been carefully reviewed by a committee of the American Scientific Affiliation members and by the Executive Council of the same group and has been found, in general, to be dependable and accurate in regard to the scientific material presented. The mathematical analysis included is based upon principles of probability which are thoroughly sound, and Professor Stoner has applied these principles in a proper and convincing way.[6]

Mr. Stoner states that we find that the chance that any

man might have lived down to the present time and fulfilled all eight prophecies is 1 in 10^{17}. That means that if you were a betting person you would have one chance out of 100,000,000,000,000,000 for eight prophecies to be fulfilled in one man's life. To make this a little more graphic, Mr. Stoner asks us to imagine that:

> We take 10^{17} [to the seventeenth power] silver dollars and lay them on the face of Texas. They will cover all of the state two feet deep. Now mark one of these silver dollars and stir the whole mass thoroughly, all over the state. Blindfold a man and tell him that he can travel as far as he wishes, but he must pick up one silver dollar and say that this is the right one. What chance would he have of getting the right one? Just the same chance the prophets would have had of writing these eight prophecies and having them all come true in any one man, from their time to the present time.[7]

It is rather obvious to any thinking person that the prophecies and their fulfillment in the life of Christ are no coincidence. And we have only examined eight of the prophecies. If we apply the probability test to just 48 of the prophecies which Christ fulfilled, the probability factor jumps up to 1 chance in 10^{157}—that is a 1 followed by 157 zeroes for those of you who have been out of school for a while. The science of mathematics, rather than scarring the prophecies, elevates them to a higher level of credibility. It also cannot be argued that the New Testament writers made the script fit the prophecies, because of the historical accuracy with which the writers recorded the gospels.

If the writers fictitiously created the life of Christ, there is nothing to suggest this in the 24,000 manuscripts discovered. It would have required a humanly impossible effort to get all the manuscripts written by different writers to match up to the same fraudulent story.

Another explanation that might be given is that Jesus deliberately orchestrated the events in His life so that they would match up to the 60 prophecies and over 270 ramifications detailing the life of the Messiah to come. This was not possible, however, because Jesus could not determine his place of birth, his family lineage, and so forth. Even if he could, by the law of statistics this is considered impossible. Dr. Duane Tolbert Gish, who received his Ph.D. in biochemistry at the University of California and served on the research staff of the Upjohn Company, one of the nation's largest pharmaceutical firms, states that when one deals with a probability factor of 10 to the seventh power or higher—from a scientific viewpoint—it is considered impossible. To say that Jesus could have controlled the family lineage, place of birth, being preceded by a forerunner, betrayal by a friend for thirty pieces of silver, burial in a rich man's tomb, and death by crucifixion is considered mathematically and scientifically impossible. (*The Fakers* [Grand Rapids: Baker Book House, 1981], pp. 135-142).

Perhaps the following simple but clear illustration will help to illustrate the powerful impact of fulfilled prophecy.

The Application

We have briefly stated some of the compelling evidence for the Bible and for Jesus Christ. Can we identify Jesus Christ beyond the shadow of doubt as being what He claimed to be? Please consider the evidence one more time. God will not force you to believe. You must make that final and forever choice. But to fail to act on that evidence and receive Jesus Christ as your Saviour will result in you spending an eternity in Hell, and that breaks my heart for you.

When I was a sailor, I had several "blind dates." Suppose for this particular blind date, I agree to meet her in Philadelphia, Pennsylvania at the Greyhound Bus Station, 464 Liberty Street, at 8:00 P.M. tonight. She is one-legged, and wears a peg-leg on her left leg which she has painted florescent yellow with a blinking red light bulb in it to keep folks from stumbling over her leg. She also has a matching florescent yellow patch over her right eye, which she lost in the same accident in which she lost her leg. Also, she is missing the little finger on her right hand. She will wear a pink stocking on her one good leg and a maroon and white saddle oxford on her one good foot. She will wear a green hat and a lavender dress and will carry a purple purse. She says she is 5 feet tall and weighs about 200 pounds. Do you honestly think I would have any trouble identifying the right girl at the Greyhound Bus Station at 8:00 P.M.?

Remember, the *time* of Jesus Christ's birth was foretold centuries in advance (Dan. 9:24-26). This does away with the otherwise possible objection sometimes made that one could make *any* prophecy and something would eventually occur which could be labeled as the fulfillment of that prophecy. The time element destroys this objection.

I only gave about 13 or 14 marks of identification concerning this girl. However, the chances are millions to one against there being another girl with these identification characteristics in that particular bus station at 8:00 P.M.! God gave 333 *marks of identification* about Jesus concerning His birth, life, death and resurrection. Each mark of identification was perfectly fulfilled in Jesus, so there could be no doubt about identifying Him WHEN He came, and SINCE He has come! Remember, everything Christ said came true. He said Hell was real and forever, just as Heaven is. A miilion years from now you will be alive somewhere. Will it be in Heaven or will it be in Hell?

Remember, the fulfilled prophecies about Jesus and the illustrations identify Him as the God He claimed to be. He alone is the Saviour of men (John 14:6). Every prophecy of the Bible is always accurately, literally fulfilled. To get the full impact of this, suppose some prognosticator predicted 100 things that would happen to you in the coming year. Many of these predictions are very detailed. The first prediction is that you will stub your toe on a chair leg on January 1st at 12:35, just past midnight. You will fall on a glass on the kitchen table, which will shatter and cut a U-shaped wound on your chin. This jagged wound will require 13 stitches. It will be sewn up by a new doctor in town named McGuire, your doctor being unavailable at the time. To your chagrin and amazement, when January 1st comes, this is *exactly* what happens, right down to the most minute detail!

Then, throughout the year, 99 of these prophecies are literally, actually, perfectly fulfilled in every detail. 99 of the 100, with 1 more to go! This last prophecy is for the last day of the year. It declares that if you drive downtown to 5th and Main at 5:00 P.M. you will be in a fiery car crash that will leave you blind and crippled and badly burned. You will be in excruciating pain. You will be hospitalized for 6 months and finally die.

Tell me, would you deliberately drive down to 5th and Main at 5:00 P.M. on the last day of the year if you had a choice? Would you consider it a safe, sane, intelligent risk when 99 prophecies have come true without a failure, which would be virtually impossible mathematically by chance alone?

Now let us round Bible prophecies off to 100, 99 of which have already been perfectly fulfilled. The 100th prophecy is that if you ignore or refuse to accept Jesus Christ as your personal Lord and Saviour, you will die without hope and spend eternity in the Lake of Fire spoken of in Revelation chapter 20 as the destiny of the lost. A billion years from now your agony and despair and lostness from His love will barely have begun. Since the other Bible prophecies came true in literal and absolute fact, would it be intelligent to gamble your destiny forever that this last and final prophecy will not also come true?

Beloved friend, it is so good to have Jesus and His abundant life and peace even now, in this life, as well as settling your destiny forever to be sure of being in Heaven with Him! How unutterably sweet it is to have your sins forgiven, to be saved and know it, to lay your head on your pillow at night absolutely sure that you will be in Heaven with Jesus forever.

Jesus loves you so much. He proved it on the bloody cross when He died for you in your place.

Notes

1. Paul E. Little, *Know Why You Believe* (Wheaton: Victor Books, 1984), p. 103.

2. S. Maxwell Coder and George F. Howe, *The Bible, Science and Creation* (Chicago: Moody Press, 1965), p. 39. Used by permission.

3. Alexander Keith, *Evidences of Prophecy,* p. 8.

4. Many have made an effort to foretell the future—not one, outside the Bible, has ever succeeded. "The extreme difficulty of framing a prophecy which shall prove accurate, may be seen in that

familiar but crude rhyme known as 'Mother Shipton's Prophecy.' Some years ago it appeared as a pretended relic of a remote day, and claimed to have predicted the invention of the steam locomotive, the rise of D'Israeli in English politics, etc., etc. . . . For years I tried to unearth and expose what seemed to me a huge imposture, and I succeeded. . . . I traced the whole thing to one Charles Hindley (of England) who acknowledged himself the author of this prophetic hoax, which was written in 1862 instead of 1448, and palmed off on a credulous public. It is one of the startling proofs of human perversity that the very people who will try to cast suspicion on prophecies two thousand years old, will, without straining, swallow a forgery that was first published AFTER the events it predicted, and will not even look into its claim to antiquity" (Dr. A. T. Pierson, *Many Infallible Proofs*, pp. 44, 45.)

5. Keith, *Evidences of Prophecy*, p. 8.

6. Peter W. Stoner and Robert C. Newman, *Science Speaks* (Chicago: Moody Press, 1968), p. 366.

7. Ibid., p. 112.

CHAPTER THIRTEEN

The Ultimate Evidence

Jesus Christ—God's Living Word

". . . and the Word was God" (John 1:1-3, 14).

The Bible claims that Jesus Christ is the Son of God. The Bible also claims that the Son Himself is God, who took upon Himself human flesh, and visited earth on a dramatic rescue mission to save men from sin, death, and Hell. Isaiah 9:6, for example, says, "For unto us *a child* is born, unto us *a son* is given, and the government shall be upon his shoulders; and his name shall be called Wonderful, Counselor, *The Mighty God, The Everlasting Father, The Prince of Peace*"; 1 Timothy 3:16 states, "And without controversy great is the mystery of godliness: *God was manifest in the flesh,* justified in the Spirit, seen of angels, preached unto the Gentiles, believed on in the world, received up to glory" (italics added). The Bible speaks of Jesus' Second Coming as ". . . the glorious appearing of the *great God and our Saviour, Jesus Christ*" (Titus 2:13, italics added).

Jesus Himself claimed to be one with God. "He that hath seen me hath seen the Father" (John 14:9). Jesus is also called the Creator, the Resurrection and the Life, the

Alpha and Omega, and possesses the names, attributes and titles of God. The apostle Thomas recognized Him as his Lord and his God (John 20:28). Jesus was worshiped as God. He performed miracles that only God could perform.

As C. S. Lewis said, "A man who was merely a man and said the sort of things Jesus said would not be a great moral teacher. He would either be a lunatic—on a level with the man who says he is a poached egg—or else the Devil of Hell. You must take your choice. Either this man was, and is, the Son of God: or else a madman or something worse. You can shut him up for a fool, you can spit at him and kill him as a demon, or you can fall at his feet and call him Lord and God. But let us not come with any patronizing nonsense about his being a great moral teacher. He has not left that open to us. He did not intend to." In the remainder of this chapter powerful evidence will be given to authenticate Jesus Christ as being God, as He claimed. At the same time this evidence gives strong testimony to the Bible as the Word of God.

Consider the Miracle of Jesus' Life

Never was a man born like this man. As was prophesied approximately seven hundred years before His birth, He was born in Bethlehem of a certain tribe and family of the Jews (Mic. 5:2), born of a virgin (Isa. 7:14), and born at the exact time in history that the Scriptures said He would be born (Dan. 9:25, 26). An entire nation awaited His birth, something that never happened before or since to any person in history.

Never did another man live like Him. Christ's whole life was foretold in detail: His birth, purpose, life, method of death, ministry, and resurrection. He lived the only un-improvable life that anyone has ever lived. All the good characteristics of all the great men that ever lived could not be combined to make one Jesus. He and He alone was absolutely flawless, without sin. He asked those who hated him to identify one sin he had committed, but they could not.

Never did another man make such stupendous, specific claims. He claimed to be the "door" (John 10:9), and "the way, the truth, and the life" (John 14:6), the only way to heaven, to the Father. He claimed to be God in the flesh (John 8:58), forgave sins as God (Matt. 9:2-8), and accepted worship as God (e.g., Matt. 28:9).

Never did another man die as this man died. As was foretold in the Bible hundreds of years before the fact, Jesus died pierced on a cross. This was an unknown and unused method when the predictions were given (see, e.g., Ps. 22:16). Over three hundred predictions were literally, precisely, and perfectly fulfilled in His birth, life, death and resurrection; and thirty-three of them were realized on the very day He was crucified. We have covered these predictions in detail in the preceding chapter. No wonder Dr. Stoner concludes, "Any man who rejects Christ as the Son of God is rejecting a fact proved perhaps more absolutely than any other fact in the world."

Never did any other man die for such a purpose as this man. As God's Word in the Old and the New Testaments makes clear, Jesus came to die for us, to take our place, to shed His blood on the cross for us. Through His tears and His pain on the cross, Jesus said, "Father, forgive them" (Luke 23:34). No one ever loved us so, and if we cannot trust Jesus, who died for us, who can we trust?

No other man ever rose from the grave, conquering death. The founders of the world's religions, Buddha, Confucius, Muhammad, are all dead, their bodies long since decayed. Only Jesus Christ arose from the grave. Only Jesus had power over death. His tomb is empty!

Various Arguments Against the Resurrection

Consider briefly various arguments given by some of the world's most intelligent men who have tried to deny the resurrection.

1. *"The disciples stole the body."* In truth, however, the chief priests and elders bribed the soldiers with money to say that the disciples stole the body while the soldiers were asleep (Matt. 28:11-15). The frightened disciples had fled the horrors of the cross! Would they then defy the power of Rome for a dead body? Would all the soldiers have slept simultaneously knowing that their very lives would be at stake if this had truly occurred? How could the disciples have moved among them and moved the huge rock that sealed the tomb without awakening the soldiers? Besides, if the soldiers had been asleep, how would they have known that the disciples stole the body?

2. *"The soldiers stole the body."* Why? To risk their lives? Absurd. These tormentors and persecutors of Christians could have demolished Christianity and the disciples' claims about Christ's resurrection simply by producing the body—if they had stolen it. And, if true, why would the disciples lie about the resurrection and even risk their lives for something that never happened?

3. *"Jesus swooned, was put in the tomb while yet alive, revived, pushed the stone away, and came forth."* Jesus

was killed, pierced, and mutilated with a spear thrust through his side to his heart, so that the blood and water ran forth. The Roman soldiers did not even break His legs, as they did the legs of the two thieves, because He was already dead. So how could Jesus, mortally wounded, freely bleeding, and left alone for three days in a tomb, remain alive? How could He walk on nail-pierced feet, or move a huge rock with wounded hands and stagger past the soldiers without disturbing them? How could Joseph of Arimathaea, who wrapped Jesus in a clean linen cloth, not notice that he was alive? (Nicodemus and Joseph had wrapped one hundred pounds of spices around the body of Jesus in the wrapping cloth, which tended to glue and harden, so escape would have been impossible [John 19:38-42]). It takes far more faith to believe nonsense like the swoon theory, than to simply believe the truth! Jesus arose from the dead!

4. *"The disciples suffered from hallucinations: they wanted to see Jesus so much that they had a vision of Him."* In that case the soldiers must have had hallucinations also. Otherwise, how can one explain the angels and the empty tomb? The fact remains, the *body* of Jesus Christ was gone! Besides that, imagine five hundred people having the same hallucination at the same time in broad daylight (1 Cor. 15:6). For people prone to hallucinations, the hallucinations usually increase in intensity and frequency, but the very opposite happened when Jesus Christ ascended into heaven after appearing to His disciples. The fact is that the disciples saw the risen Christ, and went forth to tell the good news. They were freed from doubt and fear of death and rejoiced to suffer shame and even death for Jesus Christ. Nothing can account for the

dramatic sudden change in their lives except the bodily resurrection of Jesus Christ!

Several other speculations attempt to explain away the resurrection, such as mistaken identity, the body dissolving into gas, and the disciples going to the wrong tomb. But these efforts are futile, foolish, and factually unfounded.

Let us carefully consider a few more facts about the resurrection. Jesus Christ was undeniably dead. The Roman centurion was an expert on death. He was not only made a centurion for his bravery in battle, his effectiveness in killing the enemy, and his astuteness. One of his tasks, as pointed out by a lawyer-pastor friend, Dr. Bob Topartzer, was to check on the dead after a battle to see if they were really dead, or just playing possum. In Mark 15:44, Pilate, recognizing this expertise, asked the centurion about how long Jesus had been dead. The centurion had examined Jesus. He knew He was dead. The soldiers knew Jesus was dead. They did not even break his legs. (And thus unwittingly fulfilled prophecy! Not a bone of Him was to be broken!) Remember, as we pointed out previously, one soldier had thrust a spear into his side, rupturing the heart sac, and blood and water had run forth. The disciples knew he was dead. They had heard Him say He would die and rise again, and the horror of His death had begun to cause them despair. The women, including Jesus' mother, knew He was dead. Later they brought spices to embalm the body. Pilate knew he was dead, as did the Jewish officials. They demanded a seal for His tomb. Joseph of Arimathaea knew He was dead, as did Nicodemus. They are the ones who took the body and wrapped it in linen with 100 pounds of spices, and put it in Joseph's tomb. Jesus was dead.

Jesus Christ was undeniably buried in a rich man's

tomb belonging to Joseph of Arimathaea. Joseph of Arimathaea knew Jesus was buried. It was his tomb. Nicodemus knew it. He helped Joseph of Arimathaea bury Him. The women knew it (Mark 15:47). They watched His burial. The soldiers knew it. Their very lives depended on the body staying in the tomb. It would be exceedingly naive to believe that they did not thoroughly check the body before they sealed the tomb. Jesus was buried.

That leaves only one real alternative. Resurrection. The bodily resurrection of the Lord Jesus Christ. The tomb was and is empty!!

Think of it! The disciples were proclaiming the resurrection of one condemned as a criminal. They proclaimed this at a time when the population of Jerusalem was believed to be crowded with at least a million people. They grew bolder and bolder in declaring the message, especially after Pentecost. Bible scholars estimate that at least 125,000 Jews were converted to Christ in Jerusalem the first year after the resurrection! The evidence, the empty tomb, was *right there!*

The disciples knew all Jerusalem was thoroughly aware of the crucifixion of Jesus and his burial. By publicly declaring that he had conquered death and had risen from the tomb, they virtually dared any skeptic, *anyone,* friend or foe, to walk the short distance to the tomb and see for themselves! No one could deny that the body had been in the tomb. No one could say that Jesus Christ had not been buried. No one, not even the most bitter enemies of Christ, even tried! They would have been branded as fools. Jesus had been dead. He had been buried in the tomb. Now the body was gone. The tomb was empty. Both the friends and enemies of Christ agreed on this. They had no choice.

It was an established fact. Thousands could verify it then. Millions can and have since. The tomb is still empty.

The appearances of Jesus Christ, again and again, to the disciples, to the women, to over 500 people at once, solidified the evidence.

Over 500 people watched the ascension of Jesus Christ into the clouds (compare Luke 24:33 with Luke 24:50, 51, 1 Cor. 15:6, and Acts 1:9). This event had to have happened or it would never have been included in the scriptures. Many of the disciples, many of the 500 who were there were still alive when these scriptures were written. They would have denied the ascension of Jesus and destroyed the credibility of the Bible, had the event never occurred. They knew. They were there!

The event foreshadowed and predicted in the Old Testament hundreds of years before had come to pass. Not only the death, but the Resurrection of Jesus Christ. Among many other things, it was foretold in Isaiah 53 that Jesus would die in intense suffering for others, but in other scriptures it was plainly declared that He would reign forever. Impossible . . . without the resurrection, which is exactly what was being predicted. In Leviticus 14:1-7, God directed that a bird was to be killed in sacrifice, picturing Christ's death on the cross, and the blood of that bird was to be sprinkled on a living bird which then was to be set free! The living bird symbolized Christ's resurrection! This was a picture of the death and resurrection of Jesus Christ! Then Jesus Himself told His disciples that He would die and rise again the third day. He did.

Another tremendous testimony to the resurrection of Jesus Christ is found in Leviticus 23:9-11 with 1 Corinthians 15:20. In Leviticus God instructs the children of Israel to remember that when they begin to reap the harvest, they are to bring a sheaf of the FIRSTFRUITS of the harvest to the priest. The priest was to wave the sheaf of firstfruits ON THE MORROW, AFTER THE SABBATH, to be accepted as an offering for them. 1 Corinthians 15:20 informs us that the firstfruits is CHRIST. The Jewish *Sabbath* was *Saturday!* The MORROW AFTER THE SABBATH IS SUNDAY. It was God's way of introducing a new day honoring the resurrected Christ! God had given very specific instructions to the Jews concerning keeping the Sabbath. It was part of the covenant with God, of the whole Sabbath structure involving letting the land lay idle one year out of seven. This included the Jubilee year, measured by 7x7 Sabbatical years. Debts were rescinded, houses and possessions returned, servants set free in this glorious 50th year. The loss of any part of the structure decimated the whole. The Sabbath was given particularly to the Jews. Death could be the penalty for breaking it, or not observing it. The fact that converted Jews *risked their lives by celebrating Sunday in place of Saturday is a strong witness to the resurrection of Christ!*

Special celebration days have historical significance. We celebrate July 4th in honor of the signing of the Declaration of Independence. July 4th celebrates a historical fact. So it is with other special days. As Josh McDowell well says, "Sunday is the only day (he knows), that celebrates a historical fact 52 days a year!" That fact is the resurrection of Jesus Christ!

As we have said, one of the powerful testimonies to the fact of the resurrection of Christ is that thousands of Jews, at the risk of all they owned, even of their lives, began to worship God on a new day, Sunday!! Jews were the first

converts. Imagine the courage and conviction it took for
them to step out and change their day. This was done in
spite of centuries of Sabbath keeping, in spite of families
and loved ones, in spite of certain loss. Nothing can account for this change but the resurrection of Jesus Christ!

All of this brings us to the indisputable fact that the disciples were transformed from mice to martyrs by the resurrection of Jesus Christ. Why would they suffer the loss of
homes, families, and careers for a lie? Why would they
suffer loneliness, hunger, cold, and torture and death, for a
lie? Why would they even rejoice in their losses, and die rejoicing? They had *everything* to lose, and *nothing* to gain,
unless the resurrection of Jesus Christ was a FACT! Nearly
all, if not all, of the disciples of Jesus Christ died a martyr's
death. They knew the truth about His death and resurrection. Since then, it is estimated that some 66 million Christians have been martyred for Christ.[3]

The FACT is the disciples saw the risen Christ, and
flamed forth to tell the good news. They were freed form
doubt and fear of death and rejoiced to suffer shame and
even death for Jesus Christ. Nothing can account for the
dramatic, sudden change in their lives except the bodily
resurrection of Jesus Christ! They saw Him. Jesus conquered death. His claims are true!

The Miracle of Changed Lives

"Therefore if any man be in Christ, he is a new creature: old
things are passed away; behold, all things are become new"
(2 Cor. 5:17)

The power of the cross, of Jesus Christ, to change lives in-
stantaneously, to wash away sins, and to transform hate to

love, was illustrated so graphically in the case of five young Christian martyrs in Ecuador. Missionaries Nate Saint, Ed McCully, Jim Elliot, Roger Youderian, and Peter Fleming had flown into the domain of the savage aboriginal Auca Indians to bring them the gospel of Jesus Christ. On 8 January 1956 at least five Aucas brutally speared and slew them, and destroyed their plane.

Frank Drown, a fellow missionary who almost went with them, told me about going to get their bodies, and how it broke his heart! He knew them all and loved them. Imagine the shattering news to their young wives and children, parents and families. Yet, in unbelievable love and forgiveness, God worked.

Nate Saint was the missionary pilot of the plane. Rachel Saint, Nate's sister, went to these Auca Indians who had killed her brother, lived among them, and shared the gospel with them as she mastered their language. After two years four of the Indians received Christ. A little later the fifth was saved and was baptized by Phil Saint, the brother of Nate and Rachel. The wives of these Auca men also opened their hearts to the forgiving, life-changing Lord Jesus Christ. Who can change the attitudes and habits of a lifetime in a moment? Only Jesus. What a Savior!

President Lyndon B. Johnson visited Anchorage, Alaska while I lived there. A fourteen-year-old girl shook hands with him, and although she had previously shaken hands with the Beatles, she said this was even better. She was *never* going to wash that hand again! But, with all due respect to the President, if this girl had serious moral problems or crippling habit patterns *before* she met the President, she still had them *after* she met him. But an encounter with Jesus Christ is life-changing.

One night in Anchorage I counseled Ed Perry. Ed was a very heavy drinker, a rough, ungodly man. A professing agnostic, he was embittered by a physical tragedy in the family. He was also a former semipro football player. When I finally got an opportunity to talk alone with him he firmly resisted the Gospel.

To Ed's and my surprise, I abruptly interrupted our verbal sparring and said, "Ed Perry, you are going to be saved in five minutes." I marched over to his side, opened the Bible, and showed Ed how to become a Christian. Ed was saved, his bitterness gone forever, and his whole pattern of life radically changed. If you find this story hard to believe, ask the Rev. Ed Perry, now a pastor in Everett, Washington. Ed could add many other things to this story, for his life was sick with sin and shame until Jesus delivered him. What else can change a man like that but *Christ!*

No man can change lives like Jesus Christ. "Therefore if any man be in Christ, he is a new creature; old things are passed away; behold, all things are become new" (2 Cor. 5:17). Saul, the religious bigot and persecutor, became Paul, the mighty missionary for Jesus Christ from an encounter on the Damascus road with the risen Christ. Life-changing conversions have happened to millions since who have put their trust in Him. I have never met a prostitute, an alcoholic, or a drug addict who has said to me, "I met George Washington the other day, and he changed my life!" But I have met many who have said simply, and often with tears of joy, "I met Jesus Christ the other day, and He changed my life!" Why? Because He is alive!

Since Christ has come into my heart and changed my life, I recommend Him to you with all my heart. This personal relationship with Him is beyond price. He has given peace when life has tumbled in; answered prayers miraculously in impossible situations; answered prayers for food when we were hungry and isolated in a remote place; displayed His mighty power and presence in danger, trials, and countless other predicaments. He is real and alive and He loves you and will take care of you, both here and hereafter.

One Solitary Life

Nearly two thousand years ago in an obscure village, a child was born of a peasant woman. He grew up in another village where he worked as a carpenter until He was thirty. Then for three years He became an itinerant preacher.

This Man never went to college or seminary. He never wrote a book. He never held a public office. He never had a family nor owned a home. He never put His foot inside a big city nor traveled even two hundred miles from His birthplace. And though He never did any of the things that usually accompany greatness, throngs of people followed Him. He had no credentials but Himself.

While He was still young, the tide of public opinion turned against Him. His followers ran away. He was turned over to His enemies and went through the mockery of a trial. He was sentenced to death on a cross between two thieves. While he was dying, His executioners gambled for the only piece of property He had on earth—the simple coat He had worn. His body was laid in a borrowed grave provided by a compassionate friend.

But three days later this Man arose from the dead— living proof that He was, as He had claimed, the Savior whom God had sent, the incarnate Son of God.

Nineteen centuries have come and gone and today the risen Lord Jesus Christ is the central figure of the human race. On our calendars His birth divides history into two eras. One day of every week is set aside in remembrance of Him. And our two most important holidays celebrate His birth and resurrection. On church steeples around the world His cross has become the symbol of victory over sin and death.

This one Man's life has furnished the theme for more songs, books, poems, and paintings than any other person or event in history. Thousands of colleges, hospitals, orphanages, and other institutions have been founded in honor of this One who gave His life for us.

All the armies that ever marched, all the navies that ever sailed, all the governments that ever sat, all the kings that ever reigned have not changed the course of history as much as this *one solitary life*.

Over the centuries milions have found a new life of forgiveness from sins and peace with God through faith in Jesus Christ. Today He offers this life to all who will believe. "I am the way, the truth, and the life," Jesus said, "no man cometh unto the Father, but by me." "He that heareth my word, and believeth on him that sent me, hath everlasting life, and shall not come into condemnation, but is passed from death unto life" (John 14:6; 5:24).

Has the Lord Jesus Christ changed your life?[4]

Ask Him . . . *Trust* Him . . . *He Will!*

Notes

1. Peter W. Stoner and Robert C. Newman, *Science Speaks* (Chicago: Moody Press, 1968), p. 112.

2. See Luke 24:33, 50, 51; Acts 1:9.

3. See John Foxes, *Book of Martyrs* for more information.

4. "One Solitary Life," author anonymous. Used by permission of Good News Publishers, 9825 W. Roosevelt Road, Westchester, Illinois.

CHAPTER FOURTEEN

Facing the Exciting Evidence

Simon Greenleaf was a famous lawyer, a Harvard law professor, and author of an authoritative work on evaluating evidence. He knew empirical evidence, and he knew infallible evidence, and evidence totally convinced him that Jesus Christ had risen bodily from the tomb. He became a committed follower of Jesus Christ, and wrote a book entitled *The Testimony of the Evangelists*. Irwin W. Linton studied earnestly the evidence for the resurrection of Jesus. Irwin was a lawyer also. His doubt fled. He accepted Jesus Christ as his Lord and Savior and wrote a tremendous book, *A Lawyer Examines the Bible*. Frank Morrison was a thoroughgoing skeptic. As a lawyer, he knew how to evaluate evidence. A careful study of the resurrection won his heart for Jesus Christ. He wrote, *Who Moved the Stone?*

Bob Ingersoll, an infidel, challenged his friend Governor Lew Wallace as he entertained Lew with one of his diatribes against Christ, the Bible, and Christians. Though not a Christian, Lew, the author of *Ben Hur,* decided to investigate the Bible and the resurrection for himself. Consequently, he converted to Christianity.

Charles Finney, a lawyer with an analytical mind, decided to face head-on the testimony of Jesus Christ. Eventually, he became a mighty evangelist, making an impact upon America for his Savior.

Josh McDowell was a brilliant young man. He had, however, a very sad childhood and was an unhappy young man. His father was a town drunk. His friends laughed at his father's drunken escapades. When Josh's friends came over, he would even take his father out to the barn and tie him up. Then he would park the car near the silo and tell his friends his father was not home! While laughing on the outside, Josh cringed on the inside. In a small town, few things are worse than having your father be the town alcoholic.

Josh was generally an angry young man, but he especially hated his father. On one occasion he had seen his mother lying in the manure behind the cows in the barn. Josh's father had beaten her so badly that she could not even get up. One can only imagine the rage and hate that filled his heart.

Slowly the years passed. Josh went off to college and met some genuine born-again Christians. He saw in them something for which his hungry heart longed, yet his intellect was not ready to accept. So Josh purposed to "intellectually refute" Christianity and the resurrection of Jesus Christ. He dug determinedly into the evidence. The battle for his mind and heart was monumental. Finally, convinced but still reluctant, Josh did what he felt was the only honest thing he could do. While alone in his room, he invited Jesus Christ into his heart and life on December 19, 1959 at 8:30 P.M. It was a quiet unemotional conversion, based on evidence and the reality of the risen Christ. But what began as a relatively uneventful conversion, later became an explosive transformation. Josh said he was debating the head of the history department in a midwestern university when the professor challenged him to name some concrete changes

Christ had made in his life. Forty-five minutes later the professor asked him to stop!

Some of the changes that Jesus Christ made in Josh McDowell's life involved taking away his fierce temper, giving deep peace to his restless mind, removing his bitterness, and replacing his insecurity with assurance. God also gave Josh a passion to reach other people for Jesus Christ.

Josh experienced another astonishing change after he had accepted Christ. Slowly but surely God began to replace the burning hatred in his heart for his father. About five months after receivng Christ, the love of Christ so overpowered Josh that he looked his father in the eye and told him, "Dad, I love you!"

Sometime later when Josh was at home his father came into his room and asked Josh how he could possibly love a father like him? Josh told his dad that just six months earlier he had despised him! Then Josh told him about how Jesus Christ had come into his life. He told his dad that Jesus had turned his hate into love, and that now he truly loved his dad. Forty-five minutes later, Josh experienced one of the greatest thrills of his life. His dad, who had known Josh and his hatred, simply said, "Son, if God can do in my life what I've seen Him do in yours, then I want to give Him the opportunity." Then and there a miracle occurred. Josh's alcoholic dad prayed with him, and trusted Christ as his Lord and Savior. The life of Josh's father changed from night to day. No longer was he an alcoholic. He was truly a new creature in Christ.

Since then Josh McDowell has become internationally famous. Some of his books such as *Evidence That Demands a Verdict* and *More Evidence That Demands a Verdict* are classics and contain a mass of historical evidence for the Christian faith and Scriptures. Josh has spoken in more than six hundred universities. He has debated skeptics, atheists, and unbelieving religious leaders all over the world.

Mike Warnke tells a bittersweet story in his book, *The Satan Seller.* Mike and his fellow Satan worshipers were discussing how to welcome two new members into their coven. Mike said that according to the Satanist's manual, they were supposed to rape a virgin on the altar for the fertility rites. They agreed to do this. Their only concern was how to keep the woman from talking after they released her. (At this point they were not yet quite into human sacrifice, although considerable evidence exists that some human sacrifices have been used in Satanic rites.) Someone suggested that if the girl witnessed an authentic demonstration of demonic power, she would not dare talk.

Mike and his cohorts cruised the streets of San Bernadino looking for a likely prospect. Two strong-arm men for the group, Bert and James, found a girl named Mary who they deemed suitable for their purpose. They hustled her into the car and took her to an isolated barn where their altar to Satan and other Satanic paraphernalia was set up. They directed the girl to take off her clothes. She refused, so she was forcibly undressed and placed on the altar—still not fully realizing what awaited her.

As the ritual continued, she heard Mike declare that it was time for the fertility rites. What was about to happen to Mary finally dawned on her. She fought hopelessly, desperately. Once she even escaped from Bert and James, the two men who held her. She began to cry, pleading desperately, "Please, don't!"

After considerable torture, Mary yielded, begging

them not to hurt her anymore. She was then brutally gang-raped. Finally, the indescribable horror and humiliation was over. The "guys," as Mike described these fellow Satanists, took Mary to a doctor for which Mike was paying. Mary would have little help from this doctor other than patching her up, but Mike felt that this strategic move, along with the demon manifestations Mary had seen, would prevent her from reporting the brutal incident.

Some time later Mike was walking around the campus of Valley College. A woman came toward him, and as she got closer, he became alarmed. It was Mary. "Kidnap, rape," he thought to himself. What would she do to him?

Mary approached Mike and said, "I know you." She began to walk along beside him. Bracing himself for the worst, Mike asked what she wanted from him. To his absolute astonishment, Mary smiled at him. This girl who had been kidnapped, terrorized, and raped smiled at him! Then she said, "I don't want anything. I just came over to tell you that I love you." Seeing the unbelief and agony in Mike's eyes, she repeated, "I said, I love you. I've accepted Jesus as my Savior. And I love you."

This experience shattered Mike Warnke. In fact, he almost committed suicide. Later, in the Navy, two sailors continued the impact of the love of Christ on him and showed him the way of salvation from the Bible. Mike Warnke—onetime dope addict, Satanist, sinner—accepted Jesus Christ as *his* Savior and became a new creature in Him. Today, he carries the gospel all over the world—leading others from the darkness in which he once lived to the light of Jesus Christ in which he now lives.

When you are thinking about the reality of Jesus Christ and His resurrection, please think seriously about Mike

Warnke and Mary. Nothing can so change people and replace hate and revulsion with love and forgiveness except the living Lord Jesus Christ!

Herbert Vander Lugt shares a thrilling story of the transformation Christ can make in a person's life:

> I had no idea what my grandson meant when he told me he wanted a Transformer. Then he explained that it is a toy that can be changed from robot to tank to truck and back to robot again. Seeing one helped me understand how it got its name. But it also made me think about life's ultimate transformation—the one that Jesus Christ produces in the lives of all who trust Him.
>
> Oscar Cervantes is a dramatic example of Christ's power to transform lives. As a child, Oscar began to get into trouble. Then as he got older, he was jailed 17 times for brutal crimes. Prison psychiatrists said he was beyond help. But they were wrong! During a brief interval of freedom, Oscar met an elderly man who told him about Jesus. He placed his trust in the Lord and was changed into a kind, caring man. Shortly afterward he started a prison ministry. Chaplain H. C. Warwick describes it this way: "The third Saturday night of each month is 'Oscar Night' at Soledad. Inmates come to hear Oscar and they sing gospel songs with fervor; they sit intently for over 2 hours; they come freely to the chapel altar. . . . What professionals had failed to do for Oscar in years of counseling, Christ did in a moment of conversion."
>
> In Mark 5 we read that Jesus Christ turned a raging, demon-possessed maniac into a docile, normal man. The same power that changed the maniac and Oscar Cervantes is available to all who trust Jesus. He is the Master Transformer. Has He changed you?[1]

As Dr. Josh McDowell has pointed out in his dynamic book, *More Than a Carpenter,*[2] Jesus Christ had to have been either a liar, a lunatic, or the Lord God. It is impossible that Jesus Christ was a liar. He was the epitome of honesty, and demanded that people be honest at any cost. Everything He said came true. He gave his own life for what He said was true.

He was no lunatic. Rather He was the essence of sanity and tranquility under intense pressure, false accusations, persecution, and death. His impeccable character and serene demeanor negate this possibility.

The only other viable alternative? Jesus Christ *was* and *is* the Lord God! Tens of millions have testified that Christ has changed their lives, answered their deepest needs, satisfied their longings, and given them peace. These transformed individuals include former White House special counsel Chuck Colson, scientists Dr. Henry Morris and Dr. Duane Gish, pro football players Steve Largent and Roosevelt Grier, Dallas Cowboy head coach Tom Landry, ice skater Janet Lynn, pro basketball player "Dr. J." Julius Erving, scholar Josh McDowell, some sixty-six million martyrs who have been tortured and slain for Jesus, and millions of other "ordinary" people. From them and others the cry of praise goes up, "Jesus died for me, and I love Him, and He is alive. He loves me, He has saved me, He dwells in me, and He has changed my life!"

Has He changed your life?

Notes

1. Reading for 10 March 1987, vol. 32, no. 1 in *Our Daily Bread* (Grand Rapids: Radio Bible Class, 1987).

2. Josh McDowell, *More Than a Carpenter* (Wheaton: Tyndale House, 1980).

CHAPTER FIFTEEN

The Verdict . . . Your Response

Suppose you are driving down an unfamiliar highway en route to a town called Bunkersville. You come to a fork in the road, with two roads continuing in the general direction of Bunkersville. One road is marked "Closed," and the other is marked "Bunkersville." Which road would you take?

The sensible action would be to take the road marked "Bunkersville." But suppose for some reason—or for no particular reason—you doubt the signs. You hesitate, uncertain what to do. Then you notice something. Driving back out of the road marked "Closed," you see a continual stream of traffic, cars battered and drivers haggard. Some of them now go down the "Bunkersville" road, but others shake their heads sadly and say that there simply is *no way* to Bunkersville. Though you point out the sign that clearly indicates the way, they refuse to take the right road. Some drivers even contend that *there is no Bunkersville,* because they could not reach it on the road marked "Closed!"

Meanwhile, some drivers passing by tell you with great assurance that they have already tried the road marked "Bunkersville" and that it really does lead there. What would be your judgment then about the only intelligent action for you to take?

God's "road sign," the Bible, says that the only door that

leads to Him is marked "Faith." He says man's wisdom never leads to Him. That door is marked "Closed" (1 Cor. 1:21). (God does say, "Come now and let us reason together" [Isa. 1:18]. He will give any willing mind more than sufficient evidence to make faith credible. But He will not give such overwhelming proof that no faith is required, because He has established faith as the route to God.) After thousands of years no one has ever found God by wisdom. Not Plato, nor Socrates, nor Paul, nor Bertrand Russell, nor Einstein. God declared it impossible, and men have found it so.

God's Word declares, "But the natural [unsaved] man receiveth not the things of the Spirit of God; for they are foolishness unto him, neither can he know them, because they are spiritually discerned" (1 Cor. 2:14). Just as there are sounds the human ear cannot hear, and sights the human eye cannot see, so there is a spiritual dimension which human wisdom cannot comprehend.

Those who have sought to find God by wisdom and failed have had various reactions. Some, like the genius Pascal, have switched to the road of faith and found God. Others have said there is no way to find God, and still others have said there is no God to find. Meanwhile, many have testified that they have sought God through faith as the Bible says to do and have found Him.

Consider my scientist friend Duane and his wife Corky. Duane was an aticulate, well-read atheist, who delighted to discredit Christianity. His wife was an agnostic. Some friends coaxed them out to church with the promise of a turkey dinner, and arranged for me to interview them after dinner. Duane gave the usual arguments for atheism, with some of his own twists.

"Duane," I marveled, "I just wish I had as much faith

as you have!" (I knew well that many atheists despise faith, considering it beneath the dignity and intellect of an educated man.)

"What?" he said in surprise.

"Do you agree with many scientists that matter is not eternal, and that therefore everything in existence must have come out of nothing?" I asked.

"Of course," he answered.

"You do not believe in God, so nobody created the universe; it simply evolved or happened?"

"Right!"

"Duane, do you realize you are saying that *nobody + nothing = everything!* What a tremendous amount of faith it must take to believe *that!* Yet you ridicule the Christian faith, which is based on solid, substantial facts! To find a watch on a wilderness trail and assume its intricate design just happened or evolved apart from outside intelligence is no more foolish than to look at the great universe in its infinite design and precision and declare there is no Designer. Someone has said that it would be easier for a monkey to write a novel by tossing the letters of the alphabet up and down than it would be to create the universe by pure chance. What about known laws which regulate our universe? Have you ever known of a law without a lawgiver? Then consider the human body. George Gallup, the famous pollster-statistician, contends that he could prove God statistically. He says that the human body alone, with all of its many and complicated functions, could not possibly just happen by chance, that this would be an impossible statistical monstrosity."

This got Duane's attention. Soon we were in the Bible. First, we considered the prophecies and their fulfillment, and then we zeroed in on the death and resurrection of Christ, the greatest attested fact in history. Within three hours, this sharp young scientist-atheist and his wife had received the Savior. Tears of pure joy swelled up in the eyes of both Duane and Corky as Jesus took their sins and doubts away and gave them everlasting life.

What happened? Duane had tried to find God by wisdom, but failed and gave up. He had declared that God did not exist and had read everything he could find to reinforce his position. Then he decided to go God's way to find God. Duane found Him, and so can you.

"Christian faith is wishful thinking"

Suppose you live in France and want to send a letter to George VanderMeer, 321 Oak Street, Centerville, Oregon, USA. When you write "USA" on the envelope, you eliminate over one hundred other countries. You write "Oregon," and that eliminates forty-nine other states. "Centerville" eliminates every other village, town, and city in the state of Oregon. You write "321 Oak", his street and street number, and so eliminate perhaps dozens of other streets in town, as well as all other numbers on Oak Street. You write "VanderMeer," eliminating scores, perhaps thousands of other people in Centerville, Oregon. Then you also write "George," his first name, thereby eliminating all other VanderMeers in that area.

What happens? By a simple system involving six or seven processes of elimination, your letter goes to George VanderMeer, 321 Oak Street, Centerville, Oregon, USA. Out of six billion people on the face of the earth your letter finds its way to exactly the right person!

If human beings can design a simple system that can deliver mail, can't God the Designer of the universe send Jesus Christ, His "special delivery" love gift to us? He can, and He has!

Let us consider just one miracle recorded in all four Gospels (Matt. 14:15-21; Mark 6:32-44; Luke 9:10-17; John 6:1-14). Jesus fed 5,000 people from a little boy's lunch of five loaves and two fishes (John 6:9). This miracle was impossible to fake and totally impossible for any human being to do.

Several years ago in Anchorage, Alaska, I met Ian Drummond, a chef at the plush Captain Cook Hotel. Though a young man, Ian had been a chef in six different countries, and had cooked for Queen Elizabeth once. He had considerable experience in feeding large groups of people. We estimated the quantity of food that it would take to feed a crowd of 5,000 men, not including the women and children. Five loaves and two fishes were approximately enough for one small boy. The people had hiked and climbed a mountain and had not eaten for quite some time. Their hunger was probably ravenous. Thus it would have taken 25,000 loaves and 10,000 fishes for only the men to have as much as the boy. And it may have required twice this amount to feed all of the women and children. Even if only one-tenth of this amount of food were needed (2,500 loaves and 1,000 fishes), a stupendous miracle was still required.

Jesus sat upon an open mountain (John 6:3), in broad daylight, and fed all of these people. He divided only five loaves and two fishes, and yet all of the people and His disciples had plenty to eat. Then they gathered twelve baskets full of leftovers! This miracle aptly portrayed Jesus Christ as the Bread of Life. It proved that He was the Creator

(John 1:3), and it also showed His compassion for the hungry multitude.

Ian and I agreed that it would take thousands of pounds of food, perhaps a *boxcar,* full of food to feed that many people. If it was a hoax, where did Jesus hide the food? In His robe? To suggest that it was faked either accuses the Son of God of deception or accuses the four Gospel writers of collusion and duplicity. These disciples and others who later followed Jesus gave up everything for Him, in some cases their very lives. Would they have shown such devotion for a known faker?

This account was published during the lifetime of many who were there. If the event had never occurred, the fraud could and would have been exposed by friends, disillusioned disciples, or Jesus' bitter enemies. To have included such a sham in the Gospel record would have immediately discredited the New Testament during its circulation. Yet Jesus *did* perform a miracle, which demonstrates His claims about who He is and what He has done for our salvation.

Please consider the evidence. Men who know nothing about electricity do not hesitate to turn on the switch and use the light. They would think you eccentric if you stood in the dark and argued that the whole idea of electricity sounded weird, that you didn't understand it fully, and that you were not about to turn the switch until you did.

Yet many men still approach God's miracles on this basis. God will not cram you with so many facts that you are forced to believe against your will. That would violate your free agency and leave no room for faith (Heb. 11:6). He *does* provide us with abundant evidence so that faith is resting on the credible promises of God.

Since He will not force you, physically or mentally, *you* must make the final choice. But to ignore the evidence and say there is none while believing countless other things with little evidence, may haunt you for an eternity in Hell!

What if you saw a man painting a burning house, oblivious to his danger and to the rapidly lessening chance of saving his house and its contents? When you urgently inquire as to why on earth he is painting a burning house, he looks at you as if *you* were crazy, and calmly goes back to painting his house!

It is just as ridiculous to concentrate totally on the things of this present life if there really is a Heaven to win and a Hell to shun. How insane to ignore eternity as if it didn't exist or had relatively little importance if a million years from now we will still be alive somewhere—either in Heaven or Hell!

Not all the money, not all the prestige, not all the pleasure, not all the popularity, not all the food, not all the sex, not all the drinks, not all the success, not all the kicks, not all the luxury, not all the comfort in the world, will mean a thing to a person after five minutes in Hell!

"It costs too much to be a Christian"

You may have heard of the atheist who challenged the teenage boy about his conversion to Christ. The atheist chided the boy for his foolishness in believing "mythology," and called his conversion nonsense.

The teenager listened to him and then responded: "Sir, if you are right and I am wrong, we will go to the same place when we die. So I've lost nothing. Besides, now that I believe in Jesus, I'm immeasurably happier with a better life and higher purpose even if it is only for this life. But suppose that I am right and you are wrong. I'll be in heaven with Christ and you will be in hell forever. Mister, *I can't lose, and you can't win!*"

That is so true, and yet Christianity is not just playing the odds. Our faith rests in the certainty of a risen Lord and living Savior. Beloved friend, let Him prove His reality to you. It is foolish to refuse Him, His love, and the hope of heaven, especially when the alternative is an eternal hell apart from God.

"I will try religion some day"

During the great Alaskan earthquake of 1964 a terrifying tidal wave swept in and devastated part of Seward. Can you imagine a man running *toward* that vast and lethal wave screaming, "Save me, save me, please save me"?

What would you think of a person on the roof of a burning hotel who is running toward the flames of the fire, and away from the approaching firemen, all the time yelling for them to save him? Yet many people treat God this way. They run desperately from His salvation, and frantically toward damnation. They even avoid people who could help them find God.

A tough ex-semipro football player I led to Christ told me that normally he would have beaten me up or run me off if I had spoken to him about Christ. Yet he said that many a dark night he cried out to God to make Himself known if He were real and if He cared. He fought the hardest against what he wanted most.

Some years ago I took my dog Sneezer to the vet to be treated for the mange. Instead of putting him to sleep for the treatment, the doctor asked me to hold him. Sneezer fought tooth and nail, exhausting both the vet and me. Finally, the exasperated vet said, "You know, the more intelligent a dog is, the quicker he realizes that I am trying to help him. Then he quits fighting and starts cooperating." I gathered that he classed poor Sneezer as a canine moron.

Is it really an intelligent decision for you to fight against the God who loves and wants to save you?

"I'm just not sure what to do"

Sometimes a person hesitates because he/she doesn't know exactly how to accept Christ and receive assurance of heaven. You can choose against your doubts and for Christ. He will reinforce that choice and prove Himself irrevocably to you. He did this for me and He has done it for thousands of others. Jesus said, "Him that cometh to me I will in no wise cast out" (John 6:37). That's true whether you come with doubts or not.

No one else will give you the answers to life and death, heaven and hell, except the One who loved you enough to die in your place, and who conquered death for you in His resurrection body. He is alive, real, and waiting for you. Will you pray the following simple prayer and receive Him right now?

> "Lord Jesus Christ, cleanse me from all my sin by your shed blood. Come into my heart and life, and make me a child of God. Give me your free gift of everlasting life and let me know that I am saved, now and forever. I now receive you as my own personal Lord and Savior. In Jesus' name, Amen."

God promises, "For whosoever shall call upon the

name of the Lord shall be saved" (Rom. 10:13). Did you call? If so, did He save you? Or did He lie? He had to save you or lie, and He *cannot* lie! Never mind *feeling*. Do you believe His Word? Would He love you enough to die in agony for you and then refuse you?

I didn't particularly feel married after I said "I do," but my marriage license declared that I was married. I have many other reasons to know that I am married now, including feelings, and so it is with real salvation, but it is faith that saves you, not feelings! Your marriage license to Jesus is the Word of God. You can *know* you are saved the moment you ask Jesus to save you, because His Word says so!

You have changed your mind ("repented") about going your own way as the master of your life, and have now given Jesus Christ the opportunity to save you and change your life. Now he has become the Master of your life.

Believe and memorize John 3:36a: "Whoever puts his faith in the Son has [right now] eternal life" (NIV). This is true assuming you believed with your heart—the ruling, governing center of your being. Thank God for giving you everlasting life now, for saving you forever, and for giving you assurance of heaven. The Bible promises it!

As Dr. Bob Jones, Sr. once said, "Dying men have said, 'I am sorry I have been an atheist, an infidel, an agnostic, a skeptic, or a sinner.' No man ever said with his last breath, 'I am sorry I have lived a Christian life.'"

(For further and more detailed information on how to become a Christian and know it, see the chapter, "Contact With the Ultimate.")

CHAPTER SIXTEEN

The Beautiful Side of Death

Physically, it had been a nightmare. Burning, agonizing pain. At times, intense thirst. A ruptured appendix and the spreading poison of peritonitis. Many internal organs had been covered by this deadly poison, and some had disintegrated. Blocked bowels. Separation from dearly loved children. Days and weeks in a coma, or semi-coma. The agony of being able to hear doctors discuss her hopeless condition, of having loved ones near and not being able to open her eyes or respond. Yes, I am referring again to the story of Betty Malz, then Betty Upchurch.

Betty is a tall, dynamic woman, very striking in appearance. Last week, over TV, I heard her refer to herself as "5 feet 12 inches."

At the time of the death, or out-of-body experience we are writing about, Betty was a patient in Union Hospital, Terre Haute, Indiana. She had wasted down to 80 pounds.

Dr. Bherne declared that in 18 years experience, he had never seen such a gangrenous mess inside anyone. He could only find small pieces of the exploded appendix; the poison had spread everywhere. Betty went through four rounds of operations and steadily worsened.

Betty had supposedly accepted Christ at 13, after one of her godly father's messages on the second coming of Christ. However, it was as she lay on her bed, eyes closed, unable to respond, but conscious of all that went on around her, that God really worked in her heart. As her father prayed, deep, moving, personal prayers in which he called repeatedly on Jesus, Betty marveled at the intimate personal relationship her father obviously had with Jesus, and realized that she did not have it. Then and there, Betty repented, realizing the difference between her former mental assent and heart belief, and sought the Savior with all her heart. Then and there a deep, sweet, personal relationship began. This turned even the physical agony, and the humiliation of body exposure, and painful, foul elimination forced by two rubber-gloved, probing nurses into an incredible experience of the love of Christ! Joy and love flooded Betty's soul, even under this most dreaded and degrading circumstance.

At 5 A.M. one bleak morning, Betty died. The life support system was removed from her body. All bodily organs had ceased to function. A sheet was pulled over Betty's body and face. She had been pronoucned dead.

The transition was beautiful, painless, tranquil. Betty found herself walking up a long hill with a strong, masculine presence walking close beside her. The sky was so very blue! The grass was a different shade of vivid green than any she had ever seen on earth. The touch of it was like velvet. Betty felt so *good* inside and out, so clean, so whole. It was sheer ecstasy! It seemed much like early spring. She saw no sun, but everywhere was caressed by light. There were flowers, trees, and shrubs. Then she became aware of singing, such as she had never heard before. Betty was an organist, but she had never heard music like this before, harmonious, and in many different languages! She came to a gate of luminous pearl. She saw streets inside with the appearance of gold, overlaid with glass or water. Then she became conscious of a light, a Presence, a Person, Jesus! She was aware of warmth and loving energy. Then the communication came to her clearly, though unspoken, asking her if she wanted to go in?

Betty longed to . . . but there was also a desire to go back and find her father. She expressed that desire. Suddenly she found herself on the way to earth again as she walked down the hill. Terre Haute, Indiana came into focus. Then the hospital, and room 336 . . . her room. She saw her body on the bed with a sheet pulled over it. In a moment she was back in her body, but marvelling over translucent ivory words two inches high, shimmering past her bed and on into the room. "I am the resurrection and the life; he that believeth in me, though he were dead, yet shall he live." Betty shoved the sheet aside and sat up. Her beloved father had come into the room just after five. It was now 5:28 A.M. Betty's broken-hearted, but submissive-to-God's-will father, was uttering one precious, powerful name, over and over again, "Jesus . . . Jesus . . . Jesus!" It was his prayer that Betty had been conscious of, even in the entrance to the beautiful city. She claims her father's prayers had brought her back!

Several interesting things Betty brought out about her experience. She saw Jack Holcomb in heaven. He was a gospel singer she loved and admired. At the time, she did not know that he had died, and did not find out about it until some time later! She also saw people working on many dwelling places, as if expecting a great host of people to come up at one time!

The experience, not just the 5 A.M. to 5:28 experience, but the whole episode, especially of coming to know Jesus in a real and personal way, changed Betty's life. She had disliked, perhaps even hated, minorities. Now she loved them. She was a manipulator, in control, wanting her own way. Now she wanted God's way. She disliked her mother-in-law, and resented her interference in her husband John's and her life together. Now she began to really love her, though this was tested and deepened in the months ahead. Her relationship with Jesus and spending time with Him became the most important thing in her life. She had a deep desire to share Him, as evidenced by her public testimony of Him again and again since that time.

Incidentally, when Betty sat up, near pandemonium occurred in the hospital. Her father was delighted, but stunned. So was her husband and her mother when they arrived later to take care of the corpse!

Betty was not only healed spiritually, but physically. The nurse insisted on putting her back on the life support system. Betty politely, but firmly refused. She had eaten almost nothing in weeks. She was scheduled for a dreaded colostomy as her bowels were blocked off, some organs apparently destroyed. She asked the astonished doctor for a big meal. He refused, saying graciously that he would allow her to try a 7-Up on ice. Imagine Betty's delighted surprise when the nurse came in with two pork chops, applesauce, cottage cheese, lemon cake and a pot of tea. She ate every crumb. An error had been made. A meal ordered for a Mrs. Underwood had been delivered to Mrs. Upchurch (Betty's name).

The nurse shot in with a mobile unit! Obviously, this was an emergency. Betty would have to have her stomach pumped out! Betty begged her not to, and finally gently but firmly refused. Reluctantly, the nurse left. Shortly afterward, Betty had to go to the bathroom. She was thrilled to know that her plumbing worked just fine!

A word of warning just here. This kind of experience is not necessary to believe the Word of God. I am reminded strongly of Luke 16:27-31, where the rich man in Hell begged that someone rise from the dead and go tell his five brothers, that they might not come to that awful place. He was told that they should instead believe Moses and the prophets. At this time, that would have to be referring to the written Word of God. The rich man thought that this would not be enough to convince them. It hadn't convinced him! Then he was told, "If they hear not Moses and the prophets, neither will they be persuaded, though one rose from the dead." Doubting Thomas who *insisted* on seeing the risen Jesus and examining his wounds in order to believe, was told by Jesus of a *better* way. "Blessed are they that have *not* seen, and yet have believed" (John 21:29). God wants our faith to be based on the Word of God: that is the only sure anchor and that is what brings the greatest glory to God.

Betty Malz's story is recorded in her book, *My Glimpse of Eternity*. One other thing needs to be said. Though God in His mighty wisdom and love may occasionally lift the curtain a tiny bit on eternity as he did with the apostle Paul (2 Cor. 12:1-7), none of these experiences, until death actually occurs permanently, are really death experiences. They are near-death experiences. Some out-of-body experiences occur in people with mental or emotional problems, some are induced by drugs, some by experiences with the occult, etc. There are some, however, such as Betty's, that bear the mark of God's work, insofar as we can determine. Whereas most experiences lead to denying the judgment of

God against sin, or even that man is a sinner, and ignore the unique Deity of Jesus Christ, Betty's experience only enhanced her love for the Word of God. The presence of the Lord Jesus Christ and His love became the heartbeat of her life. However, the validity of these experiences being from God is an open question the reader will have to struggle with on his own.

Sometimes things are best seen in contrast. Notice carefully the following observations by Dr. Nelson recorded in his book, *The Cause and Cure of Infidelity.* Dr. Nelson was a thoroughgoing infidel, skeptical in the extreme of God, Christ and Christianity. As head of a hospital for years, he carefully noted those who were skeptics, atheists or agnostics, and he also noted those who professed faith in Christ, those who were Christians. He watched them when they thought they were going to die, when some of them had out-of-body or near death experiences. Then he observed them when they really did die. There was an amazing difference. There *is* a beautiful side of death for those who have accepted Christ. In spite of the somewhat stilted language of Dr. Nelson's day, his message comes through loud and clear.

As written in *A Lawyer Examines the Bible,* pp. 200-202, Dr. Nelson declared:

> I was surprised to find that the condition of mind in the case of those who were dying, and of those who only *thought* themselves dying, differed very widely. I had supposed that the joy or the grief of death originated from the fancy of the patient, one supposing himself very near to great happiness and the other expecting speedy suffering. My discoveries seemed to overturn this theory. Why should not the professor of religion who believes himself dying, when he really is not, rejoice as readily as when he *is*

departing, if his joy is the offspring of expectation? Why should not the alarm of the scoffer who believes himself dying, and is not, be as uniform and decisive as when he is in the river, if it comes of fancied evil or cowardly terrors? The same question I asked myself again and again. I have no doubt there is some strange reason connected with our natural disrelish for truth which causes so many physicians, after seeing such facts so often, never to observe them. During twenty years of observation, I found *the state of the soul belonging to the dying was uniformly and materially unlike that of those who only supposed themselves departing.*

1. There was a man who believed himself converted, and his friends, judging from his walk, hoped with him. He was seized with disease, and believed himself within a few paces of the gate of futurity. He felt no joy, his mind was dark and his soul clouded. His exercises were painful and the opposite of every enjoyment. He was not dying. He recovered. He had not been in the death stream. After this he was taken again. He believed himself dying and he was not mistaken. All was peace, serenity, hope, triumph.

2. There was man who mocked at holy things. He became seriously diseased and supposed himself sinking into the death slumber. He was not frightened. This fortitude and composure were his pride and the boast of his friends. The undaunted firmness with which he could enter futurity was spoken of exultingly. It was a mistake, he was not in the condition of dissolution. His soul never had been on the line between two worlds. After this he was taken ill again. He supposed as before that he was entering the next state, and he really was; but his soul seemed to feel a different atmosphere. The horrors of these scenes have been often described and are often seen. I need not endeavor to picture such a departure here. The only difficulty in which I was thrown by such cases was, Why was he not thus agonized before, when he thought himself departing? Can it be possible that we can stand so precisely on the dividing line

that the gale from both this and the coming world may blow upon our cheek? Can we have a taste of the exercises of the next territory before we enter it? When I attempted to account for this on the simple ground of bravery and cowardice I was met by two following facts.

First, I have known those—the cases are not infrequent—who were brave, who had stood unflinchingly in the battle's whirlpool. They had resolved never to disgrace their system of unbelief by a trembling death. They had called to Christians in a tone of resolve saying, "I can die as coolly as you can." I had seen those die from whom entire firmness might fairly be expected. I had heard groans, even if the teeth were clenched for fear of complaint, such as I never wish to hear again; and I had looked into countenances such as I hope never to see again.

Again, I had seen cowards die. I had seen those depart who were naturally timid, who expected themselves to meet death with fright and alarm. I had heard such, as it were, sing before Jordan was half forded. I had seen faces where, pallid as they were, I beheld more celestial triumph than I had ever witnessed anywhere else. In that voice there was a sweetness and in that eye there was a glory which I never could have fancied in the death spasms, if I had not been near.

The condition of the soul when the death stream is entered is not the same with that which it often becomes when it is almost passed. The brave man who steps upon the ladder across the dark ravine, with eye undaunted and haughty spirit, changes fearfully in many cases, when he comes near enough to the curtain to lift it. The Christian who goes down the ladder pale and disconsolate oftentimes starts with exultation and tries to burst into song when almost across.

The contrast here given by Dr. Nelson is astonishing. There *is* an *ugly* side of death for unbelievers in Christ.

Dr. Nelson and others record some of the horrible

deaths of those who were not Christians. I have read, from this source and many others, of those who scoffed at Christianity, and did not believe in God, Christ, heaven or hell. Some screamed and twisted uncontrollably on their death bed, frantic because they said they experienced slipping inexorably into a burning Hell! Some were already in the flames, groaning and pleading in inexpressible agony and fear. I remember one book, documenting some of these experiences, was called *Voices on the Edge of Eternity.* Dr. Maurice Rawlings listed several experiences with his dying patients that underlines these foretastes of an eternal Hell the Bible warns about.

I recall reading about the death of the defiant atheist, Voltaire. Some of his last words, or rather screams, were pitiful. He offered his doctor half his fortune if his life could be prolonged six months. In unadulterated terror he said he was sinking down into Hell, and screamed over and over again, "O God . . . O Jesus Christ," begging, apparently too late for mercy.

This is the *ugly* side of death. It is what the Bible says awaits every unbeliever, whether they believe it or not. That is why this author, and the others involved, are producing this book. Jesus wept over Jerusalem, and then gave His life on the blood-stained cross, that neither they, or anyone else might go to Hell. God spoke from the depths of His heart, when He said the He was not willing that *any* should perish! (2 Peter 3:9). Neither am I! God declared that He takes no pleasure in the death of the wicked, but desires that he should turn from his wicked way and live (Ezekiel 33:11). Paul, filled with the love and compassion of Christ, cried out, "Brethren, my heart's desire and prayer to God for Israel is, that they might be saved."

Also, ". . . that I have great heaviness and continual sorrow in my heart. For I could wish myself cut off from Christ for my brethren, my kinsmen according to the flesh" (Rom. 10:1; Rom. 9:2, 3). In some small measure we share this passion, this deep burden, for our fellow men without Christ.

Remember, it does not matter in the least whether one believes in Hell or not. It is the ultimate, final and forever end of those who do not know Christ. One may not believe in the law of gravity, but if he steps into space from the top of the Empire State Building, his unbelief will not affect the law of gravity one iota. So it is with the reality of Hell.

Unfortunately, although we are told in Luke 16 of the rich man in Hell pleading for a drop of water to cool his tongue, and in Revelation 14:11 that the "smoke of their torment ascendeth up for ever and ever: and they have no rest day nor night . . ." and in Revelation 20 that all un-believers are cast into the "lake of fire," that is not all of the awfulness of Hell. Separation from the God of the Bible forever is the epitome of this unspeakable horror. Since God is the one spoken of in James 1:17, "Every good gift and every perfect gift is from above, and cometh down from the Father of lights, with whom is no variable-ness, neither shadow of turning," not one good thing will ever again happen to those who have chosen to be their own gods, live by their own Bible, and ultimately be pup-pets of Satan. Never again will they thrill to a beautiful sunset, a rainbow, or lovely flowers. Never again will they listen to beautiful music. Never again will they enjoy the embrace of a loved one. Never again will they taste good food, or water. There will be no God there, no loving, caring Jesus Christ. No Christian will ever again bother them about salvation. There is no hope. There is no love. There is no recreation, no parks, no trees, no animals, no birds, no pleasure ever, of any kind, no enjoyment whatsoever—nothing but utter despair, loneliness, hopelessness, hate, anger, cursing, pain, unbearable heat, and eternal misery. Not even an aspirin, not a moment of relief, physically, spiritually, or emotionally—nothing but eternal regret. A day may seem like a year, a year like a century, a century unthinkable, and yet Hell goes on and on and on forever, and there is no escape. *This* is what Jesus died on the cross to save men from. This, and the sins which take them to Hell, especially the greatest sin of all, unbelief in Him, coupled with "going one's own way, being one's own god, being self-centered instead of Christ-centered."

It is with great relief that we turn from the indescribably ugly side of death to *the beautiful side of death* again!

In the *National Enquirer* recently, reporting on Dr. Billy Graham's book *Angels—God's Secret Agents*, Billy wrote, "I believe that death can be beautiful. I have come to look forward to it, to anticipate it with joy and expectation." He went on to say that to realize and accept death as just the entrance to a new life can transform our life here and now. That is certainly true, but only for a Christian. Billy also wrote, as reported by the *National Enquirer*, in "The Secret of Happiness," that as his mother began her passage to Heaven, she came face to face with Jesus Christ. When she actually died, she sat right up and shouted out to the Lord! He notes that there will be no fear, failure or fatigue in Heaven. We also know that there will never, ever, be any sorrow, any heartbreak, any burning, unfulfilled desires. We will love and worship Jesus, and enjoy Him and each other forever, in the most beautifully prepared place imaginable. As a dear friend of mine, Lee Millay, used to say: "I am looking forward to death. The door, physical death itself, may be full of splinters. I am not looking forward to that. But that is only for a moment. Then I will be in Heaven with Jesus forever, where there is no more death. No matter how rough the entrance may be, it is nothing in comparison!"

Just recently a godly, well-known Baptist preacher in Virginia became ill with terminal cancer. He was, I believe, in his early 60s. Many had been won to Christ by this much-loved man, and many others helped and encouraged on the rough road of life. His own life reflected generosity, love, kindness, and purity. He suffered terribly. His agony nearly broke the hearts of his family, and those who knew and loved him. Finally, mercifully, he died.

The fellow pastor who preached his funeral was approached by a confused and puzzled man. With perhaps some anger and resentment, as well as sorrow, he asked if this was the way God rewarded His servant after years of faithful service for Him? The pastor wisely replied something like this. "Reward!? My friend, this was not his reward! It was just his final test!"

We were not called to follow Christ by being carried through life and on to Heaven on a silk pillow. Mark 8:35b says, ". . . Whosoever will come after me, let him take up his cross, and follow me." Yet it is still true that Christ not only promises Heaven hereafter for those who put their trust in Him, but a full and abundant life here and now (John 10:10). And He delivers! Though many have been and will be martyrs for Him, He gives such peace and joy and satisfaction. All the basic questions of life are settled in

Him. He then goes with us through the most agonizing of life's valleys, even the valley of the shadow of death! So true is this, that I have heard many enraptured with Christ say that even if there were no Heaven and no Hell, they would still rather be Christians and follow Christ, because it is so wonderful to know and follow Him! All this and Heaven too, for those who know Him!

A judge's wife down in Texas was a professing Christian. She had an abnormal fear of death, even as a Christian. (Normally, as many Christians can tell you, God takes away their fear of death, except sometimes the physical aspect.) One sad day, the judge's wife was taken ill, and informed by her doctor that she only had a short time to live. She was in great distress. Then she began to die. Her sad countenance brightened. She spoke of dear friends she saw. She asked those round about her bed if they did not hear the exquisitely beautiful music she heard. They did not. Then she became aware of Heaven and her precious Lord Jesus. The fear was gone. She cried as she was dying, "If this is death, it is beautiful!" Then she passd on over to the other side.

How great it is to know that with Jesus, we are never alone.

A friend of mind, Dr. Leslie Flynn, tells this story in his fine book *The Sustaining Power of Hope,* pp. 81-82.

A boy living in Idaho would never forget a lumber buyer named Benham who stayed a week in his home. An outspoken atheist, Benham could repeat persuasively the major arguments of agnostic Robert G. Ingersoll. He stated openly that he spent most of his money and time proving God did not exist. Irrevocably he held there was no afterlife, no heaven, and no hell.

Twenty years later the boy, grown to manhood, was attending a convention in St. Paul, Minnesota when he noticed a familiar gentleman. It was Mr. Benham, who also recalled the youth and invited him to lunch. It was soon evident that the atheist had lost his poise. He acted like a man facing a death sentence.

Now 71, Benham explained that he had an incurable blood disease, and less than half a year to live. He then launched into an incident about an elderly lady who lay at death's door in a local hospital where Benham had gone for a check-up. While there, he had been enlisted by a nurse sent out by the dying woman to get three witnesses to a deathbed will she could not sign because of a paralyzed arm. Entering the lady's room, he was mesmerized by the utter serenity of this woman who, bedridden for several years, was now facing the end with a smiling countenance. The nurse scribbled with whispered instructions of the stricken woman for the disposal of her property. When all three witnesses had signed the paper, the lady smiled, thanked them and said, "And now I am ready to leave this pain-wracked body to meet my Maker, my husband, my father, my mother, and all my friends who have gone before me. Won't that be wonderful!"

Tears started down Benham's pale, wrinkled cheeks. "Look at me," he said in a hoarse whisper. "I've lain awake many nights since I learned my days were numbered, staring at the ceiling with nothing to look forward to except that my life would end in a handful of ashes. That's the difference between me, an atheist, and the lady I've described. She, believing, faces her final days with a smile. Here am I, a nonbeliever, with every moment a nightmare, facing nothing but a cold tomb." He hesitated a few moments, then added, "I would shove my hands into a bed of red-hot coals if by so doing I could secure a belief in a Supreme Being and an afterlife!"

In a church God enabled me to start as a Conservative Baptist missionary in Alaska some years ago, was a sweet and wonderful Christian woman named "Noby" Davis. She and her husband played the organ and piano for us. One day to my consternation, I heard that Noby had been rushed to the hospital and suffered a double mastectomy. She was eaten up with cancer, and was only given a short time to live. A younger sister, 23 years old, had recently died just after a similar operation. Noby was given about six months to a year. She had two boys in Moody Bible Institute, a loving husband, and a church that loved and needed her dearly.

I rushed to the hospital to pray with and comfort her. I prayed God would give me real words of comfort, not some parroted, unfeeling phrase. My sorrow and discomfiture was obvious. To my incredulity, Noby laughed out loud at me!

"Brother, 'Mac'" she said, "This cancer doesn't bother me any more than if it were a wart!" She went on, "Please pray that before I die, God will give me strength to go back to Missouri and take a much anticipated trip to California with my Dad."

That is exactly what I prayed. God answered. Noby got the strength to take that cherished trip to California with her Dad! Some time later I got word from her husband. "Brother, Mac, Noby died today. Just as she died, she sat up in bed and said, 'Take me, Lord Jesus' and she was gone."

Over twenty years rolled by. A lady in our church who had been very neurotic, very fearful about death, called my wife and me in Washington, long distance from Alaska. She was going in for a dreaded operation, cancer suspected, in her jaw. I braced for her fear and depression, and prayed God would help me to help her. I said, "Katy (not her real name) are you afraid?"

Remarkably, I heard her say firmly, clearly and distinctly, "NO!" I asked her, "Why?" She said three simple words, "I remember Noby!"

She knew that what Jesus had done for Noby He would do for her!

D. L. Moody was a powerful evangelist for the Lord Jesus Christ. God used him to rock two continents for Christ. Once he was asked if he had "dying grace." Moody replied that he did not. He said in effect that he had living grace. But he added that when the time came to die, he would have dying grace. Indeed he did.

Many years later, as Moody began to die he said triumphantly, "Heaven is opening . . . earth is receding . . . Jesus is coming."

Beloved friend, which way do you want to die? With Jesus Christ, death ushers in a glorious new world for you. Death can be beautiful. Will it be for you?

We have appealed both to your heart and mind. We can do nothing. We cannot possibly verbalize the glory and wonder of Jesus Christ, but if the Holy Spirit of God takes this stumbling effort and reveals the reality of Christ to you so that you *want* Him, we will be happy beyond words. Only God's Spirit *can* reveal Christ to you, and then only if you are *willing* to see. Jesus warns, *now* is the day of salvation. *Today*, if you hear His voice, harden not your heart.

Perhaps, as you read you felt either vaguely or acutely uncomfortable. You may have felt "pressured." Beloved, it is hard to do a "soft" sell, to awaken your wife and child when you know the house is on fire. Paul Revere had little time for social chitchat on his wild night ride, however less offensive it might have been. The message was urgent, and *far more so* is the message of the Cross.

When I was in the Navy and suicide planes were attacking us off Okinawa, I noticed a peculiar reaction, much like Pavlov's dog. We had a buzzer which signaled the alert for action time and time again on various occasions. After awhile, we sailors experienced knots in the pit of our stomachs, dry mouths, and intense reactions when the *buzzer* sounded, usually long before planes were sighted. We began to actually resent the *buzzer!* Yet had we put ear plugs in our ears, or ignored the buzzer we would be dead today, as many times our instant response to the buzzer got us in position to defend our ship and our lives before the enemy came. The buzzer was our best friend and actually startled us into saving our lives.

The gospel alarms one out of his apathy, mental or moral. One can then either apply ear plugs, ignore the alarm of conviction, the nagging uneasiness, or quickly respond and honestly confront and then accept the risen Christ, who then secures us against all enemies. Sometimes there is but one alarm, and that may be but faintly heard amidst the strident clamor of the world.

No one *ever* cared for you—like Jesus! Religion won't do. I've led Bible teachers, Bible School graduates, even missionaries, to Christ or to assurance of their salvation. Only really knowing Him will ever satisfy and suffice.

In a way, it's much like the little boy said to the atheist who was deriding him because he was so happy that his alcoholic Dad had accepted Christ. The atheist chided the boy for being so naive as to believe the myth of the Bible and that old-fashioned stuff about being "saved." He closed his statement by exclaiming, "Boy, you're dreaming!" The boy replied aptly, "Mister, Dad used to come home and beat and kick me. I'd hide in terror when I heard him come staggering home. He cursed and beat my dear Mom and we were often cold and hungry and short of clothes, and Mother cried a lot. Now Dad buys nice clothes for Mother, and kisses and hugs her. He takes me on his lap and tells me stories and tells me he loves me. Our home is warm and snug and we all love Jesus. Mister, if I'm dreaming, please don't wake me up!"

Friend, Jesus frees from enemies more subtle and deadly than alcohol ever was—doubt, insecurity, hopelessness, dread, fear, anguish, purposelessness, uncertainty. He frees from sin and Hell. Through Him you can know and experience "The beautiful side of death!"

From all of us who wrote this book, we have one desire—to point you to Jesus *now!* It was His heartbeat you felt, my friend, and from the bloody cross, the empty tomb, and now at your heart's door He pleads with you. Eternity—one heartbeat away—so long, oh dear God, so long—so endless. "Let me into your heart and life. I, Jesus Christ, love you, love you, love you. . . !"

Just in case it is *still* not clear exactly how to be saved, how to accept Jesus, to believe savingly on Him, and *know* for *sure* that you have been saved, please read the next chapter, "Contact with the Ultimate."

CHAPTER SEVENTEEN

Contact with the Ultimate

Introduction

Many who read this book may not be familiar with the basic message of the Bible. For this reason, we include a very brief summary of God's plan for mankind as recorded in the Bible, God's proven source book. This clear, simple summary is taken from the narration of a soon to be released film by Jeremiah Films.

These Bible facts along with the remainder of this chapter may enable the reader to make an intelligent decision to personally receive the Lord Jesus Christ.

> In the beginning, God created the heavens and the earth. . . . He created every living thing. . . . In the day He created man, He made him in the likeness of God.
>
> He created them male and female, and blessed them and called them Mankind in the day they were created.
>
> Then God saw everything that He had made, and indeed it was very good.
>
> The scriptural record then states that Adam and Eve, having been tempted by the fallen angelic being, Satan, sinned against God, causing Him to bring them and all physical creation under judgment.
>
> Everything changed at that point. Mankind died spiritually, that is, cut off from the communion he formerly had with God. A sin nature replaced former

innocence. Physical death followed. All of creation, that which was good, became degenerate.

Yet, though the human race was now separate from the Creator and under a curse, God made provision for man's redemption and reconciliation through His Son, Jesus Christ.

Mankind's separation from God and sin nature degenerated into such a state of wickedness that God's judgment on such rebelliousness came in the form of a catastrophic worldwide flood.

Following the flood, God prepared a people through whom He would send His Messiah, who would be God incarnate, who would pay the debt for sin that God's perfect justice demanded, a debt that sinful man could not pay.

Two thousand years ago Jesus Christ was crucified, died, and was buried. His death was the atonement for the sins of mankind. His resurrection demonstrated that He was no mere man, but God come in the flesh.

The Scriptures state that salvation is for those who will accept Christ's death in place of their own.

The Bible also declares that Christ will come again, and His final coming to earth will be preceded by a time of worldwide rebellion and holocaust—a time in which God will pour out His wrath. Many Bible scholars believe Christ's coming and these events may be very soon.

Yet, at the height of the unprecedented tribulation, Christ will intervene "or no flesh would be saved," and reign on a renewed earth for a 1,000 years.

Following that, final judgment will take place— after which there will be a new creation, new heavens and earth into which sin will not enter.

Those who have accepted Christ will live forever with Him and those who have rejected Him will be separated to everlasting punishment.

Five Steps for Contact with the Ultimate

Step One: One God

God loves you and wants you to know that there is only *one God, a personal God separate and distinct from us and the rest of his creation.*

This *one God* created and is *Lord* over all the universe, stars, planets and all.

"In the beginning God created the heaven and the earth" (Gen. 1:1).

". . . before me there was no God formed, neither shall there be after me" (Isa. 43:10b).

God was never a man, and man will never be God! As the eternal God he became the God-man Jesus, to die for us, but for all eternity he was God, not man.

". . . from everlasting (that's eternity past) to everlasting (that's eternity future) thou art God! (Ps. 90:2b).

God never progressed, earned or attained His way to being God, *He was always God.* (The Bible mentions false gods, but to believe that other gods really exist is pagan polytheism, not Christianity.)

Clearly, there is not now, and never will be, any other God on this planet or any other "world" or planet. There is forever only *one* God. Men cannot become Gods—none ever has, none ever will!

". . . for I am God, and there is none else; I am God, and there is none like me" (Isa. 46:9b). ". . . before me there was no God formed, neither shall there be after me" (Isa. 43:10b).

Step Two: The Saviour, Jesus Christ, Who is Eternally God

"For unto us a child is born, unto us a son is given: and the government shall be upon His shoulders, and His name shall be called Wonderful, Counselor, The mighty God, The everlasting Father, the Prince of Peace" (Isa. 9:6). Within the nature of God there are three eternal distinctions: God the Father, God the Son, and God the Holy Spirit; there is only *one* God. Since Jesus is repeatedly called God, we must accept Him as God, or we accept another Jesus. In the Bible the "Word" means Jesus (John 1:14). "In the beginning was the Word, and the Word was with God, and the Word was God" (John 1:1). "Beginning" here simply means, "from all time." As God was God *from all time,* so was Jesus Christ God, *from the beginning, from all time!* Jesus never progressed, worked, or attained His way into being God, *He always was God* (Mic. 5:2).

God forbade forever the worship of any other god (Exod. 34:14), yet Jesus accepted worship as God on many occasions. "And as they went to tell his disciples, behold, Jesus met them saying, All hail. And they came and held Him by the feet and worshipped Him" (Matt. 28:9). No wonder Thomas cried out to Jesus, "My Lord and my God" (John 20:28).

Step Three: The Sin Problem—Our Sin Nature

An apple tree is an apple tree *before* it bears apples. It bears apples *because* it is an apple tree.

So, we sin *because* we have a sin nature. An apple tree is just as much an apple tree by nature, whether it bears one apple or a thousand! So it is with a sinner.

One sin or a thousand is not the point! The point is, we *all* have a sin nature that must be changed.

Beating the apples off the tree does not change the nature of the tree! So, getting rid of some sins does not change our nature!

"Ye must be born again" (John 3:7). John 1:12 tells us how. "But as many as received Him to them gave He power to become the sons of God, even to them that believe on His name."

We are *not* by nature children of God. We must receive Christ in order to *become* the children of God.

We are sinners by nature and choice. Sin is the fruit of our sin nature, of each of us as sinners. Sin is "going our own way" (Isa. 53:6). It is being the God, Manager, Boss, Lord of our own life. It is being self-centered instead of Christ-centered.

"For by grace are ye saved through faith; and that not of yourselves: it is the gift of God: Not of works, lest any man should boast" (Eph. 2:8, 9). "There is none righteous, no, not one" (Rom. 3:10b).

"Now to him that worketh (for salvation) is the reward not reckoned of grace, but of debt. But to him that worketh not, but believeth on Him that justifieth the ungodly, his faith is counted for righteousness" (Rom. 4:4-6).

Salvation is not by works, it is a *gift*. Personally receiving Christ, trusting Him alone to save us, is God's way of salvation. "For the wages of sin is death, but the gift of God is eternal life through Jesus Christ, our Lord" (Rom. 6:23).

We cannot make ourselves "worthy" of the grace of God. Salvation is a free gift for the unworthy, the undeserving, which we all are. Christ died for the "ungodly" (Rom. 5:6).

A dog does not bark in order to become a dog. He barks

because he already is a dog. His barking helps demonstrate the fact! Just so, we do not do good works in order to become Christians (be saved). We do good works *after* we are saved (become Christians) to demonstrate the fact that we have been saved.

Remember that God's Word says, *before* salvation, "All our righteousness are as filthy rags" (Isa. 64:6b). We all have a sinful nature. We are sinners by nature and by choice. "For all have sinned and come short of the glory of God" (Rom. 3:23). This means we are all *lost* sinners. Besides, how many *good works* can a *dead* man do? As natural men we are all "dead in trespasses and sins" (Eph. 2:1b).

Although salvation is not by works, true salvation always produces a changed life. Christ comes in by personal invitation as Lord and Savior to change our life, and live His life through us.

The Good News is . . . the blood of Jesus Christ, God's Son, cleanses us from all sin (1 John 1:9).

Step Four: The Time is Now

After death it is too late. Now is the time to be saved. ". . . now is the accepted time; behold, now is the day of salvation" (2 Cor. 6:2b). There is no chance after death. "And as it is appointed unto men once to die, but after this the judgment" (Heb. 9:27). There is *no* general salvation for all men because of Christ's death, but *only* individual salvation for those who believe. ". . . he that believeth not the Son shall not see life; but the wrath of God abideth on him" (John 3:36b). All men are resurrected, but the unsaved dead are resurrected to damnation, not salvation (John 5:29; Rev. 20:3-6).

"And whosoever was not found written in the book of life was cast into the lake of fire" (Rev. 20:15). Nowhere in the Bible is anyone ever said to have been saved after they died. Today is the day of salvation.

"Enter ye in at the strait gate: for wide is the gate, and broad is the way, that leadeth to destruction, and many there be which go in thereat. Because strait is the gate, and narrow is the way, which leadeth unto life, and few there be that find it" (Matt. 7:13, 14).

According to God's Word, the vast multitude of men are on the road to Hell, and to the resurrection unto damnation (John 5:29) unless they personally invite Christ into their life as Lord and Savior. Death ends all hope for the lost.

Because of our sin nature all men are sinners, both by what we are and what we do. That is why Jesus said, "Ye must be born again" (John 3:7).

Suppose a pig tried to become a sheep by *acting* like a sheep. Suppose the pig were clothed in sheep wool, ate sheep feed and even learned to bleat like a sheep. Would that *change* its pig nature and make it a sheep?

Would it matter whether or not the pig was "good" or "bad" by pig standards? So it is with trying to *act* like a Christian in order to become a Christian! It takes a miracle—the new birth. Just as it would take a miracle from God, a new birth, for a pig to become a sheep, so it takes a miracle from God, the new birth, for a sinner to become a child of God, a Christian.

"But as many as received Him, to them gave He power to become the sons of God, even to them that believe on His name" (John 1:12). This is the new birth.

Step Five: The Way of Salvation

Jesus alone can cleanse us from sin and change our nature. "Who His own self bare our sins in His own body on the tree . . ." (1 Pet. 2:24). Not just Adam's sin, but our own personal sins. This is why He died on the cross for us, why He shed His blood for us, to pay the debt for our sins.

We need cleansing from sin and a new nature in order to become a Christian. Jesus took our place and shed His blood to cleanse us from sin. No amount of "good works" could wash away one sin or change our nature. "Just as I am without one plea, but that thy blood was shed for me."

Good News! Salvation is instant! The moment we repent, turn to Jesus from our sins, He saves us. Christ said to the unbaptized, unsaved, no good works, thief on the cross, in instant salvation response to the thief's believing call: "Today shalt thou be with me in paradise" (Luke 23:43b). (The place Paul saw as the Heaven of God, 1 Cor. 12:2-4). *Instant* salvation for a harlot: "Go thy way, thy faith hath saved thee" (Luke 7:50b). *Instant* salvation in response to the publican's believing call: ". . . this man went down to his house justified" (Luke 18:14a).

Saul the murderer was changed to Paul the Apostle from one vital encounter with the living Christ. Salvation includes accepting Jesus Christ as both Lord (*our* God, Lord, new manager) and Savior. It involves heart (the ruling, governing, choosing, center of our being) belief. "That if thou shalt confess with thy mouth the Lord Jesus, and shalt believe in thine heart that God hath raised him from the dead, thou shalt be saved" (Rom. 10:9).

We thus turn from our sins, our self, and our way to God's way. When we believingly call on the Lord Jesus, in faith and repentance, He enters our life, cleanses us from sin, makes us children of God by the new birth, and gives us the free gift of salvation, with new, abundant, everlasting life. Heaven becomes our certain home, and His peace our possession.

There is no magic in the few puffs of air emitted from our vocal cords as we call on Christ. Yet He said, "Out of the abundance of the heart the mouth speaketh" (Matt. 12:24). If our call is from the heart, using our God-given power of choice to believe in Christ, *God always responds and saves! He promised!*

Salvation is simple. "For whosoever shall call upon the name of the Lord shall be saved" (Rom. 10:13). We must personally call *believingly* on Jesus to save us. This is *how* we receive Him. If we do so call, He must save us or God would be lying, and God cannot lie. If Jesus loved us enough to die in bloody agony to save us, would He then turn us down when we called on Him? Of course not!

Remember! "God commendeth His love toward us, in that, while we were yet sinners, Christ died for us" (Rom. 5:8). God *loves* us, and wants us to come to Christ just as we are. God loves *you* and wants *you* to be saved. Would you like to receive Jesus as your Lord and Saviour right now? Just pray, *if you mean it,* the best you know how, with all your heart, this prayer, or a similar one.

> "Lord Jesus Christ, come into my heart and life. Cleanse me from all sin by your shed blood. Make me a child of God. Give me your free gift of everlasting life, and let me know that I am saved, now and forever. I now receive you as my very own personal Lord and Savior. I place my complete trust in you alone for my salvation. In Jesus' name, Amen."

Did Jesus save you or did He lie? According to Romans 10:13 he had to do one or the other if you called believingly on Him. "For whosoever shall call upon the name of the Lord, shall be saved."

Salvation is certain! You can *know* you are saved, not just by *feeling,* but because God's Word says so! Memorize John 3:36a. Read it three times. "He that believeth on the Son hath everlasting life." What do you have right now according to God's Word? Where would you go if you were to die right now, according to God's Word?

If you *know* that Jesus has saved you, according to His Word, please thank Him out loud for saving you.

"These things have I written unto you that believe on the name of the Son of God, that ye may know that ye have eternal life" (1 John 5:13a).

As a help to you, to further nail down this definite decision, you may wish to sign your name to the following statement:

> I have today received Jesus Christ as my Lord and Savior. I am claiming by faith His promise of sins forgiven and His gift of eternal life.

Signed: _____

Date: _____

Choose to believe Christ, feelings or no feelings, and He will prove His reality to you as you step out in faith that He has kept His word and saved you.

Note this important illustration. Three men step aboard an elevator bound for the third floor where they all want to go. One is laughing, one is crying, one is poker-faced, unemotional. All three of them get to the third floor, regardless of their feelings, because they *believed* the elevator would get them to the third floor, *acted* on their belief, and *committed* themselves to the elevator. So it is with trusting Christ, feelings or no feelings.

The reality of your salvation will be shown in your love-response in obeying and following Jesus Christ. ". . . If a man love me, he will (not if, maybe and/or but) keep my words" (John 14:23a). To work *for* salvation shows unbelief in the sufficiency of Jesus Christ alone to save us. However, true salvation, true faith, always produces good works! "But wilt thou know, O vain man, that faith without works is dead?" (James 2:20).

Apple trees do not have to produce apples in order to become an apple tree! Apples are products of the tree and prove that it is an apple tree. So, good works never *produce* a Christian, they merely *prove* he is one. "Therefore, if any man is in Christ, he is a new creation, old things are passed away; behold, all things are become new" (2 Cor. 5:17).

We must have salvation in order to demonstrate it, just as we must have a car before we can demonstrate it! True Christians produce good works.

Believe Him for His victory, thank Him, step out in faith, and He will prove His victory in your experience.

In the next chapter some guidelines and helps for new believers are introduced and explained.

CHAPTER EIGHTEEN

The Test of Reality

"Jesus answered and said unto him, If a man love me, he will keep my word: and my Father will love him, and we will come unto him, and make our abode with him" (John 14:23).

For quick reference this list with Bible verses for you to study is given. A discussion of each of the eight items listed is given in this important chapter.

1. Be baptized. Acts 2:41, 10:47-48; 16:31-33.
2. Confess Christ before men. Luke 12:8-9; Rom. 10:9-10.
3. Attend church faithfully. Heb. 10:25; 1 John 3:14.
4. Read the Bible daily. Study it, and memorize special verses. Joshua 1:8; Ps. 1:2; 119:1; Col. 3:16-17; 2 Tim. 2:15; 1 Pet. 2:2. Start in the New Testament with John, then 1 John, and then go to Matthew. Read straight through the entire New Testament, then read the Old Testament.
5. Pray daily . . . and more often. Jeremiah 33:3; Matt. 18:19; 21:22; Rom. 8:32; 1 Thess. 5:17; 1 John 5:14-15.
6. Confess sin instantly, honestly, and avoid it. Proverbs 28:13; 1 John 1:9.
7. Share Christ . . . Witness . . . Win the lost. Psalms 126:6; Proverbs 11:30; Luke 5:10; 19:10; John 20:21; Acts 1:8.
8. Let Jesus live His life through you. 1 Cor. 15:57; Gal. 2:20; 5:16; Col. 3:1-4. Live not by feeling, but by faith. Faith-root, feeling-fruit.

About Your Decision

The definite decision for Christ is necessary and important.
Life or death, Heaven or Hell, hinge upon this decision.
That is why we stress the need of crystallizing belief into a
concrete act of accepting Christ. We are told in the Bible to
call, to receive, to be born again, to open the door.

Agrippa believed the prophets, Paul said, but was not a
Christian; he did not personally receive the risen Christ.
The devils believe and tremble, God says, but they are
doomed to Hell forever. Obviously then, there is a belief
which falls short of saving faith in Christ, short of the act
of receiving Him as Savior and Lord, unconditionally.

A young man can love a young woman and she can return that love; yet they can remain apart in deepest frustration and sorrow until death. They do not belong to each
other until in the simple act of marriage each consents to
receive the other and forsake all others. So it is with Christ.
One may profess to believe in Him, to love Him, and yet
never receive Him, call on Him, open the door to Him for
salvation. Saving faith then requires the act of calling on
and receiving Christ and being born into the family of God.
Then we are new creatures with new desires, new power,
and new life (2 Cor. 5:17).

Regardless then of how much we convince ourselves
we love Him and believe in Him, we must call on Him, receive Him, open the door to Him, invite Him in by a definite
decision or act of faith as the Bible says. "For whosoever
shall call upon the name of the Lord shall be saved" (Rom.
10:13). We trust you have made this definite decision!

If you *did ask* Jesus believingly to save you, WEL-
COME TO GOD'S FAMILY! Congratulations! You have

just become a child of God! You have just been born again, born from above, born of the Spirit of God into the forever family of God! You are a new creation in Christ. Your sins are washed away by His shed blood. You have a new future, a new family, and a new Father! We have just shown you from God's Word how you can be saved and know it for sure from Romans 10:13. Check also John 3:36 and 1 John 5:13 (we suggest you memorize these verses). You can rejoice with all your heart that Jesus is yours and you are His forever, that Heaven and not Hell is your eternal home, and that He will be with you in a new and vital way now and forever. Salvation is instant, the results last forever! God says you are now a "new creature in Christ." How delightful! How exciting! (2 Cor. 5:17)

Now let me share with you how to begin and continue with your new life of love-response, obedience and growth in Christ. As a real child of God, I know you will be ready to obey the Lord Jesus Christ, just as God's Word says you will in John 14:23. "Jesus answered and said unto him, If a man love me, he will keep my words: and my Father will love him, and we will come unto him, and make our abode with him."

1. Be Baptized

The waters of baptism cannot wash away one sin. That was done the moment you were saved by the shed blood of the Lord Jesus Christ. But God commanded that we be baptized as soon as we have been saved. Just as the approximately 3,000 converts in Acts 2:41 were baptized the day they were saved, and the jailer in Philippi was baptized the very night he believed and was saved (Acts 16:31-33), so

we should be baptized as soon as possible after we are
saved. Baptism is an outward picture of an inward cleansing. It comes after salvation; before salvation it has no
value or meaning. It pictures on the outside what Christ has
already done on the inside. Even more important, bibli-
cally, it pictures our death to the old life with Jesus, identifies us with His death for us, identifies us with His burial
for us as we go down under the water of baptism, and identifies us with His risen life as we rise from the water of baptism as He bodily arose from the grave. We are thus publicly forever declaring our identification with the Lord
Jesus Christ, our death to the old life, and declaring our
new life in Him. Acts 10:47 clearly shows the order: salvation, then baptism (see also Rom. 6:1-4).

I believe baptism is by immersion since that is what the
original word meant, and it alone fulfills the picture of
death, burial, and resurrection, a picture of our identification with Christ. Good Christians from other denominations may hold to different views.

When we have been saved, God counts it that we died
with Christ in His death, were buried with Him, and rose
with Him to new life. Baptism pictures this! Beautiful! *Do
it,* not in order to be saved, but because you have *already*
been saved, and now want to fully love and obey Him!!

2. Confess Christ Before Men

"Also I say unto you, Whosoever shall confess me before
men, him shall the son of man also confess before the angels of God: But he that denieth me before men shall be
denied before the angels of God" (Luke 12:8, 9).

Open, public confession of Jesus Christ is Biblical evidence and confirmation of salvation. That is why many of our churches give public invitations so that before a friendly, loving crowd praying for just such miracles, you may acknowledge Chirst. *God* commanded confession before men. If those early disciples in Jerusalem had declared that salvation was a private thing between them and God only, and had refused to confess God before men, often hostile, murderous men, the gospel would have never spread beyond Jerusalem. So *confess Christ before men,* in church as a good beginning, and wherever God leads. It is tremendously strengthening!

3. Attend Church Faithfully

> "Not forsaking the assembling of ourselves together, as the manner of some is, but exhorting one another; and so much the more, as ye see the day approaching" (Heb. 10:25).

"Assembly" and "church" have virtually the same meaning in this context, so God is saying not to forsake the "churching" of ourselves together. The New Testament knows nothing of a true Christian living in isolation from the local church. We immediately become part of the body of Christ upon our salvation. Each of us have gifts to share with one another; we form different but essential parts of the body of Christ. We attend church both to give and receive. God gave godly men with special gifts to serve the church, officers called pastors to oversee and feed us, and also deacons. He carefully created the church and gave special ordinances to the church, Baptism and the Lord's Supper. He is not about to ignore His beloved church, and meet with some disobedient Christian gone A.W.O.L. in the woods or in some "spiritual" fellowship that bypasses His church. Frankly, to despise the local church is to despise the Lord of the local church, whether one is aware of it or not. The Bible says that Christ is the head of the church, and the church is His body. Just as it would be nonsense to marry a person's head and have nothing to do with their body, so it would be nonsense to "marry" Christ (be joined to Him eternally through conversion), and have nothing to do with His body, the church. It is true there are sometimes hypocrites in the church, but that only proves the Bible true, for Christ predicted such in His parable of the tares and wheat. He will tend to that in due time.

The thrilling thing is that you are now a part of the family of God, filled with brothers and sisters with whom you will spend eternity! Sharing their joys and burdens, being discipled to be more and more like Jesus Christ, to His glory!

So, attend church faithfully! This is one of the surest evidences that you have truly been saved. "We know that we have passed from death unto life, because we love the brethren" (1 John 3:14). If we love Jesus and the brethren we will be delighted to be with them in church.

Be sure to find a church that clearly believes the Bible, and the Bible only, to be the inspired, infallible Word of God. Find a church that believes that Jesus Christ's blood cleanses from sin and is dependent on Him alone for salvation.

4. Read the Bible Daily

"As newborn babes, desire the sincere milk of the Word, that ye may grow thereby" (1 Peter 2:2).

As food is to you physically, so the Word of God is to you now spiritually. Ask God to help you understand each time you read it, and He will. Start with the gospel of John, then read 1 John, then the New Testament, and then the Old Testament. God's Word gives growth, strength, helps you to avoid sin (Ps. 119:11), illuminates your daily walk with God, brings peace, knowledge and wisdom, heightens joy, and lessens danger of stumbling in the Christian walk (Josh. 1:8; Ps. 1:2; Col. 3:16-17). If possible, it is best to read your Bible and pray early in the morning before facing the day, just as it is best to tune your instruments before playing in the orchestra; but any time is acceptable. It has been well said, "This book will keep you from sin, or sin will keep you from this book." *Memorize special verses!* (See also 2 Tim. 2:15.)

5. Pray Daily . . . and More Often!

"Pray without ceasing" (1 Thess. 5:17).

You now have a hot-line to heaven through the Lord Jesus Christ. God *promises* to answer prayer (Jer. 33:3; Matt. 18:19; 21:22; 1 John 5:14-15). Reading the Bible is God talking to you, prayer is you talking to God (although He speaks to your heart as you pray also) and witnessing is you talking for God. Praise God, worship Him, thank Him, and ask Him for your needs believingly every day. It is very important to tell the Lord Jesus Christ, preferably out loud, every day, that you love Him and thank Him for dying on the cross for you and giving you eternal life. It is amazing what this will do for you, in warmth, love, and abiding fellowship. It turns your mountains into molehills!

Together, prayer and Bible study form the essence of our communication with Jesus. Love in its practical application is spelled T-I-M-E. The quintessence of our love for God is expressed and enhanced by the times we spend with

Him in prayer and Bible study. Those who profess to have no time for prayer and Bible study may call into question the reality of their relationship with Jesus Christ. A person claiming that he has no time for Bible study, prayer, and to live for God, is like a bird declaring that it doesn't have time to fly, or a fish claiming it has no time to swim. For this they were created. To love God, spend time with Him, get to really know Him and serve Him—for this we were created. At the very least, neglect insures leanness of soul, defeat and heartbreak instead of triumph and joy. Through prayer and Bible study we tap God's love and power, and grow into mature Christians established in doctrine and practice and most of all Christlikeness. The fruit of the Spirit—love, joy, peace, longsuffering, gentleness, goodness, faith, meekness, temperance—will flow from us to His glory and attract others to Him! (Gal. 5:22, 23). Besides, what a thrill it is to see the God of the universe answering your prayers.

It is probably true that no Christian is any stronger, better, or greater, than his prayer life! It is doubtful if anything worthwhile has ever been accomplished except by prayer . . . often much prayer. Even as a new babe in Christ, like the first call of a baby to its mother, your prayers are very precious to God. Begin the habit of prayer and Bible study right now. Perhaps the greatest reward of all is that as you daily focus in on Christ through prayer and Bible study you become like Him! (2 Cor. 3:18). As a plant looks to the sun and is transformed by photosynthesis, so let us look to Jesus in prayer and Bible study, and we will be transformed into His likeness by Christosynthesis! Christ now actually dwells in you and intercedes for you! Pray in confidence and boldness in His name.

6. Confess Sin Instantly, Honestly, and Avoid It!

"He that covereth his sins shall not prosper, but whosoever confesseth and forsaketh them shall have mercy" (Prov. 28:13).

Christians can still sin because although we have a new nature, we still have the old basic, human sin nature, but God has made provision in Christ. "If we confess our sins, he is faithful and just to forgive us our sins, and to cleanse us from all unrighteousness" (1 John 1:9). Instant confession, of the thought before the deed is done, avoids much sorrow and heartbreak. But thought or deed should be confessed to God for instant forgiveness and virtually unbroken fellowship. We turn by His strength from that which caused us to stumble. Remember, a Christian can sin, but a true Christian cannot live in sin. This is true for several reasons.

First, when we came to Christ we repented of our sins (changed our minds about sin, self and the Savior) turning from self and sin as the Lord of our life. "That if thou shalt confess with thy mouth the Lord Jesus (literally, *Jesus as Lord*), and shalt believe in thine heart that God hath raised Him from the dead, thou shalt be saved" (Rom. 10:9).

Secondly, though we are sometimes surprised by sin, 1 John 3:9 tells us, "Whosoever is born of God doth not commit (habitually practice or continue in) sin." To illustrate, a pig and a sheep could be taken, washed, perfumed, beribboned, petted and kept in one's home. But if someone left the door open, the pig would head for the first mudhole and wallow happily in it; that is the pig nature. The sheep might fall into the same mudhole (I've seen some very dirty sheep), but would get out as quickly as possible. It is not a sheep's nature to wallow happily in a mudhole. So it is with the true Christian. He can never again wallow happily in sin, and will seek to flee from temptation and avoid sin, even though he can still sin.

Thirdly, we are told, "Love not the world (not speaking of trees, birds, etc. but the wicked world system presided over by Satan), neither the things that are in the world. If any man love the world, the love of the Father is not in him" (1 John 2:15). Sin and the world are what Jesus saved us from. The Bible says we have passed "from death to life," and these are the things of death. Nevertheless, when we do sin, instant confession and instant forgiveness are the answer. Sonship can never be broken; fellowship can, and sin breaks fellowship between us and God. Agreeing with God about our sin honestly in instant confession restores that sweet fellowship. (See God's promise in 1 Cor. 10:13!)

7. Share Christ . . . Witness . . . Win the Lost

"But ye shall receive power, after that the Holy Ghost is come upon you; and ye shall be witnesses unto me both in Jerusalem, and in all Judaea, and in Samaria, and unto the uttermost part of the earth" (Acts 1:8).

Matthew 4:19 tells us "And He saith unto them, 'Follow me, and I will make you fishers of men.'" (Those not fishing, call into question the reality of their following.) We are saved to be conformed to the image of Christ, to bring glory to Him. However, the very heart of this is sharing Christ and winning others to Him.

Purpose: ". . . henceforth thou shalt catch men" (Luke 5:10b). (Actually, win them, not just fish for them.)

Promise: "He that goeth forth and weepeth, bearing precious seed, shall doubtless come again rejoicing, bringing his sheaves (the harvest, souls) with him" (Ps. 126:6). "The fruit of the righteous is a tree of life; and he that winneth souls is wise" (Prov. 11:30). (See Dan. 12:3; Ezek. 33:8.)

Priority: "For the Son of Man is come to seek and to save that which was lost" (Luke 19:10). His priority and purpose now becomes our priority and purpose! "Then said Jesus to them again, 'Peace be unto you; As my Father hath sent Me, even so send I you'" (John 20:21). May we also, by His loving grace, be consumed like Paul with a passion for the lost. Paul's great heaviness and continual heart sorrow caused him to cry out, "For I could wish that myself were accursed from Christ for my brethren, my kinsmen according to the flesh" (Rom. 9:3).

Winning souls! This is the one thing we can do to make Jesus and the angels of Heaven rejoice (Luke 15:9-10). There is also the rejoicing in the hearts of those reached for Christ, and the rejoicing in our own hearts and in the church!

God's command and Christ's love within compel us to witness and win souls to our Savior. Also, more souls being saved and more people being conformed to His image brings *more glory to Him.* Other motives include the joy of sharing the good news, seeing messed-up lives transformed and made abundant here and now in this life, the desire to share heaven with as many as possible, the growth and joy that occur in oneself as we witness and share Him, the demonstration of the power and compassion of Christ, and above all *saving precious lost souls from the awfulness of an eternity in the lake of fire!* Truly, if salvation is the most important thing ever to happen to us, and it is, and if we "love our neighbors as ourselves" as God commands, then love constrains us to share Christ with them to deliver them from sin and Hell. This is the most wonderful privilege and purpose known to man—sharing Christ, and winning the lost to glorify Him forever!

Begin by sharing what Christ has done for you and tell those to whom you witness how it can happen to them. Share the Bible verses that brought you to salvation and assurance in Christ. You will become more and more effective as you revel in His love, learn His word, and share Him more and more with others.

8. Let Jesus Live His Life Through You

"But thanks be to God which giveth us the victory through our Lord Jesus Christ" (1 Cor. 15:57).

We cannot live the Christian life in our strength. Christ clearly said, "without Me ye can do nothing," but we can live it in *His* strength. Letting Jesus daily live His life through you, being filled and controlled by His Holy Spirit (Eph. 5:18) takes much of the strain out of the Christian life. Thus we can consider ourselves to be "dead indeed unto sin, but alive unto God through Jesus Christ our Lord" (Rom. 6:11). And we can "walk in the Spirit, and ye shall not fulfill the lust of the flesh" (Gal. 5:16). We are not to live by *feelings*, but by *faith, and as we step out on God's Word, feelings or not, we will find His Word true, His presence real, and the feelings ultimately will follow, as the fruit* never the *root* of the Christian life. Now that you are His, bought by His blood, you will want to give Him, cheerfully and willingly, *first*, yourself, *followed* by your time, talents and treasure. Love is the compelling motive in the Christian life, not legalism, which can be a slavish, mechanical obedience to stated laws out of fear or force, bringing constraint and unhappiness.

Thus a young wife could obey a list of rules posted daily by her husband. Yet love, a higher motive, would cause the young wife to seek ways to please her husband, rules or no rules. Something he expressed that she knew would please him would bring a joyous response. This response would be done in complete freedom and bring happiness and peace. So it is with the Christian and Christ. Obeying is not legalism. It is the *attitude,* the motive, toward rules, toward obedience, which determines whether it is legalism or love-obedience. The grace of God will cause us to love and obey Jesus.

This is what the true grace of God, the unmerited favor, the free flow of His marvelous love on undeserving sinners really does. "For the grace of God that brings salvation has appeared to all men. It teaches us to say 'No' to ungodliness and worldly passions, and to live self-controlled, upright and godly lives in this present age, while we wait for the blessed hope—the glorious appearing of our great God and Savior, Jesus Christ, who gave himself for us to redeem us from all wickedness and to purify for himself a people that are his very own, eager to do what is good" (Titus 2:11-14, NIV).

Beloved, when you met Jesus, you met the Living God, for He *is* God. He is risen bodily. He is alive, and He is God (John 20:28; 1 Tim. 3:16). He is now your life (Col. 3:1-4). He can meet all your needs (Phil. 4:13, 19; 1 Peter 5:7; John 14:1-3, 27).

The shimmering splendor of His life—new life, eternal life—is yours forever! Love Jesus, love His people, love the Word, and love the lost for Him! God bless you! 1 John 5:13.

Last Words in His Love

Many Christians have found their lives gloriously transformed by Christ. He has fulfilled their deepest needs, calmed their fears, curbed their restlessness, taken away their guilt, lifted their burdens, given them His sweet and abiding peace. Their life is full and abundant, they revel in His love, they enjoy the Christian life, and love other Christians. Jesus is all in all to them, His life is now their life, and they love it.

Unfortunately, many others, though they say the same things about Jesus, and claim they know Him and love Him, are still wallowing most of the time in defeat and discouragement. They are still restless, unfulfilled, often swallowed up in troubles, bad habits, sin, self-pity. They are barely able to keep their heads above water in the Christian life, much less bring any glory to Christ, grow, mature and be faithful as Christians, lead others to Christ, or be real pillars in the church.

Some, of course, have never been truly saved, profession or not. However, many others are like a person who goes to the doctor, gets a prescription with eight ingredients in it, and scratches out one or several of the ingredients before he gives it to the druggist to be filled. Then, after less than desirable or even disastrous results, he blames the doctor or the druggist for the medicine not working. He may even lose faith in the doctor, or claim he is a fraud. Tragically, some do this in the Christian life. We must do what the Great Physician prescribes to enjoy and grow successfully in the Christian life. Love, loving Jesus, is the bottom line, but we must not take lightly 2 John 6a: "And this is love, that we walk after his commandments."

You may find these following scriptural principles helpful:

1. Victory is a gift basically, as salvation was (2 Cor. 15:57).
2. Know that you are dead to sin (Rom. 6:11). Sin is not dead to you! You are, however, alive to God! (Eph. 2:1).
3. Yield yourself to Jesus as one alive from the dead (Rom. 12:1-2).
4. Believe, accept, reckon, rely on, claim, and live these facts by *faith* not *feeling*.
5. This is all true because of your identification with Christ in His death, burial and resurrection.
6. Claim His control, the filling of His Holy Spirit, by faith (Gal. 5:16; 2:20).

We must exercise the power of the Holy Spirit in our lives by faith. While *He* provides the power *we* do it by faith that He is working in and through us. As Charles Ryrie well said, "God's working is not suspended because I work; neither is God's working always apart from my working."

Perhaps the greatest secret of that new life is to really believe and claim Romans 8:28 and to *show that* confidence in Christ constantly. How? Practice always the following verses by faith, not feeling—for all things "good" and "bad":

"And we know that all things work together for good to them that love God, to them who are the called according to his purpose" (Rom. 8:28).

"In everything give thanks, for this is the will of God in Christ Jesus concerning you" (1 Thess. 5:18).

Another tremendous, life changing truth is that God sees us as perfected forever in Jesus Christ! This is our *position* in Christ. "For by one offering he hath perfected forever them that are sanctified (saved)" (Heb. 10:14).

Claim this truth, rejoice in it, and your *practice* will begin to reflect your *position* as a true child of God! May God bless you in your new life!

CHAPTER NINETEEN

The Way to a Higher Plane

The church you attend is going to have a great deal to do with your growth, perception of God and His purpose for you and your outreach. The following is a list of things you should look for in a true New Testament church.

1. Find a church that believes the Bible, and the Bible only, to be the inspired, infallible (without error) Word of God.

2. A church that believes and teaches that the blood of Jesus Christ, God's Son, cleanses from all sin. A church that clearly tells you that depending on Jesus alone is the way of salvation. Any church that claims to be "the one true church," flee from *immediately!!* There are many fine Christians in many different churches and denominations. No church saves you or helps save you. Only Jesus can do that!

3. There are false churches, nevertheless . . . the Bible calls them "Synagogues of Satan." Be careful and prayerful and trust God to lead you and give you peace when you have prayerfully and scripturally searched for and found a Bible-believing and living church. He will!

4. Be sure the church talks much, freely and with joy, about the precious shed blood of the Lord Jesus Christ (1 Pet. 1:18-19). Read the church's statement of beliefs and constitution. Check with people and pastor. See if the church agrees with the Bible. This is *the* most important test!

5. Find out what the church teaches about being born again. If it is anything other than receiving Jesus Christ, as Lord and Saviour, leave!! Salvation is not by works, or baptism, or anything else. This comes *after* salvation, to demonstrate your salvation. Never *before* salvation in order to help Jesus save you. That would be heresy! (Check chapter 17, "Contact with the Ultimate.")

6. Be sure the church believes in the virgin birth, sinless life, death on the cross for our sins, and bodily resurrection of the Lord Jesus Christ. Ask! Accept no hedging!

7. Be sure the church believes in instant salvation (Luke 7:50; Rom. 10:13), and that they believe John 3:36a, "He that believeth on the Son hath everlasting life. . . ."

8. Be sure the church believes that there is now, always was, and always will be one God, existing as three eternal distinctions in what the Bible calls the Godhead, God the Father, God the Son, and God the Holy Spirit—One God.

9. Be sure the church believes in an eternal heaven and an eternal hell.

10. On the practical level, see if the church is bearing the fruit of the Holy Spirit—love, joy, peace, long suffering, gentleness, goodness, faith, meekness, self-control. See if there is a genuine friendliness, a concern, love for one another. No church is perfect, expect that! But there should be progress in this direction even when failures occur, as they surely will!

11. Be sure they are trying to reach the lost. Be sure also that they have a missionary program. See if the leaders in the church, and many of the people, give evidence that God has changed their lives through Jesus Christ.

Reading is so vital to your life as a Christian. Get acquainted with your Christian bookstore. Ask your pastor or a mature Christian to study with you. It may be helpful to join a Bible study group such as Bible Study Fellowship (write 19001 Blanco Road, San Antonia, TX 78258 for information). I suggest you take several good Christian magazines such as *Moody Monthly*. Reading the Bible is more important than reading all the other books put together. However, support books are extremely vital, as God has gifted some in the body of Christ to write in specific areas to help you grow, win others, and glorify Him. Here is a partial list. Get them and read them if you can. Very helpful for every serious Christian is a concordance to locate every word or verse in the Bible, with clear definitions: Strong's, Young's or Cruden's concordance. A Bible dictionary such as *The New Bible Dictionary* by J. D. Douglas, published by Eerdmans, is one of the best, or a smaller, less expensive one. A good commentary is needful, such as Matthew Henry's, or one by Jamieson, Fausset and Brown, or something like the Pulpit Commentaries, for those who wish to dig deeper. W. E. Vine's *Expository Dictionary of New Testament Words* is very valuable. *Word Studies in the Greek New Testament* by Kenneth Wuest is tremendously helpful. I remember reading through Strong's *Systematic Theology* a few weeks after I was saved. Most of it was helpful and delightful. Get it at least to refer to.

For Apologetics: (Evidence for the Bible)

Evidence That Demands a Verdict and *More Evidence That Demands a Verdict* by Josh McDowell
Science Speaks by Peter Stoner
Countdown by G. B. Hardy
The Seal of God by F. C. Payne
Know Why You Believe by Paul E. Little
You Must be Joking by Michael Green
Mere Christianity by C. S. Lewis

Who Moved the Stone? by Frank Morrison
Basic Christianity by John Stott
Why I am a Christian by Terry Winters
The Messiah in Both Testaments by Fred John Meldau
A Lawyer Examines the Bible by Irwin W. Linton
The Genesis Flood by Morris and Whitcomb
Therefore Stand by Wilbur Smith
Alleged Discrepancies in the Bible by John Haley
The Reason Why by R. A. Laidlaw
The Twilight of Evolution by Henry Morris
The Harmony of Science and Scripture by Harry Rimmer
Also several books by Francis Schaeffer

Prayer:

Power in Prayer by E. M. Bounds
Prayer, Asking and Receiving by John R. Rice
How I Know God Answers Prayer by Rosalind Goforth

Bible:

The Inspiration of the Scriptures, God-Breathed by
  L. Gaussen
The Inspiration and Authority of the Bible by Benjamin B.
  Warfield
Our God-Breathed Book—The Bible by John R. Rice

Books for Help and Outreach:

The Christian's Secret of a Happy Life by Hannah Whitall
  Smith
Your Reactions are Showing by J. A. Petersen
The Trinity in the Universe by Nathan Wood
Things to Come by Dwight Pentecost
The Cult Explosion by Dave Hunt

Through Gates of Splendor by E. Elliott
Athlete and Pioneer by C. T. Studd
Evangelism Explosion by James Kennedy
Discipleship Evangelism by Ken Stephens
Loving God by Chuck Colson
Dare to Care Like Jesus by Leslie Flynn
Peace, Prosperity, and the Coming Holocaust by Dave
  Hunt
The Act of Marriage by Tim LaHaye
Know the Marks of Cults by Dave Breese
James Dobson's books on *Marriage and Family*

A few of these books are out of print. Check with Christian bookstores, or second-hand bookstores.

Are You Really Ready?

Beloved friend, Jesus came the first time just as God's Word foretold. God's Word says He will soon come again for His own at any time. The situation is ripe for His coming. World conditions, the Jews returning and reestablishing their nation, Russia becoming a mighty nation and becoming involved in the Middle East are all foretold in scripture. These events create the exact picture God's Word gives that will exist when Jesus comes.

Are you ready for the coming? The Book of Revelation pictures the horrors, now and eternally, for those who are not ready. Revelation also pictures the unalloyed joy His coming will be to those who are ready, now and forever.

We have only given a very brief sketch with a handful of prophecies concerning the end times and Jesus Christ's return. Yet, calculating the fulfillment of prophecy mathematically or by common sense, His coming is assured by any honest reckoning. His soon coming is overwhelmingly indicated. Please accept Him, and please do it right now if you haven't already. Turn again to the chapter on "Contact with the Ultimate," and make very sure you are His, now and forever.

ATTENTION PLEASE to all the readers of this book. The purpose of this book, *The Beautiful Side of Death,* is to penetrate society and reach multitudes, as God enables, for our Lord Jesus Christ. Multitudes are interested in the occult, the Force, life after death, world unity and man's potential, and other related subjects.

For this reason we have endeavored to use mankind's interest in these subjects as a starting point. Our heartfelt prayer is that once interest is aroused, the gospel can be introduced and receive a fair hearing. The actual answer to all of our gropings are in Jesus Christ. Where we came from, why we are here, and where we are going, can be fully answered only in Christ. Our motive is not profit. Our motive is to reach souls for our Lord Jesus Christ and to penetrate an unbelieving and unheeding world in a new, fresh and powerful way. For further information on ordering books economically in quantity or for distribution in other languages, please contact Gospel Truths Ministries, Box 1015, Grand Rapids, Michigan 49501.

Please contact this address for any other information or personal help you may need after reading this book. We would be very happy to have you share your decision for Christ with us. There is absolutely no obligation, nor will anyone in any way invade your privacy.

CHAPTER TWENTY

New Horizons

We have traveled a long road together. I trust that by this time we have become good friends.

In the company of the astute medical doctor, Dr. Maurice Rawlings, we have looked at "The Ugly Side of Death." His insights into the spirit world were very illuminating. Since he has been at the deathbed of many patients, his contributions were especially valuable. He has walked through the dark shadows with them—at times has seen the sunlight, at other times the gathering darkness. He has recounted their voyages into this mysterious netherworld with great fidelity. Dr. Maurice Rawlings has the unique opportunity to know things about death firsthand that many of us only wonder about. He has been a reliable, bonafide expert.

With Johanna Michaelsen we encountered virtually irrefutable evidence that non-human entities do indeed exist in this world. Johanna accompanied us as we encountered some of the most fascinating of these spirit entities. Especially gripping was her account as the assistant of Pachita, the psychic healer. Pachita's operations with a rusty knife and scissors *graphically* involved us in the action that Johanna experienced. We came to distrust her spirit guides and eagerly anticipated the breathtaking climax to her spiritual journey.

Dr. Koch, a world-renown authority on the occult, added interesting personal experiences to the unfolding story, as did Mike Warnke and others. Their live encounters with spirit beings gave authenticity to our convictions that a spirit world really does exist.

In the case of Uri Geller we also discovered that latent powers beyond that of which we were aware may reside within human beings. We also found that tremendous power, apparently outside of man, can be tapped for good or evil. We have investigated various aspects on our trip, whether Ascended Masters, a "God-of-whom-we-all-are-a-part," an impersonal force, a person's God potential, or a personal God outside of a person.

A worldwide movement for the inner development of human beings, for a worldwide "togetherness" based on a person's love and need for fellow humans, seems to exist. This "togetherness" is motivated also by common dangers such as nuclear war. To some extent the New Age movement for universal unity and peace, for one world, and for one world religion has attempted to channel this movement.

How refreshing it was when renown author and researcher Dave Hunt provided the Master Plan, which helped us to discover where these spiritual detours came from and where they led. We used the truths and insights that he provided to cut our way through the jungle, clear the road, and resume our journey again. Having traveled in and/or done research in some forty nations, he knows his way very well through the jungle.

Finally, we emerged into the sunlight again, and sped on our way. We happily left "The Ugly Side of Death" and experienced what makes it beautiful.

We trust you have enjoyed the journey. We thank you for your companionship, and trust that your eyes too have seen New Horizons as you contemplated with us "The Beautiful Side of Death."

Bon voyage! to all who travel this road and to those who may endeavor to take this rewarding trip!